MYSTERY CULTS
of the
ANCIENT
WORLD

HUGH BOWDEN

MYSTERY CULTS
of the
ANCIENT
WORLD

Princeton University Press

Princeton and Oxford

For Jill

HALF-TITLE
Detail of the tauroctony from the Walbrook
Mithraeum in London, with the zodiac in
a circle around the central scene.

FRONTISPIECE
Vase decorated with a Dionysiac scene:
women dance while wine is ladled from
amphorae into drinking vessels.

TITLE PAGE
A marble relief from Rome, interpreted
as a scene of Dionysiac initiation.

THIS PAGE
Detail of the mosaic of grades in the
Mithraeum of Felicissimus in Ostia.

Published in North America in 2010 by
Princeton University Press, 41 William Street,
Princeton, New Jersey 08540
press.princeton.edu

First published in the United Kingdom in 2010 by
Thames & Hudson Ltd, 181A High Holborn,
London WC1V 7QX

thamesandhudson.com

Copyright © 2010 Thames & Hudson Ltd, London
Text copyright © 2010 Hugh Bowden

Library of Congress Control Number 2009938050

ISBN 978-0-691-14638-6

Printed and bound in China by Toppan Leefung

10 9 8 7 6 5 4 3 2 1

Contents

Introduction

I reached the boundary of death, and set foot on the threshold of Proserpina, and then I returned, carried through all the elements; in the middle of the night I saw the sun blazing with bright light; I approached the gods below and the gods above face to face, and worshipped them from nearby.[1]

With these words Lucius, the hero of Apuleius's Latin novel *Metamorphoses*, also known as the Golden Ass, describes the experience of being initiated into the cult of Isis in the Greek city of Corinth. He has reached this moment of heightened perception after a period of preparation including purification and fasting, when he has been left alone in the heart of the sanctuary of Isis.

Although Lucius is a fictional character, the experience he is attempting to put into words was one shared with thousands of real people in the Greco-Roman world, not only in the cult of Isis, but also in the Bacchic cult in honour of Dionysus, in the Eleusinian Mysteries held in honour of the 'Two Goddesses', Demeter and Kore, and in a number of other religious rites which are generally referred to as mystery cults. This book is about these ecstatic experiences – where and when they took place, what they involved, and what they meant to those who underwent them.

To learn about mystery cults we need to consider all kinds of evidence. Works of Greek and Latin literature can tell us something, but we will also look at ancient art, including wall paintings, sculpture and painted pottery, and we will need to look at the archaeological evidence of the sites where rites took place. This evidence covers a period of over 1,000 years and comes from all over the Mediterranean region and beyond. But to make sense of this material we need first to have some understanding of the nature of religion in the ancient Mediterranean world.

Religion

Religion in the ancient Mediterranean before the age of Christianity was different in a number of important ways from what is usually meant in the modern world by the term religion. To make sense of it we should forget about sacred texts like the Bible or the Qu'ran and the idea of a central religious organization claiming authority in its interpretation of doctrine. Such things did not exist. Instead it is better to start with something the ancient Mediterranean cultures had a lot of, which was gods [1].[2]

Every individual and every community in the ancient world had to concern themselves with their relationship to the invisible supernatural beings whose actions were believed to determine the course of their lives. Although the powers themselves were invisible, their effect on communities was easily seen: gods were held responsible for the success or failure of the harvests, for storms and earthquakes, diseases and their cures, and for victory or defeat in wars. All the areas of life beyond human control were considered to be the realm of the gods.

But these gods were not simply invented as a convenient albeit naive explanation for what we would now call natural events. People living in the ancient world sometimes felt the presence of gods near them and would respond emotionally to this presence, whether with fear or elation or simply an awareness of something unusual. These are the conclusions of anthropologists studying the role of evolution and cognition in religion. Human beings have evolved strong instinctive reactions to certain situations, such as the potential presence of dangerous predators or corpses. These reactions, which developed to help human beings survive in a

1 Assembly of Gods on an Athenian hydria (water jug) of c. 550–500 BC. From left to right: Heracles, Athena, Hera, Zeus, Aphrodite, Hermes and Ares.

2 The Virgin Mary being carried in procession through the streets of Seville in Semana Santa (Holy Week). Compare this with the procession in honour of the Mother of the Gods [75].

hostile natural environment, make certain notions that we would call religious particularly influential. These include the idea of powerful but invisible supernatural beings and also certain kinds of rituals, such as ritual purification to ward off pollution. The emotional power of these beliefs and rituals is evident from the fact that even in Christian societies, in particular in the Mediterranean world, there are widespread local cult practices, including offerings at shrines, the wearing of amulets, and rituals for warding off the evil eye, which carry on sometimes with, but often without, the support of the Church hierarchies [2]. These practices are sometimes referred to as folk religion, or less politely as superstition, but they have proved impossible to suppress: their durability is evidence of the strong emotional rather than intellectual drive behind them.[3]

Gods and Mortals in the Greco-Roman World

This understanding of supernatural powers underlies both the personal and the public religious practices of the communities of the Greco-Roman world. Those of the Greeks have been studied in most detail, and this is where most of the cults discussed in this book have their origins.

The Greek world was initially the area of the Greek mainland and the Aegean Sea, including the west coast of Asia Minor. In the period from 750 BC onwards, Greek settlement spread across the eastern Mediterranean to southern Italy and Sicily, North Africa and the Black Sea area.

In Italy the Greek cities developed alongside other indigenous communities including Latins and Etruscans, and most particularly the city of Rome. The Greek world was always in contact with civilizations to the east, including the empires of Mesopotamia and Egypt. It is argued that some of the stories that are now referred to Greek myths had their origins in stories from other Near Eastern societies, and even in the fifth century BC the Greek historian Herodotus could claim that the Greeks acquired their knowledge of the gods from the Egyptians.[4]

Towards the end of the fourth century BC Alexander the Great, whose father had brought the Greek mainland under the control of Macedonia, led a campaign into Asia that ended with Alexander as ruler of what had been the Achaemenid Persian empire, which reached as far east as the borders of India and included all of Iran, Mesopotamia, the Levant and Egypt. Within this vast territory Alexander founded new settlements, many named Alexandria after himself, to act as administrative centres or garrisons and as homes for his veteran soldiers. After Alexander's death his empire was divided into competing kingdoms in which the Greco-Macedonian rulers supported both Greek and indigenous practices. The Ptolemies, who ruled Egypt for three hundred years until the death of Cleopatra in 30 BC, controlled their kingdom from Alexandria in Egypt, one of the most important centres of Greek culture in this period, but presented themselves to the Egyptian population through hieroglyphic inscriptions and traditional Egyptian statue forms [3].[5] The Seleucid rulers of Persia and Mesopotamia used cuneiform in their documents and maintained many of the court practices of their Persian predecessors [4].[6]

In the following centuries this Hellenistic world became a part of other empires. The territories to the east of the Euphrates were gradually taken over by the new Persian empires of the Parthians and later the Sasanians. At the same time the territories west of the Euphrates were eventually absorbed into the Roman empire, as the power of the city of Rome spread first through Italy and then across the whole Mediterranean.

3 Ptolemy I, a Macedonian who became the founder of the dynasty that ruled Egypt for nearly three hundred years, presented in the traditional style of Egyptian sculpture.

4 Cuneiform document from Babylon describing the participation of the ruler Seleucus III in the New Year Festival of 224/3 BC.

5 State inscription from the Athenian Acropolis from the early fifth century BC, referring to cult practice in the temples there.

The earlier phase of Greek settlement overseas, alongside similar activity by the Phoenicians and the later creation of new settlements under Alexander, had turned the Mediterranean basin into a world of city-states, local self-governing communities with their own laws and traditions; and this became the basis on which the Roman empire functioned. Communities within the Roman empire were self-governing. They had their own laws and customs, and as long as these did not conflict with the interests of Rome, they were encouraged to maintain them.

These laws and customs included all matters to do with religion. Every community had its own gods, its own festivals in their honour and its own regulations about how worship should take place [5].[7] The travel writer Pausanias, in his description of Greece in the second century AD, shows it to be a world full of gods, with thousands of religious sites marked by temples, altars and statues, some of which were major centres of pilgrimage while others were almost abandoned. The situation in Italy was similar to that in Greece, and as Roman influence spread to places such as Gaul and Britain, new urban centres with their own religious structures developed there along the same lines.[8]

Religious Practices in the Greco-Roman World

Because every community was its own religious authority, there was a great deal of variety in their individual cult practices, but there were also rituals that were shared across the whole Greco-Roman world. These common practices were the result of a shared understanding of the world, and of the relationship between men and gods, that was the inevitable result of the constant contact between communities and individuals in the Mediterranean basin.

The most important religious practices included prayers to the gods and festivals in their honour. Festivals might include processions and performances of various kinds and animal sacrifice, which was a central feature of much public and personal religious cult [plate III]. Gods were usually worshipped at their own sanctuaries, which were areas set aside for them in cities or in the surrounding countryside. Sanctuaries would generally contain an altar where sacrifices and other offerings could be made. Usually, but not always, the god would be represented by a cult statue. Some cult statues were small enough to be moved, and they might be carried in processions or used in other ritual activity, but in major cult centres in large cities, cult statues could be vast: the gold and ivory statue of Athena on the Athenian Acropolis was some 10 metres (33 ft) high [plate II].[9] Temples were built to house cult statues, and cult activity generally took place in the open air in front of the temple.

As we have already noted, gods were understood to be powerful beings, capable of causing great harm to humans but also of bringing them great benefits. As a result, ancient religion is generally understood as transactional, that is to say that human worshippers made offerings to the gods in the hope that the gods would return the favour.[10] The practice of communities dedicating to the gods a proportion of the harvest, or part of the booty after a military victory, is evidence of this aspect of religion, and dedications to gods by private individuals are also a common feature of ancient religious life [39].[11] But relations with the gods were not understood purely in these commercial terms. Festivals were occasions in which gods and mortals could be understood as enjoying events together. The central scene of the east side of the Parthenon frieze from the Athenian Acropolis probably shows the annual offering of a *peplos* (a form of dress) to Athena. The human figures carrying out the ritual are depicted flanked by twelve thrones on which the gods are seated, joining the Athenians on the Acropolis itself [6].

Animal sacrifice might also be understood in terms of a meal shared between men and gods. In Greek sacrifice as described by Homer, writing in the early seventh century BC, when the victim – usually a sheep or an ox – had been slaughtered, bones wrapped in fat were burned on the altar with small pieces of meat, while the rest of the carcass was cut up and cooked for human consumption. This can be interpreted as a shared meal, in which gods and men each received an appropriate part of the animal. Reserved for the immortal gods were the long-lasting parts of the animal, namely the bones, and the fat with its preservative properties. While these were burning, the smoke would rise into the air for the gods to appreciate. Meanwhile the meat, which would soon rot, was eaten by mortals, who would themselves eventually die.[12]

This is not the only way in which sacrifice can be understood, and it is a feature of a number of the rituals which were a common part of ancient religious practice that they are open to different interpretations at different times and in different contexts.[13] This points to the important notion that, like the gods themselves, many religious rituals were not consciously invented by human beings to serve specific purposes. The origins of sacrifice, and of many other rituals, are lost in time, but they most likely came into being because they fulfilled an emotional, instinctive need rather than as a result of practical calculation.

Knowing about the Gods

BELOW
6 Athena's new robe (*peplos*) is received by her priest at the climax of the Panathenaic processionn Athens, while she and the other Olympian gods look on, as depicted on the frieze of the Parthenon, now in the British Museum.

OPPOSITE
7 Athena wearing her aegis, in a sculpture from c. 480 BC. The sculptor is interpreting the description of the aegis with gorgon's head at the centre from Homer's *Iliad* book 5.

The gods were invisible and generally inaudible to mortals, and this posed a considerable problem in maintaining good relations with them. Central to an understanding of religion in the Greco-Roman world is the notion of the unknowability of the gods.[14] Although it might be assumed that an event had been caused by a god, it was not often possible to identify which god was responsible. If the event occurred in or near a temple or sanctuary, it was generally thought that the god whose sanctuary it was had been involved in it. But it was not always that simple, and there were other basic questions that could not easily be answered. What did the gods look like? What were their names?

One solution was to rely on the superior knowledge of ancient poets. Thus Herodotus suggests that it was Homer and his near-contemporary Hesiod who taught the Greeks the names and attributes of the gods.[15] Certainly the descriptions of the gods in the Homeric poems influenced the way they were depicted in later artistic representations – and then these images might in turn have influenced later literary depictions [7].

Here we face the complex question of the relationship between myth and religion.[16] Tales commonly referred to as Greek myths are stories we know through the works of poets and the depictions of artists. Some of these stories offer explanations for the origins of rituals and the founding of sanctuaries, while some describe the relationships between different gods and help to explain why particular gods became associated with their various spheres of interest. Some of the stories may also reflect the traditions of specific communities passed down over generations, but it is clear that many are the invention of poets adapting material to make new and better plays or poems, and many are the work of mythographers — collectors and arrangers of myths to make coherent sense. Writers such as Pausanias and Herodotus invoke myths to explain contemporary religious practices, but in some cases the myths are stories they have found in poems written at other times and in other places. They are interpretations which these writers bring to the communities they are describing, rather than interpretations that the writers have learned from them.[17] Using myth to understand religious practices requires caution. We will see this most clearly in the case of the Eleusinian Mysteries (Chapter 1).

Communicating with the Gods

Although it was very difficult to understand what the gods were like, it was much easier to discover what they wanted. Divination, attempting to obtain answers from the gods, was a basic element of ancient Mediterranean religious practice. At every sacrifice, the entrails of the sacrificial victims would be examined to establish whether the sacrifice would be favourably received, and for any other information the god

might choose to reveal to the sacrificer. When armies went on campaign, sacrifices accompanied by divination would be a regular part of each day's activities. Answers to specific questions could be sought by consulting oracles. This might mean turning to collections of written oracles held by cities, such as the Sibylline Oracles at Rome, which would be read through by expert interpreters in the hope that they would indicate what sacrifices or other rituals ought to be undertaken to help the city. But it could also mean visiting an oracular shrine such as the Delphic Oracle, where questions were put to a priestess through whom the god Apollo gave his responses [8].[18]

These and other forms of divination, including astronomy, were practised by individuals as well as cities. In Christianity, with its emphasis on trusting in God rather than asking questions,[19] divination was and still is considered at best a foolish superstition and at worst an act of witchcraft deserving the severest punishment. In contrast, throughout the ancient Mediterranean, establishing the will of the gods was seen as a necessary part of maintaining good relations with them.

Nonetheless, even when Apollo spoke through his priestess, it was her voice the questioner heard: the god himself

8 A consultation of the Delphic oracle, on an Athenian vase of the fifth century BC.

remained hidden. There were stories of individuals meeting gods, but almost always the god would be in disguise and the meeting only brief.[20] During sacrifices cult statues, observing the rituals through the open doors of their temple or brought outside to be closer to them, might stand in for gods, but they were only statues, not the real thing. It was a basic understanding in most of Greco-Roman religion that the gods could only be indirectly known.

Initiation and Mystic Rites

Having looked at the general nature of Greco-Roman religion we can return to the experience described by Lucius in the *Metamorphoses*. It belongs to a category of rituals that in Greek are generally referred to as *orgia, mysteria* or *teletai*, words usually translated as mystic rites, mysteries or initiations, though the terms tend to be used somewhat flexibly in both Greek and English. The words are associated in various contexts with a number of deities, as we will see in the course of this book, but most commonly with Demeter, the goddess associated with grain and the grain harvest; with Dionysus, the god of wine and of drama; with Isis, whose sphere of interest is similar to Demeter's; and with a number of gods or goddesses referred to only by titles, such as the Great Gods, the Mother, the Mistress or the Maid. Apart from Egyptian Isis and the Mother, whose origins lie in Anatolia, these are Greek gods and goddesses, though their cults in some cases spread to Italy and other parts of the Greco-Roman world. We will be adding one other god to their number, Mithras, whose cult emerges much later under the Roman empire, but which nonetheless shares features with the Greek *orgia* and *teletai*. These cults, taken together, are what I will be referring to as mystery cults.

We will explore what we know about the individual cult practices in the following chapters. What they had in common is that they usually took place at night, and in secret. They were carried out by or for individuals or groups. They were, as far as we can tell, frightening and disorienting, involving rapid movement between darkness and bright light, with loud music and other noise [plate I]. Participants may have been blindfolded, and probably little if anything of what they experienced would have been explained. These practices also appear usually to have been open to all, rather than restricted to the citizens of the local community.

In almost all these respects, these *orgia* or *teletai* were rather different in form from the other rituals that made up Greco-Roman religion, which usually took place in the day, in the open. It is not obvious how they could have contributed to the reciprocality that we have seen characterized much religious practice – the notion of religious activity as involving transactions between men and gods. Nor were they obvious means of communicating intelligibly with the gods. To the extent that religion was about establishing and maintaining good relations between mortals and gods, these rites appear to fall outside the usual realm of religion.

Initiation and Anthropology

Just as anthropology can help make sense of ancient religion in general, so it can cast light on these mystic rites. Recent work by anthropologists has led to the idea that there are two distinct ways in which experience and understanding of the divine is transmitted through religion. These are referred to as the imagistic and doctrinal modes of religiosity. The two modes characterize different forms of social organization, and they emerged at different times in human history. They also work through different mental processes.[21]

The imagistic mode is characterized by very infrequent, but very dramatic, ritual events. It is found generally in cultures where communities are small, and there is not much of a social hierarchy. An example used to represent this mode is the religion of the Baktaman of New Guinea, a 'nation' of 183 people who had only just come into contact with the outside world when they became the subject of study of the anthropologist Frederik Barth in the 1970s.[22] Baktaman life revolves around growing taro and hunting wild pigs. The climate of the area where they live is more or less constant, so they have no experience of seasonal change and only very vague notions of time. Their counting system can reach as high as twenty-seven, but numbers above eight seem to have no function and are not generally used. Baktaman religion involves a sequence of initiations of young men – although women are involved in the rituals from the outside, they are not themselves initiated. The seven stages of initiation take place every few years, with higher-grade initiates assisting in the ceremonies of those lower down the ladder. Initiates of each stage can be identified by distinctive ornamentation, and each grade of initiation is surrounded by a different set of taboos. The rituals themselves involve considerable physical pain – beating and burning, deprivation of food and water, and so on – and they are accompanied by psychological trauma, as initiates are told that they will probably die during the process. Barth was able to undergo several stages of initiation and to observe others, and, with some hesitancy, he reveals everything he can about the rituals and their secrets, which does not amount to a great deal. One of the features of Baktaman initiation is the postponement of revelation. At the various stages connections are suggested between different elements of Baktaman life, but these are never spelled out. There is no great revelation and no obvious offer of special reward. Indeed, since essentially initiation for everyone in a particular cohort takes place together as a group, it serves to distinguish between groups within the community rather than between individuals.

The imagistic mode of religion can be contrasted with the doctrinal mode, normally associated with larger, more hierarchical communities. Mainstream Christianity is typical of the doctrinal mode, involving regular rituals repeated week-by-week or day-by-day throughout the year. Christian services involve low levels of arousal when compared to the Baktaman initiations, but they also offer clear verbal explanations of what they are about, and through them worshippers acquire an authorized account of the nature of the divine and their relationship to it.

Infrequent intense events, once experienced, are never forgotten. The memory of this kind of event is called an episodic or 'flashbulb' memory. In contrast, doctrinal religion works with semantic memory, that is, the kind of memory that allows people to carry out activities like driving a car or riding a bicycle – one remembers how to do these things not because of a single moment of revelation but as a result of habituation through repeated actions.

It is characteristic also of imagistic religious experience that it is non-verbal – those who have gone through the ritual are able to reflect on what took place, but they are generally unable to communicate the experience to others. It is suggested that this was the earliest form of religious experience and that its origins are bound up with the earliest appearance of art in the cave paintings of the Upper Palaeolithic period, around 30,000 years ago.[23]

The doctrinal mode developed later. It has been argued that the cities of the ancient Near East in the Bronze Age (around 3,000 BC onwards) provided the kind of society in which this mode of religiosity could operate, but it may have emerged rather later, in the empires of the early centuries AD.[24] Whatever its origins, the 'religions of the book', Christianity, Islam and Judaism, can all be characterized as doctrinal in this sense. Rituals of this kind, learned and then frequently repeated by worshippers, can be reproduced elsewhere, making it easy for this kind of religion to spread, in contrast to the hard-to-communicate imagistic mode.

Can we apply these anthropological models to Greco-Roman religion? The religion of city-states in the ancient world has some features that can be identified with the doctrinal mode: for example, regularly repeated sacrifices and rituals. But these are not as frequent, or as repetitive, as weekly Christian services, and those that include the slaughter of animals, sometimes in large numbers, could not be characterized as involving low levels of arousal. In any case, there is an important difference between the religion of city-states and Christianity, whether in its early days or now: in city-states it was not the religious practitioners who were responsible for encouraging the followers to maintain the rituals and the faith. Religion was rather the responsibility of the city-state itself: the political authorities were responsible for ensuring that the correct rituals were performed. In Greek cities and even in Rome priests might be elected by the citizens and could be held to account by them. And even non-elective priesthoods were often in the hands of the most powerful political figures in the cities. In these circumstances it was not necessary to develop the kind of distinctive mechanisms that sustained religions in the doctrinal mode.

While the doctrinal mode may not help to explain the nature of ancient religion, the imagistic mode seems a very useful way of categorizing mystery cults. To Lucius's account we can add another description of what it is like to experience initiation:

> Wandering astray in the beginning, tiresome walkings in circles, some frightening paths in darkness that lead nowhere; then immediately before the end all the terrible things, panic and shivering and sweat, and bewilderment.[25]

This is like the Baktaman experience, and other features of ancient mystery cults are also similar, such as the idea that the rituals cannot be explained. Lucius says of his own experience, 'I have reported things to you that, though you have heard them, you must fail to understand.' Even if we know the sequence of events in the rituals, this will not reveal their meaning. We can without too much difficulty reconstruct some of the secret parts of these rites, and these reconstructions suggest that no great piece of secret knowledge was revealed. In the mysteries of Samothrace, for example, which we will examine in Chapter 2, it seems that part of the ritual was conducted in a language incomprehensible not only to initiates, but probably also to the officiants. And it is clear that the identity of the gods whose mysteries were celebrated there was never revealed to the initiates and was presumably simply unknown.

Ecstatic Cults

The Greek terms *teletai* and *orgia* were used to refer not only to rituals of initiation such as that undergone by Lucius, but also to more frequent rituals associated with the Mother of the Gods, and especially with the god Dionysus. These rituals occurred annually, or sometimes a little more frequently, and involved groups of worshippers being led out of their city at night to the uncultivated hills around them, where they engaged in dancing and other wild activities. Participants might reach a state of ecstasy, losing any awareness of where they were or what they were doing [9]. As we will see, it is necessary to separate reality from fantasy in the descriptions we have of these Dionysiac or Bacchic rites, but there is no doubt that they took place.

Ancient writers drew connections between these ecstatic cults and the other initiatory rites, expressed in terms of the kinship between Demeter, Dionysus and the Mother of the Gods. Their rituals shared elements of disorientation and extreme emotion. When it comes to explaining how these cults fitted into the wider framework of Greco-Roman religion, we will find that both types can be explained in the same way.

9 A maenad dancing for Dionysus, from a vase of the early fifth century BC. She is holding a leopard cub and has a snake bound around her head. This is not intended to be realistic, but to indicate the wildness of the experience of worshipping Dionysus.

Ecstasy and Anthropology

Anthropological studies of ecstatic religion have tended to examine what is described as shamanism or spirit possession,[26] situations in which individuals are considered to have been entered by some supernatural power so that their behaviour is beyond their own control. This notion is found in Greek religion, generally associated with inspired prophecy. Apollo at the Delphic Oracle was believed to speak through his priestess, the Pythia. Bakis, who was considered the author of obscure verse oracles, was said to be inspired by the Muses.[27] However, the model is less useful in explaining the kind of cults we are dealing with in this book, which usually involved groups of people engaging in ecstatic ritual together.

A more useful model is Pentecostalist Christianity. Although it can claim roots in earlier Christian traditions, Pentecostalism appeared as a new religious movement in the United States of America at the start of the twentieth century and spread rapidly around the world. Those who attend Pentecostalist services hope to be filled with the Holy Spirit of God. The presence of the Spirit is revealed by various signs, of which *glossolalia*, 'speaking in tongues', is the most familiar, and this is often accompanied by healing through the laying-on of hands. Services tend to be character-ized by loud music, with drums and tambourines, and the members of the congregation calling out in response to those leading the worship [10].[28] At least one Pentecostalist tradition found among white congregations in the southern United States includes more extreme activities such as drink-ing poison and handling snakes. We will look in detail at this phenomenon in the last chapter, because it can cast light on the ancient experience of ecstatic cult.[29]

10 The pastor and his wife dance while the choir director leads the singing during a service at a Haitian Pentecostalist church in Massachusetts.

The biblical basis of Pentecostalism is the story of the descent of the Spirit on Jesus' disciples after his death and resurrection, reported in the Acts of the Apostles.[30] Although there is an emphasis on calm at the start of the story, the Spirit produced ecstatic behaviour in the disciples. Inspired by the Spirit, they went out to preach, and their words were heard by their multilingual audience in their own languages. While this impressed many, some bystanders remarked that 'they are all drunk'.[31]

Pentecostalist churches are generally autonomous, though they are bound together in various denominations. The divisions between denominations are often explained in terms of different doctrines, but they are visibly expressed not in terms of beliefs or theological understanding so much as in differing ritual practices, for example the use of different ritual formulae. The movement was born out of Methodism, a form of Christianity very much in the doctrinal mode of religiosity. Pentecostalist services, like those of the Methodists, are frequent, regular and long, with a heavy emphasis on the Bible and the reiteration of statements of belief. But Pentecostalism, following the nineteenth-century 'Holiness' movement, puts stress on worshippers having a personal relationship with God; in services the Spirit descends unpredictably on individuals, but usually with a powerful emotional impact. This fits with the imagistic mode of religiosity.

A somewhat different ecstatic ritual is a feature of Sufic Islam [11]. The *dhikr* is an act of devotion performed as a group activity by Sufi brotherhoods, often with dancing and controlled breathing:

11 'Whirling dervish': a member of a Sufic brotherhood dances during a *dhikr* in Senna, in Iranian Kurdistan.

For many *sufis*, *dhikr* is a means that will lead them to ecstasy, a state they understand as a sign of God's blessing and a fountain of mystical knowledge. Such is the power this state exercises on the imagination that, for some, *dhikr* becomes an end in itself... In many [*sufi* brotherhoods] music and singing have been added in an effort to concentrate the whole being of the performers on the task in hand: to see, so to speak, God.[32]

Meeting the Gods Face-to-Face

This examination of ecstatic worship in other religious traditions points towards one way of understanding how mystery cults fit into the broader picture of Greco-Roman religion. Lucius says of his initiatory experience, 'I approached the gods below and the gods above face-to-face, and worshipped them from nearby.' It is this idea, that mystery cults offered those who took part in them the opportunity to experience direct, unmediated contact with the divine, that makes best sense of what we know about them.

As we have seen, it was taken for granted in the ancient Mediterranean that gods were often present in the world, although they were invisible to worshippers and usually perceived only indirectly, through their actions. The issue of the visibility or otherwise of the gods is examined in a number of episodes in Homer's *Iliad* and *Odyssey*. Usually in Homer when gods wish to advise individuals they appear in disguise, taking the form of someone who might be expected to offer advice.[33] But on one occasion in the *Iliad* they become visible to a mortal: Athena tells the Greek hero Diomedes that she is going to take from his eyes the veil that prevents him from seeing the gods fighting for the Trojans on the battlefield in front of Troy, and Diomedes can suddenly see Apollo, Ares and Aphrodite, who remain invisible to the other combatants.[34] Diomedes suffers no harm from this event – Athena lifts the veil to help Diomedes avoid trying to fight a disguised god in the battle – but seeing the gods in their true form was not always so benign. Most significantly Selene, princess of Thebes and lover of Zeus, king of the gods, is tricked by Zeus's wife Hera into demanding to see him in his true form: Zeus appeared as a thunderbolt, and Selene was destroyed [plate IV].[35] Selene was the mother of Dionysus, so it is appropriate that the worship of Dionysus involved the potentially devastating opportunity of direct contact with the god.

Gods were not always so destructive in their appearance, but they were clearly frightening. In the *Homeric Hymn to Demeter*, which we will look at in the next chapter, Demeter reveals herself to the household of King Celeus of Eleusis: 'Beauty spread round about her and a lovely fragrance was wafted from her sweet-smelling robes, and from the divine body of the goddess a light shone afar, while golden tresses spread down over her shoulders, so that the strong house was filled with brightness as with light-ning.'[36] On the other hand, when Dionysus reveals himself in Euripides' *Bacchae* he does so with an earthquake, thunder and lightning.[37]

So direct contact with the gods was potentially dangerous, but at the same time greatly to be desired. And the sort of relationship between mortals and gods that this contact implied was rather different from the essentially commercial relationship considered above. The religious activ-ity of communities, and much of the time of individuals, was concerned with maintaining the goodwill of the gods by honouring and making offerings to them. This reflects a formal, slightly distant relationship, marked by respect rather than intimate knowledge. In contrast, the rela-tionship between gods and participants in mystery cults was intimate, personal and not necessarily easy to talk about.

Mystery Cults and Eschatology

It must be said that this is not the way in which mystery cults are usually understood. Scholarship on mystery cult has tended to look for the content of the cults, on the assumption that they offered initiates some kind of secret knowledge that was kept from the uninitiated masses, or some special benefit that only they shared. We need therefore to look briefly at these other interpretations.

The most common view of mystery cults is that they were concerned with life after death.[38] This is not surprising, as we will see that references to death and the underworld are found in association with several of the more prominent cults we will be examining — but not all of them. That there is a direct connection between mystery cults and experience after death might appear obvious from a number of references to the Eleusin-ian Mysteries. Towards the end of the *Homeric Hymn to Demeter*, the poet describes how the Eleusinian Mysteries were given to mortals and com-ments:

> Blessed is he of men on earth who has beheld them, whereas he that is uninitiated in the rites, or he that has no part in them, never enjoys a similar lot down in the musty dark when he is dead.[39]

These words were probably written in the sixth century BC, and we find the theme repeated in a number of later poems. The *Homeric Hymn* is concerned with the story of Persephone, Demeter's daughter, who is given in marriage to Hades, god of the underworld. All this appears to point to a focus of the cult on the fate of initiates in the underworld, but, as we will see in the next chapter, this is not straightforward, and there is another explanation of why the poet and his successors should talk about initiation in these terms.

We can see the poet's basic message in his first words: 'Blessed is he who has beheld the mysteries'. Here we have an emphasis on the rites themselves. What follows is not an explanation of what it is that makes the initiate blessed, but the additional side effects. In the *Odyssey* the Greek king Menelaus is told that when he dies he will not share the miserable lot of ordinary mortals, but he will go instead to the Elysian fields:

> There life is easiest for men: snow never falls, the winters are not long, and there are no rainstorms, but Oceanus forever sends breezes of the sweetly breathing West wind to refresh men.[40]

The reason for this is that he is married to Helen, and therefore is a son-in-law of Zeus. In the *Odyssey*, then, a better afterlife is not the consequence of any actions, but of Menelaus's personal closeness to the gods. The afterlife promised to initiates looks very similar to that of Menelaus, and the explanation for it is the same: like Menelaus, initiates have been in close contact with a god. But just as Menelaus did not marry Helen in order to reach the Elysian fields, so those who participated in mystery cults did not do so in order to have a better time after death. As we have seen, ancient religion was characterized by uncertainty about the gods – they remained generally unknowable and unknown. There is no reason to believe that attitudes to the afterlife were any different: there was no way of knowing what happened after death, aside from ideas drawn from Homer and other writers. Compared to the certainty and intensity of the immediate experience of initiation or Bacchic ecstasy, the hope of a better experience in the uncertain world beyond death must have weighed little.

Mysteries and Secrets

Several times in his descriptions of Greece Pausanias declines to talk about matters related to mystery cults. He says that he was forbidden in a dream from describing the sanctuary of Demeter at Eleusis, where the mysteries took place, and he talks about secret writings and mentions that the true name of the goddess known as the Mistress is not revealed to the uninitiated.[41] The notion that the names of certain gods were kept secret is also mentioned by other writers.[42] Several cults possessed sacred objects which were shown only to initiates.[43] Famously, there are various accounts of individuals revealing the secrets of the Eleusinian Mysteries to non-initiates and being severely punished for it by the Athenians.[44]

Mystery cults did therefore include secret elements, but this does not mean that these secrets were what the mysteries were about. Christian critics, keen to demonstrate the folly of the mysteries, have claimed to reveal the secret sacred objects of the Eleusinian Mysteries, mentioning an ear of corn or a phallus.[45] Whether or not they are right, these featured in other cult activity where no secrecy was involved; it was only in the context of the rest of the rituals that they would acquire a special meaning.

But as well as secret objects, there is the idea of secret knowledge revealed only to initiates. It is likely that some individuals who offered private initiation would have claimed to have secret knowledge, to be found in the books they possessed. We will consider these practitioners, sometimes referred to as *orpheotelestai*, 'Orphic initiators', in a later chapter. There is evidence that at least some were familiar with the work of contemporary philosophers, and Pythagoras, who was active in the late sixth century BC, was associated with both philosophy and mystery cult.[46] The fourth-century BC philosopher Plato uses the word *mysterion* to refer to secret knowledge,[47] and it is likely that it was this contact between initiators and philosophers that gave rise to the notion that mystery cults involved the revelation of secret doctrines.

Mystery Cults and Christianity

Some scholars have drawn links between mystery cults and early Christianity. They see similarities in language and rituals as well as their concern with the afterlife. As we have seen, this last comparison is probably misplaced, and it is also unclear how real the other perceived similarities are.

It was once common to study mystery cults as forerunners of Christianity.[48] It is now not unusual for historians of the Roman world to treat Christianity as an example of a mystery cult.[49] Like a number of the cults we will be examining, Christianity first appeared in the eastern Mediterranean and later spread west to Rome and beyond. It involved rituals different from those of traditional state cult, and those who participated in it separated themselves in some ways from the common mass of humanity, making claims that included the expectation of a better future after death. But these apparent similarities mask more profound differences. In particular they give too little weight to Christianity's origins in Judaism. The ideas of early Christianity may have owed much to Greek thought, but its practices owed as much to Jewish rituals. We will return to the relationship between mystery cults and early Christianity in Chapter 10.

The Limits of Knowledge

In the following chapters we will be examining in detail what we know about the actual cults. In many cases we cannot get very far, because the evidence is lacking, but this is equally true of many other aspects of Greco-Roman life that did not involve secrecy. On the other hand, we probably do know more or less what initiates experienced at Eleusis, or in Bacchic rituals, and it is unlikely that arcane knowledge was passed on. As we saw above, in the discussion of the imagistic mode of religiosity, those involved in these rites were unable to explain what they experienced. It was not that the rites should not be described, but that they could not be described.

Mithraic caves and Greek sanctuaries where mystery cults took place have been excavated, and their form can be reconstructed with some accuracy [12]. However, too much information has been lost about what happened there, and attempts to reconstruct the rituals are unlikely ever to recreate the ancient experience of initiation. On the other hand, ecstatic worship out of doors is still an element in some religious traditions, and this can offer one route to greater understanding of what participation in Bacchic or similar cults may have been like. In the last chapter we will see that some aspects of the experience of mystery cults may still be accessible to some people today.

12 Reconstruction of the Mithraeum from Carrawburgh on Hadrian's Wall.

1 *The Eleusinian Mysteries*

Even if yours has always been a sedentary life, and you have never sailed the sea, nor walked the roads of the land, you should nevertheless go to Attica, so that you may witness those nights of the festival of great Demeter. For then your heart may be free of care while you live, and lighter when you go to the land of the dead.[1]

The Eleusinian Mysteries were the most revered of all ancient mystery cults. Celebrated every autumn at Eleusis in Attica, the territory of Athens, they were in honour of the Two Goddesses, Demeter and her daughter Persephone (known as Kore, the maiden). The Mysteries were celebrated for over a thousand years, and for most of that time men and women came from all over the Mediterranean world to witness the rites and be party to their secrets. What was it like to 'witness those nights of the festival of great Demeter'? Why did men and women choose to be initiated into the cult? We know a great deal about what took place in Athens and Eleusis during the festival, and we can guess at more. In this chapter we will attempt to reconstruct both the events themselves and the meanings attached to them by initiates.

Demeter and Persephone: The *Homeric Hymn to Demeter*

Central to most interpretations of the Eleusinian Mysteries is the myth of the rape of Persephone, Demeter's daughter. Versions of this story were told across the Greek world, but the earliest surviving literary account of it is found in a poem directly associated with Eleusis, the so-called *Homeric Hymn to Demeter*, written sometime between 650 and 550 BC.[2] The Homeric Hymns are a collection of hexameter poems honouring various gods which were attributed to Homer in antiquity; however, they are of widely varying length and were probably composed over a long period.

Persephone was the daughter of Demeter and Zeus. The *Hymn* begins by describing how, with the consent of Zeus but without the knowledge of Demeter, Persephone was carried off by Hades, god of the underworld and brother of Zeus, while she was picking flowers in a meadow. The event was witnessed by the goddess Hecate, and Persephone's screams were heard by Helios, the sun. However, Demeter spent nine days travelling over the earth, carrying torches and looking for her daughter, before Hecate and Helios told her what had happened.[3]

Angry with Zeus, Demeter withdrew from Mount Olympus, the home of the gods, and wandered the earth in disguise. When she reached Eleusis she was greeted by the daughters of the king, Celeus, and offered her services as a nurse. She was invited into their house, where she declined to sit on a chair, preferring to sit on a stool covered with a fleece. She was made to smile by the jokes of a woman present there, Iambe, and, after refusing a cup of wine, accepted a drink of *kykeon*, made with barley, mint and water. Metaneira, Celeus's wife, then asked Demeter to nurse her new-born son, Demophoon. Demeter agreed to do so, but instead of feeding him, she anointed him with ambrosia and put him into the fire every night. One night Metaneira spied on Demeter's actions, but her shrieks gave her away. Demeter explained that she had been making Demophoon immortal, but that now she could not continue. She revealed her true nature and demanded that the people of Eleusis build her a temple, promising that she would reveal rites for them to perform in order to soften her anger.[4]

Demeter then stopped grain from growing across the earth. This threatened not only mortals, who faced famine, but the gods too, who would be deprived of sacrifices. Zeus therefore appealed to Demeter to return to Olympus, and when Demeter demanded as her price the return of Persephone, he sent Hermes, the messenger god, to ask Hades to release her [13]. This Hades did, but first he gave her a pomegranate seed to eat. When mother and daughter were reunited, Persephone told Demeter what had happened, and Demeter explained that because Persephone had eaten food in the underworld, she would have to spend a third of each year there. Zeus sent Rhea (his own and Demeter's mother) to placate Demeter and at last she was reconciled with the gods, and let the grain grow again.[5]

Demeter then taught the rites of the Mysteries to the rulers of Eleusis [14]:

> So the whole broad earth grew heavy with leafage and bloom; and she went to the lawgiver kings, Triptolemus and horse-goading Diocles, strong Eumolpus and Celeus leader of hosts, and showed them the conduct of her sacred matters, and taught her solemn rites, which one cannot depart from or enquire about or broadcast, for great awe of the gods restrains us from speaking. Blessed is he of men on earth who has beheld them, whereas he that is uninitiated in the rites, or he that has no part in them, never enjoys a similar lot down in the musty dark when he is dead.[6]

13 Kore (Persephone) returning from the underworld. She is led by Hermes and greeted by her mother Demeter (on the right) and Hekate, who is holding two torches.

14 Triptolemos, surrounded by other Eleusinian figures, as he is about to spread the gift of agriculture around the world. The scene, painted below a scene of gods battling against giants, emphasizes the civilizing power of agriculture and the Mysteries.

The *Hymn* ends with the return of Demeter to Olympus and a final greeting to Demeter and Persephone.[7]

The central episode, set in Eleusis itself, and the final part, in which the rites are revealed, clearly link the *Hymn* to Eleusis, and it is generally thought that the *Hymn* was composed there, probably for performance at a festival. Without these episodes, however, the story can still be understood, and other versions of the myth set it elsewhere.[8] At the heart of the myth is an explanation for the cyclical nature of agriculture: the time Persephone spends under the earth represents the barren time of the year, while the time she is with Demeter is when the earth is fertile. In the *Hymn*, Persephone's reappearance is associated with the blooming of the flowers in spring, and this is a common interpretation of the myth. However, in Greece winter was the busiest season for agriculture, and the period of Persephone's absence might originally have been thought of as corresponding to the heat of summer, the period after the harvest when the fields were dry and bare. It was common in Greece to store the harvested grain in underground silos, so Persephone might be thought to be in the underworld at that time of year, to be brought up again for the autumn sowing, the time when the Mysteries were actually celebrated.[9]

There is a lot of information about the Eleusinian Mysteries in the *Homeric Hymn to Demeter*, but it is not easy to make sense of it. We need therefore to turn to the information we have about the Mysteries from other sources of information, starting with the place itself.

Eleusis

Eleusis, where the Mysteries took place, lay in the territory of the city of Athens, some 20 km (12 miles) from the city itself, near the border with the neighbouring city of Megara. The earliest remains in the area of the sanctuary of Demeter and Kore date back to the Bronze Age, but whatever structures there were at that time were abandoned around 1200 BC, at the end of Mycenaean civilization, and the site was abandoned until the eighth century BC [15]. The evidence shows continuous occupation of the site from then until probably AD 395, when Eleusis was sacked by the Goths under Alaric. By that time Greece had long been part of the Roman empire, and Christianity had become the dominant religion of the empire. Consequently there appears to have been no attempt to rebuild the sanctuary after the sack, and this date marks the end of the Mysteries.[10]

15 The sanctuary of Demeter and Kore today. There is little left of the buildings, but the entrance is to the right of the picture, and the walls around the sanctuary are clearly visible. The square area in the centre is the site of the Telesterion, with steps at its rear cut into the rock of the hillside behind.

What Happened at the Mysteries?

The festival of which the Mysteries were a part lasted eight days. It involved public sacrifices to various gods and processions from the centre of the city of Athens to the sanctuary of Demeter and Kore at Eleusis, as well as rituals that took place behind the closed doors of the sanctuary which involved only those initiated, or being initiated, into the secrets of the cult. Our understanding of events is based on evidence drawn from a long chronological period, and some parts of the procedure may have been introduced later than others. It is likely that the festival had reached a fairly fixed form by the end of the fifth century BC and then remained constant for at least the next three centuries, and probably until at least the third century AD. Athens was sacked by the Roman general Sulla in 88 BC,

and by the Herulian Goths in AD 267, but otherwise it was generally respected by its Roman conquerors as a place of ancient learning. Eleusis was particularly honoured by the Emperor Hadrian and his successors, who were themselves initiated into the Mysteries – as Augustus had been earlier.[11]

Before the Festival

Running the festival was the responsibility of two extended families, the Eumolpidae (who claimed descent from the mythical Eleusinian king Eumolpus) and the Kerykes (heralds). Well in advance of the festival itself, members of these families were sent out to the Greek cities to announce a sacred truce that was to start on 15 Metageitnion, a date roughly equivalent to the beginning of September (a month before the start of the festival itself), until 10 Pyanepsion, in late October, thus guaranteeing safe passage to anyone wishing to travel to and from Athens for the festival.[12]

OPPOSITE
16 The City Eleusinion in Athens was on the southern slopes of the Acropolis. Although ritual activities took place here, it was administered by those responsible for the sanctuary at Eleusis.

On the day before the festival started, 14 Boedromion, at the end of September or beginning of October, a procession would leave Eleusis to bring the *hiera*, the sacred objects of Demeter, from Eleusis to Athens. The procession was led by the priests of Eleusis, and priestesses would carry the sacred objects in closed containers tied with red ribbons. For part of the journey the procession was accompanied by a military guard of young Athenian men, known as *ephebes*, which was met by Athenian priests and people at the edge of the city before finally ending at the City Eleusinion on the slopes of the Acropolis of Athens [16].

The identity of the sacred objects was one of the secret aspects of the cult, but we can make some guesses about what they might have been. Since they were carried inside containers by the priestesses in the procession they must have been quite small. It was normal for the cult statues of gods to be carried in procession at their festivals, and we can find a close parallel for this procession in the one that took place on the eve of the City Dionysia, the principal festival in honour of Dionysus at Athens. On that occasion the ancient wooden cult statue was brought from the sanctuary of Dionysus at Eleutherae, at the edge of Athenian territory to the northeast of the city, not all that far from Eleusis, to the temple next to the theatre of Dionysus beneath the Acropolis in Athens. That procession too was accompanied by *ephebes*. There were no cult statues of Demeter and Kore at Eleusis, and the *hiera* must represent the goddesses in some way. One Christian writer claims that at the height of the celebrations a reaped ear of grain was shown to the initiates.[13] As the myth in the *Homeric Hymn to Demeter* identifies the movement of Persephone between the earth and the underworld with the annual cycle of sowing and reaping grain, an ear of wheat or barley would be a very apt representation of Kore (as Persephone is called at Eleusis). How Demeter may have been represented is more difficult to guess.[14]

Preparation of Initiates

Those seeking initiation may have had to undergo some kind of rituals before they could take part in the Mysteries. There was a separate festival known as the Lesser Mysteries, celebrated not at Eleusis but at Agrae, in the city of Athens, but little is known about it. In his life of the Hellenistic ruler Demetrius, who controlled Athens for periods at the end of the fourth and the early part of the third centuries BC, the biographer Plutarch (AD 46–120) describes how Demetrius requested that he be initiated and 'received into all the *teletai*, from the least to the *epoptika* [that is, seeing the Mysteries for a second time]'. The Athenians renamed the month twice so that Demetrius could go through the Lesser and 'Greater' Mysteries within a few days of each other.[15] This does not prove that the Lesser Mysteries were a prerequisite for initiation into the Greater Mysteries: Demetrius's behaviour in Athens overall is presented by Plutarch as excessive and inappropriate, so his demands can be seen as beyond what was required. In his *Gorgias*, Plato has Socrates say to another speaker, metaphorically, 'You are fortunate in that you have been initiated into the Great before the Little: I did not think that that was permitted.'[16] But if this adds anything to our understanding it is that those who had been initiated at Eleusis would not subsequently undergo the Lesser Mysteries. According to Diodorus Siculus, writing in the first century BC, the Lesser Mysteries were instituted by Demeter so that the hero Heracles could be purified after slaughtering the Centaurs.[17] He makes no link with Eleusis, and, as we will see, ritual purification was part of those Mysteries.[18]

It has also been argued that there was some pre-initiation procedure that initiates had to undergo in the City Eleusinion at some time before the celebration of the Mysteries.[19] As with the Lesser Mysteries, we have few details. And since there was no way of ensuring that someone who had been through this procedure went on to initiation, nothing secret can have been revealed: it would not have been an appropriate moment for explaining what was to follow, beyond possibly giving the would-be initiate some basic instructions. It might be here that the initiate was assigned a *mystagogos*, someone who would lead them through the rituals, although *mystagogoi* are only mentioned in connection with the Eleusinian Mysteries from the first century BC onwards [17].[20]

OPPOSITE
17 An initiate, led by a priest holding a torch, in the procession from Athens to Eleusis.

The Public Aspects of the Mysteries

On the first day of the festival itself, the sacred herald of the Mysteries made a proclamation in Athens, inviting all who wished to come to Eleusis to celebrate the mysteries. This took place in the Athenian Agora, overseen by the Athenian magistrate responsible for the traditional festivals of the city, the *Basileus*, or King Archon. At least from the end of the sixth century BC at the latest, the invitation included all Greeks and excluded all barbarians – that is, those who did not speak Greek. Anyone who had committed homicide was excluded, as they would in any case be excluded from all aspects of civic life in Greek cities. Once Athens was part of the Roman empire, Romans were recognized as belonging to the category of Greeks rather than barbarians.[21]

On the following day those who were intending to be initiated were required to go down to the sea, taking with them a piglet, which they were to wash and then sacrifice as an act of purification [19]. Sacrificed piglets were commonly used in acts of purification, but the sheer numbers involved must have made this a rather exciting day. The number

18, 19 An initiate with a piglet (left) and
a statuette of a piglet from Eleusis (right).
The statue was found in Italy, but the
subject is Eleusinian.

BELOW
20 Asclepius, in a relief from the sanctuary
of Asclepius in Athens, which was created
after the god was brought to Athens from
Epidaurus.

of initiates is a question we will look at shortly, but at its height there may
have been several thousand people being initiated in any year. All those
piglets being carried through the city and down to the sea must have
created mayhem, especially with piglets old enough to wriggle out of their
owner's grip and escape into the streets. Pigs farrow in fairly large
numbers, but if Athenian farmers had to provide enough piglets for all the
initiates it is unlikely that all of them would have been so small as to be
easily carried around [18]. The day was known as *Halade Mystai*, 'Initiates
to the Sea'.

The next two days were the concern of the city officials rather than
the initiates. On the third day there was a major sacrifice to the Eleusinian Goddesses in the City Eleusinion, and on the fourth day, sacrifices
in honour of the god Asclepius. This element of the festival was added

in 421 BC, when a snake sacred to Asclepius was brought to Athens from his sanctuary in Epidaurus in the northeast Peloponnese. The embassy bringing the snake reached Athens during the celebration of the Mysteries, and the snake was lodged overnight in the City Eleusinion. From that year onwards, the Athenians honoured Asclepius alongside the Eleusinian goddesses [20].[22]

After this the festival moved to Eleusis itself. There were two processions from Athens to Eleusis over the next two days [21]. One was led by the priests and priestesses returning the *hiera* to Eleusis and accompanied by large numbers of Athenians, including the *ephebes*. On the following day a second procession brought the initiates themselves to Eleusis, led by a man carrying a statue of another Eleusinian god, Iacchus, who was particularly associated with the initiates. As the procession reached the outskirts of Eleusis, it crossed a bridge over the river Cephisus, where the initiates were mocked by a group of bystanders. This ritual mockery was called the *gephyrismos*. At the end of their 22-kilometre (14-mile) walk the initiates reached the sanctuary and danced for Demeter and Kore just outside its walls, by the Kallichoron Well. After this, no doubt very tired indeed, the initiates finally entered the sanctuary.

21 The Pompeion at Athens, which was by the Sacred Gate where the Sacred Way from Eleusis reached the city. It was a marshalling place for processions.

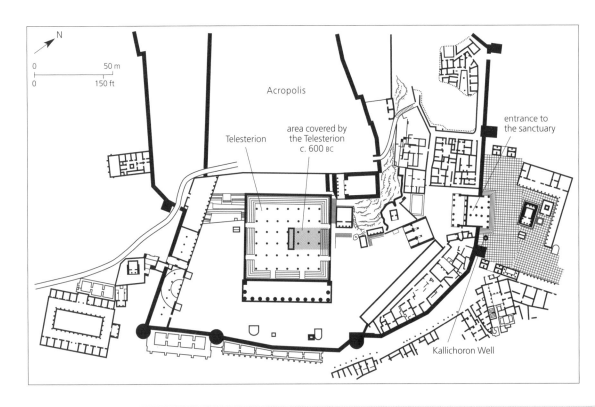

The Sanctuary at Eleusis

Archaeological excavation of the sanctuary has revealed a great deal about its development over time and can tell us quite a lot about what may have happened within it [22]. Normally we could supplement this information with the report of the travel writer Pausanias, who wrote a detailed description of Greece in the second century AD. But Pausanias claimed to have been told in a dream to say nothing about the interior of the sanctuary at Eleusis. This is further proof that the Eleusinian Mysteries continued to be revered over a long period of time, but it does deprive us of what would have been a very valuable source of information.[23]

The sanctuary was in some ways similar to that of other gods in the Greek world but in other ways very different. It was, like most sanctuaries, enclosed by a wall, and it contained a number of buildings associated with the cult. But the central structures found in nearly all sanctuaries, a temple and an altar, were absent. The altar was normally the place where animals were sacrificed in honour of the sanctuary deity, and it was normally located in front of a temple which housed the cult statue of the god. Cult activity took place around the altar, in the open air. But there was no cult statue of Demeter at Eleusis, nor anything that could be described as a temple. There was an altar just outside the sanctuary, but it seems that within the sanctuary Demeter was not generally offered sacrificial victims.[24]

The central building in the sanctuary was the Telesterion, the Hall of Mysteries, where the most secret and dramatic parts of the ritual took place [23]. This was, in its final form, a very large square building with a roof supported by a forest of columns, and with steps around its edge so that people standing at the back could see over the heads of those in front. The building was expanded in a series of stages in the course of the sixth and fifth centuries BC, by the end of which time it was capable of holding around 3,000 people. The Telesterion contained a smaller structure, sometimes referred to by archaeologists as the Anaktoron. The word means palace, referring to the house of Celeus where, according to the *Homeric Hymn*, Demeter first revealed herself to the Eleusinians. In antiquity the terms Anaktoron and Telesterion were both used to refer to the structure as a whole.[25] Elsewhere in the sanctuary were various buildings and features of significance for the Mysteries.

What Happened in the Sanctuary

On the day after their entry into the sanctuary the initiates will have rested. They probably also fasted, although it is possible that they drank *kykeon*, which was not alcoholic.[26] In the evening came what was for them the climax of the whole festival, when the secret rites were performed.

OPPOSITE

ABOVE

22 The sanctuary of Demeter and Kore (Persephone) in the second century AD. The Telesterion is much larger than it had been nearly eight hundred years earlier, and the sanctuary has been expanded, with a monumental entrance and temples just outside the wall.

BELOW

23 The Telesterion at Eleusis. In antiquity the whole area was covered by a roof supported on columns.

What precisely took place in the sanctuary has been a matter of fascination from the time of the Mysteries onwards. Various comments in the writings of ancient authors may indicate something of what went on. We have reference to *ta dromena, ta deiknumena* and *ta legomena*, 'things done, things shown and things said' as making up the Mysteries.[27] Many statements about the Mysteries stress their visual aspect: the priest of Demeter is called the *hierophant*, which means 'he who shows the holy things'; a number of ancient writers including Crinagoras, who is quoted at the beginning of this chapter, talk about the fortune of those who have actually seen the holy Mysteries.

Christian authors tell us something of what was said. At the climax of the events, when the *hiera* were revealed, the hierophant apparently said: 'A child Brimos has been born to the mistress Brimo!'[28] Initiates may also have said, to show their new status, 'I fasted, I drank the *kykeon*, I took from the chest, when I had done the deed I put into the basket, and from the basket into the chest.'[29] If these reports are reliable, they tell us something of the events, but we need to know more.

The problem that faces us is, of course, that the secrets of the Mysteries were not to be revealed to non-initiates. This prohibition is emphasized in the *Homeric Hymn to Demeter*, and, as we have seen, it was still honoured by Pausanias, writing some seven or eight centuries later. The extent of this prohibition was never clearly defined, but we can see how it was understood by the Athenians themselves from their response to an occasion when the secrets certainly were revealed to non-initiates.

24 Alcibiades. This Roman portrait is the only certain image of the Athenian general from antiquity.

The Profanation of the Mysteries

In 415 BC the Athenians were about to send a major naval expedition to Sicily. Just before the expedition set off, a group of leading Athenians were accused of profaning the Mysteries by revealing the secrets to non-initiates. Alcibiades, one of the generals appointed to lead the expedition, was accused of involvement in the profanation [24]. The events are described by a contemporary witness, Andocides, himself accused of involvement:

The Assembly had met to give audience to Nicias, Lamachus, and Alcibiades, the generals about to leave with the Sicilian expedition – in fact, Lamachus's flag-ship was already lying offshore – when suddenly Pythonicus rose before the people and cried: 'Countrymen, you are sending forth this mighty host in all its array upon a perilous enterprise. Yet your commander, Alcibiades, has been holding celebrations of the Mysteries in a private house, and others with him; I will prove it. Grant immunity to him whom I indicate, and a non-initiate, a slave belonging to someone here present, shall describe the Mysteries to you. You can punish me as you will, if that is not the truth.'

Alcibiades denied the charge at great length; so the *prytaneis* [the presiding magistrates] decided to clear the meeting of non-initiates and themselves fetch the boy indicated by Pythonicus. They went off and returned with a slave belonging to Archebiades, son of Polemarchus. His name was Andromachus. As soon as immunity had been voted him, he stated that Mysteries had been celebrated in Poulytion's house. Alcibiades, Niciades and Meletus were the actual celebrants, but others had also been present and witnessed what took place. The audience had included slaves as well, namely himself, his brother, the flute-player Hicesius and Meletus's slave.[30]

Plutarch, writing much later but with access to contemporary accounts, adds a little more information:

> They said that one Theodorus took the part of the Herald, Poulytion of the Torchbearer and Alcibiades of the Hierophant, and that the rest of his friends attended as initiates and were addressed as *mystai*.[31]

An opponent of Andocides wrote a pamphlet, which survives because it was included in the collection of speeches by Lysias, accusing him of direct involvement in the profanation, and describes his crime in these terms:

> This man donned a ceremonial robe, and in imitation he revealed the secret things (*ta hiera*) to the uninitiated, and spoke with his lips the forbidden words.[32]

All this evidence emphasizes how seriously the Athenians took the task of preserving the sanctity of the Mysteries. It is no coincidence that the accusation of profanation was aimed at someone who was about to lead a huge and controversial military expedition, and that the accusations were made just before the expedition was due to sail. In Athenian tradition those who attacked Eleusis were doomed to destruction: the Spartan king Cleomenes was believed to have been driven mad because he damaged the sanctuary when he led an army against Athens at the end of the sixth century BC, and the destruction of the army of the Persian king Xerxes when he invaded Greece in 480 BC was also considered repayment for his attack on the sanctuary.[33] Both these kings are presented as arrogant and over-ambitious, and Alcibiades, although his expedition was directed away from Athens, was also considered dangerously ambitious.[34] But our interest here is in the precise nature of the profanation.

The offence in this incident would appear to be the imitation of the words and actions of the hierophant, something perhaps easy for an initiate to do. But it would be wrong to believe that all the secret of the Mysteries amounted to was the actions of one officiant. This would hardly be enough to justify the idea that seeing the Mysteries was a life-changing event, as Crinagoras claims. We can get further if we aim, not simply to identify a secret, but to recreate the whole experience of the initiate.

The Mysteries as Experience

We do have a description of the experience of initiates in a fragment of a lost work by Plutarch. It is making a comparison between the experience of the human soul at death and that of an initiate. Although Plutarch does not explicitly say that he is talking about the Eleusinian Mysteries, it is the most likely model:

> The soul suffers an experience similar to those who celebrate great initiations... Wandering astray in the beginning, tiresome walkings in circles, some frightening paths in darkness that lead nowhere; then immediately before the end all the terrible things, panic and shivering and sweat, and bewilderment. And then some wonderful light comes to meet you, pure regions and meadows are there to greet you, with sounds and dances and solemn, sacred words and holy views; and there the initiate, perfect by now, set free and loose from all bondage, walks about crowned with a wreath, celebrating the festival together with the other sacred and pure people, and he looks down on the uninitiated, unpurified crowd in this world in mud and fog beneath his feet.[35]

To this picture we can add information from Lactantius, a Christian author writing at the beginning of the fourth century AD, comparing a rite associated with Isis with the Eleusinian Mysteries:

> The mystery of Ceres (i.e. Demeter) also resemble these, the mystery in which torches are lighted, and Proserpina (i.e. Kore) is searched for throughout the night; and when she has been found, the whole rite ends with congratulations and the throwing about of torches.[36]

And a slightly earlier Christian writer, Clement of Alexandria, says, 'Demeter and Proserpine have become the heroines of a mystic drama; and their wanderings, and seizure, and grief, Eleusis celebrates by torchlight processions.'[37]

On the basis of these descriptions, scholars have reconstructed the events of the night of the revelation of the Mysteries as a dramatic performance re-enacting the story of the rape of Persephone and her return. The following was proposed by Kevin Clinton, the American scholar who has examined the evidence from Eleusis in the greatest detail:

When it is completely dark, the initiates file into the sanctuary... When they reach the doorway... perhaps they are able to look in as they pass and see at the back of the cave, by flickering torchlight, a deeply unsettling sight: the goddess sitting on the rock in sorrow. In any case they hear lamentations coming from this cave precinct. They pass by, and walk on up to the Telesterion. Then they wander about outside the Telesterion in search of Kore, confused and disoriented as they stumble in the dark, their eyes apparently blinded by a hood, each initiate guided by a mystagogue. All the while the hierophant keeps sounding a gong, summoning Kore.

Kore's return naturally cannot be seen by the initiates. In the cave below she emerges, guided by Eubuleus [a god associated with the Mysteries at Eleusis], through an opening just opposite where Demeter is sitting. After embracing Demeter, Kore leaves the cave together with her mother, and they take the path up to the Telesterion, in the company of Eubuleus [25]. When the gods reach the Telesterion, they pause, and the Epoptai (second-year initiates) catch a glimpse of mother and daughter reunited. The Two Goddesses and Eubuleus then enter the Telesterion.

25 The Ninion Pinax, dedicated to the two goddesses at Eleusis. Interpretations vary of the scene depicted here, but the seated women on the right are probably Demeter and Kore (Persephone). The column in the top left corner suggests the scene is set indoors, and men and women carry torches and other objects.

LEFT
26 Two initiates holding staffs, and a priest holding two wands. The scene on this vase once again emphasizes the presence of torches in the rituals at Eleusis.

RIGHT
27 Triptolemos setting out on his journey. Appearing on the same vase, this image suggests that the scene with torches [26] precedes this one: Triptolemos's journey is represented as the outcome of the Mysteries.

Moments pass. Suddenly the Telesterion opens, and the hierophant stands in the doorway, silhouetted against a brilliant light streaming from the interior. The initiates enter, passing from darkness into an immense space blazing with extraordinary light, coming from thousands of torches held by the Epoptai [26].

Within the Telesterion the goddesses were probably again visible to the initiates, but now displayed on a structure which served as a platform (the structure which has usually been called the Anaktoron). Divine initiates, such as Heracles and Dionysus, we may imagine, appeared as well, and of course Triptolemus [27].

After the current year's initiates left the Telesterion, a special vision was revealed to the Epoptai. A Christian writer speaks of a display of grain and the birth of a child... The child must be Ploutos [Wealth]... As he makes his epiphany, presumably from within the structure at the centre of the Telesterion, it is probably at this moment that the hierophant displays the ear of grain.[38]

Scholarly interpretations such as this assume that everything that happens in the ritual can be straightforwardly interpreted in terms of myth, and in particular in terms of the story of the rape of Persephone. But this raises some interesting questions. We can start by noting that the description of the mystic drama outlined above does not correspond altogether with the version of the story in the *Homeric Hymn to Demeter*. For example, the *Hymn* does not mention Eubuleus, another special Eleusinian god who is given prominence in this reconstruction, and the drama does not appear to address the question of Persephone's future return to the underworld. Of course the reconstruction is based on guesswork, and the *Homeric Hymn to Demeter* was not an 'official' Eleusinian document, so there is no reason to expect the two to correspond. More fundamentally, was there an 'official' Eleusinian doctrine at all, any agreed understanding of what the Mysteries represented? Or did initiates have to interpret the sequence of events for themselves?

Mysteries and Intoxication

Before answering these questions, there is one more avenue of experience to explore. In the middle of the twentieth century the Eleusinian Mysteries were approached from the standpoint of ethnomycology, that is, the study of the role of mushrooms in human society. The poet and mythographer Robert Graves was the first to suggest that the Eleusinian Mysteries might have involved hallucinogenic mushrooms.[39] Then, in a book first published in 1978, a group of authors including Albert Hofmann, the scientist who first synthesized LSD, argued that the 'secret' of the Mysteries lay in the use of a hallucinogen related to LSD. The authors argued that the *kykeon* drunk by initiates contained psychoactive elements that were produced by the ergot fungus. The usual effects of ergot poisoning include painful convulsions, but the fungus generates chemicals including lysergic acid, and these can produce hallucinations. Although the hypothesis was not well received by classicists, it has continued to receive attention, and new studies of the theory continue to appear.[40] There are, however, objections to this approach, both practical and theoretical.

The practical objection is that it has not been possible to recreate the hallucinogenic effects that the theory proposes. Ergot poisoning tends to be painful and often fatal at levels that might generate hallucinations. If the hallucinogens cannot be produced in modern laboratories, it is difficult to see how they could have been regularly and reliably created in ancient Eleusis.[41]

The theoretical objection concerns the idea that identifying the drug somehow explains the meaning of the cult. Ancient and modern accounts of the Mysteries emphasize disorientation and dramatic visual experiences. It is conceivable that drugs might heighten these effects, but there is no reason to believe that the experience would lose its power in their absence. The cult of Dionysus was very much associated with alcohol, in the form of wine, but as we will see in a later chapter, it is not certain that wine did play a role in nocturnal Bacchic revels. The highly exaggerated account of Bacchic activity in Italy given by the Roman historian Livy (59 BC–AD 17) includes all kinds of theatrical effects, achieved by mechanical means. Athenians in the fifth century BC were able to generate spectacular visual effects in performances of tragedy and comedy that were put on in honour of Dionysus. If we are to look for an external explanation for the power of the Eleusinian experience, the theatre seems a better place to look than the kitchen or brewery.[42]

Understanding the Mysteries

To be fully initiated, participants had to experience the Mysteries twice, first as a *mystes*, then as an *epoptes*. The assumption seems to be that these two experiences would normally happen in consecutive years, but this was not necessarily a requirement. The word *mystes* is derived ultimately from the verb *myo*, which means to close the eye, while *epoptes* means viewer. Thus an *epoptes* might appear to be one who witnesses what a *mystes* experiences without seeing. While this might suggest that there were elements that only the *epoptes* took part in, it might also mean that what differentiated the experience of each group was their perspective. Studies of initiation in other societies, when those who have gone through one stage of initiation assist in the initiation of the next cohort, suggest that the ceremony is a significant experience for both groups.[43] Thus going through the Mysteries for the first time as a *mystes*, perhaps not knowing what is to happen next, and quite probably not knowing what any of the ceremony actually meant, would be a different experience from going through it a second time, when the *epoptai* would know what was to follow and would watch the *mystai* being bewildered and confused. If, as has been suggested, the *mystai* were blindfolded for some of the ceremony, the difference between the experience of *mystes* and *epoptes* will have been all the greater.[44]

But did the experience of being an *epoptes* make everything compre-hensible? Clement of Alexandria, writing at the end of the second century AD about Greek mysteries in general, not specifically of Eleusis, says this:

> For the Greeks not unreasonably purifications are the first part of the mysteries, just as a bath is for non-Greeks. After that there are the lesser mysteries which have the function of teaching, and preparation for what is to come; and then the greater mysteries which concern every-thing, where there is no longer learning, but contemplation and consideration of nature and of realities.[45]

This has been taken to show with reference to Eleusis that initiates learned what they needed to know about the Mysteries beforehand, at the Lesser Mysteries, but the passage is far from clear: it may not even refer to the Athenian 'Lesser Mysteries' of Agrae at all. And since, as we have seen, it was not necessary to go through those Lesser Mysteries before taking part in the Eleusinian Mysteries, they cannot have been an occasion when explanations for the events at Eleusis were offered.[46]

But Clement's words do suggest a way forward, with his comment that greater mysteries were occasions for 'contemplation and consideration'. As we saw in the Introduction to this book, some anthropologists have identified a particular kind of religious activity which they have called the

imagistic mode of religiosity. This is characterized by infrequent but emotionally intense religious rituals in which participants, generally described
as initiates, experienced great terror and often great pain.[47] And we saw
that Plutarch's description of the experience of being an initiate, including 'wandering astray in the beginning, tiresome walkings in circles, some
frightening paths in darkness that lead nowhere; then immediately before
the end all the terrible things, panic and shivering and sweat, and bewilderment', especially after the long walk from Athens to Eleusis, is a good
example of religious ritual of the imagistic mode.[48]

According to anthropologists, rituals which belong to the imagistic
mode have some common features, and one of these is that they lead to
'spontaneous exegetical reflection', and with it 'diversity of religious representations'.[49] In other words, the people who experience the ritual are
not given an explanation of what they have been through but have the
experience burned into their memories, and they will think over what it
might mean in the period following the ritual.

We can compare the experience of initiates at the Eleusinian Mysteries with another religious ritual to which the word mystery is also
attached, the Eucharist or Holy Communion in Christianity. As we will see
in Chapter 10, the word *mysterion* was used by early Christian writers to
refer to the secret plan of God revealed in Jesus. The whole of Christianity
was in this sense a *mysterion*, and the word came to be used to refer to
various aspects of Christian practice, including the Eucharist.[50] In contrast
to the Eleusinian Mysteries, Christianity, at least in the form that is practised by mainstream western Churches, can be considered an example of
the doctrinal mode of religiosity, characterized by frequently repeated
low-intensity rituals.[51] As with the Eleusinian Mysteries, participation in
the Eucharist requires initiation, which is achieved through baptism and,
traditionally in the Anglican Church, confirmation. Confirmation and
adult baptism are usually preceded by attendance at confirmation classes,
where Christian doctrines are taught to candidates.[52] Historically candidates would be tested by means of a fixed set of questions and answers,
the catechism. The communion service itself also explains the meaning
of the rituals it includes. There is an expectation of weekly attendance at
services, and most of the service involves words spoken by the president or
the congregation, repeated every week, which in particular reiterate the
meaning of the act of communion itself. All those who participate in
the communion are, in theory at least, able to give an agreed and authoritative account of what it means. Of course, differences in interpretation of
the Eucharist were a major part of the conflict between churches in the
European Reformation, but that makes the point clearer: each side
believed it understood the correct meaning of the communion service.

We cannot talk about the initiates at the Eleusinian Mysteries learning the authoritative meaning of the events in the way that communicants learn the true meaning of the Eucharist. There were no authoritative texts that explained the Mysteries, and there was no mechanism by which initiates could be effectively taught what they meant. Instead, as Clement suggests, each initiate would have to think about their own experience and develop their own understanding of what they had been through. Experiencing the events a second time as an *epoptes* would no doubt help with this contemplation. And the initiates, who would be familiar with the story of the rape of Persephone, would quite probably relate their experiences to that story. But there was not necessarily an agreed relationship between the events of the Mysteries and the elements of the myth.

The Homeric Hymn to Demeter Again

If this is right, then we should think of the *Homeric Hymn to Demeter* itself as an exegetical reflection on the experience of being initiated, rather than simply using it as a key to work out what happened at Eleusis. It is striking that the focus of the hymn is not on the fate of Persephone but on the experience of Demophoon and the mortal household of his family in Eleusis.

In the *Hymn* Demeter demands the construction of a temple for herself at Eleusis, and she promises to teach the Eleusinians the rites to celebrate there, at the moment when she has been prevented from making Demophoon immortal.[53] She then remains in the temple until Persephone is restored to her, and at that point, as she leaves Eleusis to return to Olympus, she fulfils her earlier promise.[54] Meanwhile the poet stresses that Demophoon is inconsolable for the loss of his divine nurse.[55] So in the poem, the Mysteries are not about Persephone at all, but about the relationship between the people of Eleusis and Demeter, and about the experience of Demophoon, who has climbed the knees of the goddess, slept in her arms, felt her breath upon him, and then been deprived of that contact and comfort.[56] It follows from this that the poet did not connect the

Mysteries directly with Demeter's role in agriculture, despite the fact that the cult of Demeter and Kore at Eleusis was very much concerned with the agricultural prosperity of Athens.

We must remember that the *Homeric Hymn* is only one poet's interpretation of the Mysteries. Despite the popularity of the *Hymn* as a poem, there is no reason to believe that its interpretation of the Mysteries was widely followed at Eleusis: Demophoon does not feature very much in Eleusinian art, nor is he named in Eleusinian inscriptions. Much later writers associate Demeter's statement that 'in future times the sons of the Eleusinians will wage war against each other for him', with a festival at Eleusis called the *Balletys*, which involved mock battles, but otherwise Demophoon is far less visible in the sanctuary than other Eleusinian figures such as Triptolemus [28].[57] Nonetheless it is striking that our earliest witness to the Mysteries identifies the theme of direct contact between a goddess and a mortal as the focus of his interpretation of them.

OPPOSITE
28 Demeter and Kore (Persephone) with Triptolemos, a youth associated with them in Athens. The relief is from Eleusis, carved around 450 BC.

Eleusis and Eschatology

In the Introduction we saw that there was a tradition of associating mystery cults with ideas about the afterlife, and this association is particularly strong in the case of Eleusis. As well as the words of the *Homeric Hymn* itself and the poem of Crinagoras quoted at the beginning of this chapter, referring to the blessings initiates would receive, we have similar comments recorded in fragments of a poem by Pindar, and a play by Sophocles:

> Blessed is he who has seen this and thus goes beneath the earth; he knows the end of life, he knows the beginning given by Zeus.[58]

> Thrice blessed are those mortals who have seen these rites and thus enter into Hades: for them alone there is life, for the others all is misery.[59]

In Aristophanes' comedy *Frogs*, which is largely set in the underworld, there is a chorus of Eleusinian initiates who are clearly having a happier time than the other characters.[60] There is also the importance of Persephone at Eleusis. She is Queen of the Underworld, and it would not be unreasonable for those initiated at Eleusis to receive special favours from her.

We have already seen in the Introduction that the references to a happy afterlife do not imply that the Eleusinian Mysteries were explicitly concerned with the afterlife. They are ways of expressing the more fundamental truth that anyone who has been in direct contact with the gods is

29 This vase shows Persephone with Plouton, but the god appears with a cornucopia and is associated with wealth (*ploutos*) rather than death. Both figures are young.

forever transformed by the experience. But we can also see that the Queen of the Underworld had little to do with the Mysteries either.

The *Homeric Hymn* tells the story of Persephone eating pomegranate seeds in Hades, and therefore having to return there for a part of each year, but it does not say anything about what she will do there. The poet takes the point of view of Demeter, emphasizing the miracle of her return to the upper world each spring.[61] We do not find Persephone depicted as Queen of the Underworld in Eleusinian art either, but always as a young woman [29], usually in the company of her mother Demeter [plate V].[62] In Eleusinian inscriptions she is never called Persephone, which is the name usually associated with her role in the underworld. Instead she is always Kore, the maid, a title that identifies her as unmarried.

Conclusion

Although it is easier for us to follow Crinagoras's advice and go to Eleusis than it would have been for his contemporaries, we can no longer witness the nocturnal rites there: the Telesterion is in ruins and the site closes before sunset. We can nonetheless to some extent imagine the experience of those who did witness the Mysteries, if we make good use not only of the ancient evidence – archaeological, epigraphic, literary and artistic – but also of the insights gained from anthropology. At one level the Eleusinian Mysteries were an occasion on which the city of Athens honoured the goddesses who guaranteed the harvests and the grain that the city needed in order to survive: sending out heralds to advertise the graciousness of the goddesses to the other Greek cities and putting on sacrifices and processions in their names. But in the middle of these public festivities was a sequence of events in which the personal experience of individuals was central. Behind the walls of the sanctuary at Eleusis they met the goddess and experienced her grace and power at first hand.

We will find this combination of public celebration and personal experience in other cults, and in most cases we have fewer clues about what happened beyond the public gaze. What we have observed about Eleusis will help us to make sense of these other cults, but they also have their own secrets to reveal.

2 *The Mysteries of the Kabeiroi and the Great Gods of Samothrace*

After Eleusis, the most respected sanctuary where initiations took place was on the island of Samothrace in the northeast Aegean, dedicated to the Great Gods. In this chapter we will look at what is known about the mysteries of the Great Gods of Samothrace and at two other sanctuaries, both dedicated to the Kabeiroi (see p. 61), one near Thebes in Boeotia and one on the island of Lemnos, not far from Samothrace. There are aspects of these cults which remain uncertain due to lack of evidence, but one of their most striking features is the extent to which initiates were themselves ignorant of basic facts. We cannot say who the Great Gods or the Kabeiroi were (for discussion see below), but nor could their initiates – not because they were forbidden to speak about them, but because they themselves didn't know. These are cults of nameless gods.

Samothrace

Visible today at the archaeological site of the sanctuary of the Great Gods on Samothrace are the remains of a collection of buildings, mostly dating from the fourth and third centuries BC. What we know about the mysteries that took place there is based on these remains, along with a number of inscriptions and artefacts excavated from the sanctuary and a few remarks in the works of ancient authors. The inscriptions that refer to initiation are later in date than the buildings, while some of the most valuable literary evidence predates the buildings. Overall, therefore, any attempt to reconstruct what actually happened on Samothrace has to draw on evidence from a very wide chronological range, and parts of what follows are inevitably based on reasonable guesses rather than certain knowledge.[1]

The Sanctuary of the Great Gods

The earliest evidence of religious activity found at the sanctuary is from sacrificial deposits dating to the early seventh century BC, and this is contemporary with the earliest evidence of Greek settlement on the island.

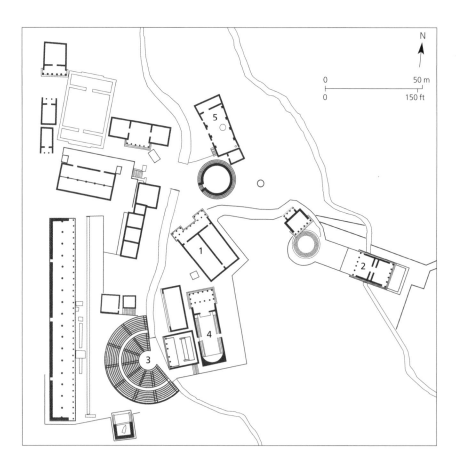

30 Plan of the sanctuary of the Great Gods, indicating the main buildings. Some of the names given to the buildings are modern, and the precise function of some is not clear.

1 Hall of the Choral Dancers

2 Propylon of Ptolemy II

3 theatre

4 Hieron

5 Anaktoron

Herodotus, writing in the fifth century BC, says that the cult was taken over from pre-Greek inhabitants of the island, whom he calls Pelasgians.[2] This suggests that to fifth-century Greeks there were aspects of the cult that were considered unusual, and probably incomprehensible, a point to which we will return later. The major buildings on the site almost all date from the fourth to the second centuries BC, and many were dedicated by Macedonian and other Hellenistic monarchs [30]. From the same period we have inscriptions recording the visits of *theoroi*, that is, sacred embassies, from many Greek cities. The embassies and public buildings are evidence that the sanctuary at Samothrace had an important public role: Greek communities and their leaders saw value in honouring – and in being seen to honour – the Great Gods. This is obviously similar to the way in which the Eleusinian goddesses were part of public worship in Athens. The mysteries, at least in this period, were not the only important element of the cult. Samothrace appears to have been valued as a regional religious centre. It was visited by Philip II of Macedon at a time when he was spreading his power across the northern Aegean – it was also said that this was where he met his wife Olympias, mother of Alexander the Great.[3] Olympias was associated in antiquity with exotic religious traditions, and this has been followed in modern scholarship; in particular there are stories that associate her with snakes, and with the cult of Dionysus, which we will look at in Chapter 5.[4] These stories add something to the mystique of Samothrace, but her presence on the island — if she was there — probably had more to do with her being the daughter of a ruler of Epirus, to the west of Macedon, than anything else. Subsequently it is the rulers of Macedon who are best represented among the Hellenistic monarchs who erect buildings there, along with Ptolemy II, ruler of Egypt from 283 to 246 BC, who did so at a time when his influence in the Aegean was at its height. One can talk about such building work as propaganda, with a political and diplomatic goal, but that is not to contradict the notion that these rulers were driven by religious motives — they were aiming to win the support not only of the Greek cities that had links to Samothrace, but also of the Great Gods themselves.

We know less about the earlier history of the island. As we will see, the mysteries date back possibly to the earliest period of cult on the island, but the northeast Aegean was relatively unimportant for most Greek cities until the late sixth century BC, and Samothrace does not seem to have been a great communal centre even after that. Indeed, once the Greek world came under Roman rule its importance as a regional centre ended, and it is clear from the epigraphic evidence that the mysteries became the main business of the sanctuary. From *c.* 100 BC onwards we start to see surviving inscriptions listing the names of initiates.[5]

The Mysteries

There is no doubt that initiation was an element of the cult at Samothrace. Herodotus implies that he himself had been initiated into the cult, and we have the inscriptions from the Roman period erected by individuals and listing the names of those who had become *mystai* and *epoptai*.[6] These terms, and indeed the word *mysteria*, were probably taken over at some point from the vocabulary of Eleusis, and it is possible that aspects of the initiation itself developed over time under the influence of other mystery cults. Most reconstructions of what happened in the mysteries assume that events took place in more than one building on the site, and we are not sure what was done before these buildings were erected.

Nonetheless we can identify significant differences between initiation at Eleusis and at Samothrace. The most obvious of these is that initiation at Eleusis happened once a year as part of a city festival, with initiates returning to complete the process in a later year, whereas, at least in the period for which we have evidence, initiation could take place in Samothrace at any time of year. Given the difficulties involved in getting to the island, compared with Eleusis, it seems unlikely that there would ever have been a large-scale annual festival involving initiates from outside Samothrace, so initiation was probably always something that could be experienced by arrangement. It seems likely too that initiates could pass through the stages of initiation over a short time – possibly in a single night – rather than waiting a year or more.[7]

Three buildings in the sanctuary are similar in form to the Telesterion at Eleusis and may have been used for rituals that required secrecy. These are the buildings referred to as the Hieron [plate VI], the Anaktoron [31] and the Hall of the Choral Dancers [32]. The Hieron is so-called because an inscription was found nearby, saying 'The uninitiated may not enter the Hieron', but the excavators are not certain that the inscription was originally put up near that building. Another inscription, found near the so-called Anaktoron but again not necessarily originally from there, states, in Greek, 'The uninitiated may not enter', and, in Latin, 'Those who have not accepted the rites of the gods may not enter' [33]. It has been sug-

gested that non-initiates were excluded from the sanctuary as a whole, but this would require, for example, that every sacred ambassador from abroad would have to be initiated before they could fulfil their responsibilities. The presence of a theatre also implies that large numbers of people were expected to meet at the sanctuary. It is reasonable to suppose that most Samothracians underwent initiation at some point, as with Athens and the Eleusinian Mysteries, but a sanctuary boasting the international profile of Samothrace in the Hellenistic period must have been accessible to non-initiates as well. It is certainly possible that the inscriptions did belong with one or two specific buildings, or perhaps an area within the sanctuary. The buildings were named by the excavators, and it is quite possible that the Hall of the Choral Dancers rather than either of the others was the heart of the sanctuary and the site of the celebration of the mysteries.

33 An inscription excluding non-initiates from some parts of the sanctuary. It is written in Latin and Greek, indicating the frequent visits of Roman officials to seek initiation at Samothrace.

We have no accounts of initiation at Samothrace, nor even any hints about what it involved. From antiquity the Great Gods have been identified with other groups of gods, including those known as the Kabeiroi and the Corybantes, and there have been attempts to use information about these cults to reconstruct what might have happened at Samothrace, but this identification is not straightforward. Herodotus says about the island:

> Samothrace was formerly inhabited by those Pelasgians who came to live among the Athenians, and it is from them that the Samothracians take their rites. The Athenians, then, were the first Greeks to make images of Hermes with an erect phallus, a practice which they learned from the Pelasgians. The Pelasgians told a certain *hieros logos* [sacred tale] about this, which is shown in the mysteries in Samothrace.[8]

The reference to statues with erect phalluses is taken to refer to herms, statues of Hermes that took the form of a square column with a head of Hermes at the top and an erect phallus on the front [34]. No 'sacred tale' survives from Samothrace, but the Greek word used, *dedêlôtai*, suggests displaying something rather than using words.

Diodorus Siculus in his discussion of the mysteries links them to the myth of the marriage of Cadmus and Harmonia.[9] Harmonia lived on Samothrace, where Cadmus was searching for his sister Europa, who had been abducted by Zeus. In one version of this story Cadmus in turn abducted Harmonia, and one ancient source indicates that initiates at Samothrace searched for Harmonia, presumably in the way that initiates at Eleusis searched for Persephone.[10] However, Diodorus says nothing about any abduction. The fullest surviving version of the story of Cadmus and Harmonia comes from Nonnus's *Dionysiaca*, an epic poem of the fifth century AD. In this version Zeus tells Electra, Harmonia's foster mother, that Harmonia must marry Cadmus; after initial reluctance, Harmonia agrees.[11] Elements of this story, most obviously the decision of Zeus to force a girl into marriage, have parallels with the story of the Rape of Persephone, and the notion that it was a significant part of the Samothracian ritual may be the result of Eleusinian influence, either on the mysteries themselves or on their interpretations.

In order to get any further in our understanding of the rites on Samothrace we must address the question of the identity of the Great Gods, and before we do that we need to turn to the other cult that is the subject of this chapter, that of the Kabeiroi.

Cult of the Kabeiroi

Two places have been excavated where sanctuaries dedicated to the Kabeiroi show evidence of initiatory activity, one on Lemnos and the other in Boeotia, west of Thebes. There was probably a further sanctuary on the island of Imbros, near Lemnos and Samothrace.[12] On the island of Delos a small sanctuary is dedicated to the Kabeiroi along with other gods, which will be discussed later, but there is no evidence of initiation. There are a number of other places where the Kabeiroi may have received cult worship of some kind, and where their image appears on coins (see below p. 66). We will concentrate on Lemnos and Boeotia, since we can be confident that mystery cult rites occurred there. There are some similarities in the development of these two sanctuaries, although, as we will see, there may have been relatively little contact between them.[13]

34 An Athenian Herm. These representations of the god Hermes were erected in Athens from the late sixth century BC on.

Lemnos

The archaeological excavations at the Kabeirion at Lemnos are still in the process of publication, but enough is known to give a broad history of the cult [35]. The evidence suggests that cult activity dates back to the sixth century BC, but there was a significant development around 200 BC, when a large building, named the Telesterion by excavators, was begun. Although never finished, it was used for the following four centuries until a similar but smaller building (called the Late Antique Telesterion) was erected nearby, which seems to have taken over its function. The form of these buildings is similar to those on Samothrace and in Eleusis, and they appear intended for people to gather inside them, hidden from the view of those outside. But it is clear that initiation predated the construction of the earlier Telesterion, and there are inscriptions referring to meetings of the 'assembly of the initiates' going back to the fourth century BC. It seems likely that the mysteries took place once a year, and that the 'assembly of the initiates' oversaw the operation of the festival – or at least reviewed it afterwards. This is the same pattern as at Eleusis, and the role of the

35 The Kabeirion on Lemnos. Evidence for sixth-century activity at the sanctuary comes from excavations in the area, to the right of the centre of the photograph. Behind and to the left is the site of the Telesterion of c. 200 BC.

36 An aerial view of the Kabeirion on Lemnos. Part of the Telesterion of 200 BC can be seen on the left, while the later, smaller, Roman building is in the centre. Both structures have similarities to the buildings on Samothrace.

assembly of initiates is similar to that of the Athenian Council which met on the day following the Eleusinian Mysteries. The similarity of procedure reflects the fact that Lemnos was under Athenian control for most of the Classical period. Vases dedicated to the Kabeiroi were found at the site, but nothing that reveals anything about them. We do not know what happened at the festival, beyond the fact of initiation. We have no descriptions and nothing on which even to base speculation [36].[14]

Boeotia

If we turn to the Boeotian Kabeirion we find a better published excavation, with more scholarly interpretation, but information about cult activity is still limited. The site is in the folds of low hills west of Thebes. There are dedications from the late sixth century BC, and the earliest buildings on the site are dated to around 500 BC. They are relatively small circular buildings which appear to have been used for seated dining, and there is also a rectangular building where diners could recline. After the earliest buildings were demolished, these functions continued in later buildings of similar form in the sanctuary. The site seems originally to have incorporated an oval hollow, the basis of the later stone theatre. At first the focus of the site appears to have been on this area, and in particular the exposed rock formation at the top of the cavea, where the spectators sat according to their place in the social hierarchy [37]. In 335 BC the city of Thebes was sacked by Alexander the Great, and the destruction of the city must have interrupted cult activity at the Kabeirion. Thebes was refounded in 315 BC, which seems to have led to a major rebuilding of the sanctuary in the following years. Then, in the later third century BC, a building named the Anaktoron by the excavators was erected in the middle of the theatre area, similar in form and date to the one erected on Lemnos. The theatre area was rebuilt in the second half of the first century BC, and the Anaktoron a century later. The site was still functioning into the fourth century AD [38].[15]

Pausanias mentions the site, but as with the sanctuary at Eleusis he declines to give any description:

> Advancing from here twenty-five stades you come to a grove of Demeter Kabeiraia and Kore. The initiated are permitted to enter it. The sanctuary of the Kabeiroi is some seven stades distant from this grove. I must ask the curious to forgive me if I keep silence as to who the Kabeiroi are, and what is the nature of the ritual performed in honour of them and of the Mother.[16]

We get what might be a description of the sanctuary from the Roman poet Ovid in his great poem *Metamorphoses*, written early in the first century AD. *Metamorphoses* retells many Greek myths and, in a sequence of stories largely about unfortunate lovers, he tells the story of Atalanta and Hippomenes. This is presented as part of a song sung by Orpheus (whom we will meet later), who in turn puts words into the mouth of Venus, the goddess of Love:

> They were passing near to a temple, deep in the forest,
> which once the hero Echion, fulfilling a vow, had built
> to Cybele, Mother of the Gods. Their journey had made them tired
> and they needed to rest awhile. It was here that, excited by me,
> Hippomenes felt an untimely urge to make love to his wife.
> Quite close to the temple they managed to find a shelter like a cave,
> dimly lit and covered above with natural limestone.
> The place was hallowed by ancient worship and filled with the numerous
> wooden statues of the old gods that the priests had left there.[17]

We shall come back to these references in both authors to the Mother, and the statues of the 'old gods' are also interesting.

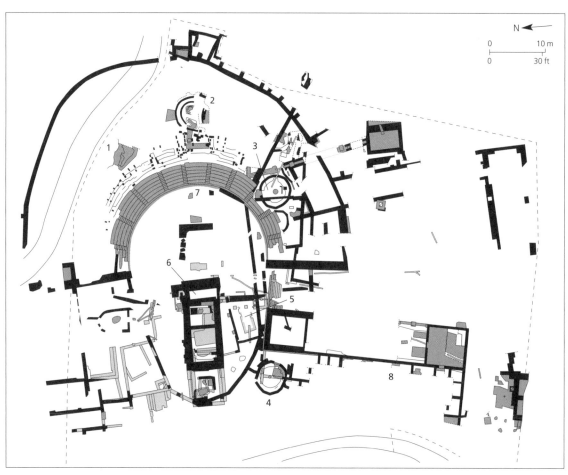

OPPOSITE
37 The theatre area at the Theban Kabeirion.
Visible near the top is the outcrop of rock
that appears to have been an original focus
for the sanctuary.

Dedications at the Boeotian Kabeirion are rather more informative than those from Lemnos, because they include images. From the Archaic period there are lead and bronze statuettes of bulls, the earliest dating probably to the last quarter of the sixth century BC, or possibly earlier [39]. Dedications of bulls continue in the fifth century BC, but terracotta replaces metal as their material. Glass beads are also common dedications. But the most interesting dedications from the Classical period are of black-figure pottery known as Kabirion ware.

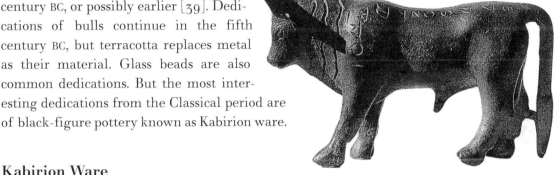

Kabirion Ware

A distinctive kind of decorated pottery has been found at the Kabeirion, as well as some examples from elsewhere such as Boeotian tombs, and at other local sanctuaries. These pots, which range in shape, are frequently decorated with scenes showing caricatured figures engaged in various activities, often involving alcohol. They date from the mid-fifth to the later fourth centuries BC, that is, up to the time of the destruction of Thebes by Alexander, and probably later.[18]

On most of these pots are human-like figures with exaggerated features, and these may be what Ovid had in mind when he described the statues of the 'old gods'. In one example we have a cart drawn by a donkey with what looks like a married couple sitting on it, accompanied by various other figures [40]. Others seem to be versions of scenes from myth, including several that might be associated with the *Odyssey* [41, 42]. These images resemble scenes of revelry in honour of Dionysus found on some Athenian pottery, which depict actors dressed in padded costumes.

It has been argued that these pots represent scenes from the mysteries performed in the Kabeirion. One pot shows a figure wearing a veil, who, it has been suggested, is a blindfolded initiate [43].[19] The donkey cart has been read as a scene from a mystic wedding. On the other hand, the fact that such pots have been found outside the sanctuary suggests that they would not show rituals that were supposed to remain secret. The resemblance to images of dramatic festivals points to another possibility. At the time the pots were made, the theatre seems to have been one of the most

OPPOSITE
38 Plan of the Theban Kabeirion.

1 outcrop of rock

2, 3, 4 early round buildings

5 early rectangular building

6 Anaktoron

7 theatre

8 later dining rooms

ABOVE
39 Bronze statuette of a bull dedicated at the Theban Kabeirion.

40 A wedding scene on a vase of Kabirion ware. Several of the figures are wearing wreaths and fillets, suggesting some kind of festival, but it is not certain how this picture relates to the mysteries of the Kabeiroi, if indeed it does.

41 Odysseus at sea on a raft made of wine amphorae. This is clearly a comic image, made more so by Odysseus's apparently padded costume.

42 A woman by a loom prepares a drink for an armed man. This is from the same vase as fig. 59 and is most likely to represent Odysseus's wife Penelope. Both images may relate to a comic drama.

BELOW
43 A scene from a vessel of Kabirion ware including a veiled figure (far left).

important features of the sanctuary, and it may well have been the site for performances of some kind. It is possible that the scenes involving grotesque figures are actually depictions of performances of comic drama or mime of some kind, which may have been open to non-initiates.

Some pots show a bearded reclining figure with a cup in his hand, surrounded by vines, who looks very similar to Dionysus. On one pot, however, this figure is identified as Kabiros, who is accompanied by a youth identified as Pais, that is, 'son' [44]. It is generally accepted that Kabiros and his son are the plural Kabeiroi of this sanctuary. Another vase shows a different pair of gods, identifiable as Hermes and Pan (son of Hermes), and they may also have been considered to be the two Kabeiroi [45]. This returns us to the question of who the Kabeiroi were – or who they were thought to be.

44 The names of the individuals on this broken pot were written by them. They include Kabiros (who looks like Dionysus) and Pais ('Son') next to him.

45 A now missing vase showed, on the left, figures with the appearance of Hermes (bearded, as befits his position as a father) and Pan, his son, with a third (female) figure. It has been suggested that this is another representation of the Kabeiroi.

Who were the Kabeiroi?

It is very clear from the literary evidence that there was no agreement about the identity of the Kabeiroi. It is not even clear how many there were. As we have already seen, Pausanias gives the impression that he knows who the Kabeiroi are, although he declines to reveal it to his readers. But then in fact he goes on to give a kind of answer:

> They say that once there was in this place a city, with inhabitants called Kabeiroi; and that Demeter came to know Prometheus, one of the Kabeiroi, and Etnaeus his son, and entrusted something to their keeping. What was entrusted to them, and what happened to it, seemed to me a sin to put into writing, but at any rate the rites are a gift of Demeter to the Kabeiroi.[20]

In this version the Kabeiroi are humans, and the mysteries are actually in honour of Demeter. In his previous paragraph the rites had been in honour of the Kabeiroi and the Mother. It would seem from Pausanias's text that he himself had been initiated at the Theban Kabeirion. The fact that his discussion of it appears rather incoherent suggests that, even so, he has not been given a clear answer to the question of what the cult was about. However, his two versions can be reconciled to some extent: the mysteries appear to involve a mother goddess (either the Mother or Demeter) and subordinate figures, the Kabeiroi, who are either divinities of some kind or the father and son who are honoured for establishing the mysteries in the distant past. The evidence of the pottery, with the depiction of Kabiros and Pais, would support the notion of two Kabeiroi, father and son, even if they appear not to be known as Prometheus and Etnaeus. As well as the two Kabeiroi and the Mother/Demeter, there may also have been a fourth figure: an inscription on a pot from an early building on the site refers to 'the Spouse', who might have been the partner of the Mother but perhaps disappeared from consideration before the Classical period.

The rather puzzling situation in Boeotia is made more puzzling by the literary evidence about the cult on Lemnos. The geographer Strabo, writing at the end of the first century BC and the beginning of the first century AD, quotes earlier writers as saying that there were three male Kabeiroi and three female Kabeirides. Other writers give them two names and still others, who thought that the Kabeiroi and the Great Gods of Samothrace were the same, give the names of four Kabeiroi. Faced with this apparent confusion, we can in fact draw a clear conclusion – that is, that no one ever knew how many Kabeiroi there were. We will return to the implications of this point later, but even if we do not know the number, or the names, of the Kabeiroi, we can draw some conclusions about the cult itself.

First there is the name Kabeiroi. Various suggestions have been given for the name, which is not of Greek origin. The most usually accepted is that it relates to the semitic word *kabir*, meaning lord. But it has been claimed that the derivation is etymologically impossible, and an alternative suggestion is that it is an Indo-European pre-Greek word of unknown meaning. This alternative would make it likely that the term came from Asia Minor, which would fit with the idea that the cult started in the northwest Aegean as, according to Strabo, 'the Kabeiroi are most honoured in Imbros and Lemnos, but they are also honoured in separate cities of the Troad; their names, however, are kept secret'.[21] It would follow that the cult spread from this area to Boeotia, and in fact the earliest material from the Boeotian Kabeirion is probably a little later than the earliest known from Lemnos. The names Pausanias gives for the founders of the Boeotian cult are also suggestive of links to Lemnos. Prometheus is the name of the Titan who stole fire to give it to mankind, and he is supposed to have stolen it from the volcano on Lemnos, where the god Hephaestus had his forge; his son, Etnaeus, is named after a volcano, Mount Etna in Sicily. Possibly the cult of the Kabeiroi was brought at some point in the sixth century BC from the northwest Aegean to Boeotia. The dramatic elements illustrated on Kabirion ware, for which there is no evidence from Lemnos, could then have been introduced by Boeotian worshippers as a way of publicly honouring the gods, rather than as part of the secret rites of the mysteries.[22]

Who were the Great Gods of Samothrace?

In his brief discussion of the mysteries of Samothrace, at one point Herodotus says, 'Whoever has been initiated into the rites of the Kabeiroi, which the Samothracians learned from the Pelasgians and now practise, understands what my meaning is.'[23] Clearly, then, Herodotus had himself been initiated at Samothrace and believed that the mysteries there were in honour of the Kabeiroi. In an anonymous commentary on the *Argonautica*, the epic poem about the voyage of Jason and the Argonauts written by Apollonius of Rhodes in the third century BC, we are told:

> The initiation at Samothrace is into the cult of the Kabeiroi, as Mnaseas says, and the names of the gods, four in number, are Axieros, Axiokersa, Axiokersos. Axieros is Demeter, Axiokersa is Persephone and Axiokersos Hades. Kasmilos, who is added as a fourth, is Hermes, as Dionysodorus relates.[24]

On the basis of this, the excavators of the sanctuary at Samothrace along with most other scholars have assumed that the Great Gods of Samothrace were identical to the Kabeiroi.

However, there are significant problems with this identification. For a start, there is no evidence from Samothrace itself identifying the Great Gods with the Kabeiroi. On the island, the Gods are referred to as *Megaloi Theoi*, 'Great Gods', in all the inscriptions, never as Kabeiroi. We also have the comment of Strabo:

> Many writers have identified the gods worshipped in Samothrace with the Kabeiroi (although they cannot even say who the Kabeiroi themselves are), just as they do the Kyrbantes and Corybantes and likewise Couretes and Idaean Dactyls.[25]

The implication is that such identifications are of questionable reliability.

The four names provided by Mnaseas and Dionysodorus may be non-Greek in origin, which would fit with the non-Greek origin claimed for both the Kabeiroi and the Great Gods, and it is possible that these were names actually used on Samothrace, although they do not appear in any inscription. The name Kasmilos, also spelled Kadmilos, has been associated with Cadmus, who, as we saw earlier, was said to have been married on Samothrace, but there is no simple explanation of this link. The names have also been taken to refer to Demeter, Persephone, Hades and Hermes, but this looks like an attempt to interpret the mysteries on Samothrace in the light of the Eleusinian Mysteries, rather than being based on any local knowledge.

But if Herodotus had actually been initiated at Samothrace, how could he be wrong on such a basic point about the cult? In answering this question, we will address issues important for our understanding not only of mystery cults but of Greek religion in general.

Identifying the Gods

In his discussion of the antiquity of Egyptian religion, Herodotus says:

> But whence each of the gods came to be, or whether all had always been, and how they appeared in form, the Greeks did not know until yesterday or the day before, so to speak; for I suppose Hesiod and Homer flourished not more than four hundred years earlier than I; and these are the ones who taught the Greeks the family history of the gods, and gave the gods their names, and determined their spheres and functions, and described their forms.[26]

What the Greeks know about the gods, Herodotus is saying, comes from the poetry of Hesiod and Homer, in which he may be including the Homeric Hymns as well as the *Iliad* and *Odyssey*.

As an explanation for how the Olympian gods were usually depicted in art and described in poetry, this is a reasonable statement, but it is clear that Greek cities paid cult tribute to many gods who do not appear in these poems, and in particular to gods, both singular and in groups, who did not have names at all as we would understand them. One example of this, Meter, or *Meter Theôn*, the Mother of the Gods, is the subject of a later chapter, but there are others, and in the next chapter we will look at the case of the Great Gods (or possibly Great Goddesses) of Andania. There are cults in Athens to 'the Hero' and 'the Healing Hero'. And there are also groups with a collective name but no individual identities, such as the Kabeiroi, Kyrbantes, Corybantes, Couretes and Idaean Dactyls mentioned by Strabo.

We might assume that the worshippers themselves must have known whom they were worshipping. It is usually taken for granted that the priesthoods would have had knowledge that they might offer or withhold, depending on the nature of the cult. It would seem obvious perhaps that in the case of mystery cults this kind of knowledge was precisely what was kept secret and passed down to initiates. So, for example, Pausanias can say of the cult of *Despoina* ('the Mistress') at Lycosura in Arcadia, which we will examine in the next chapter, that her name is not told to non-initiates.[27] But as we have seen in the case of Eleusis, the secret parts of the rituals do not seem to be concerned with the transmission of information. And in the case of Samothrace, Herodotus does not seem to be prevented from indicating his belief that the Great Gods of Samothrace are the same as the Kabeiroi – probably because he did not learn this in the ceremonies.

Gods without Myths

An alternative explanation for the lack of information about these gods and groups of gods is that nobody knew very much about them. For the Greeks who paid them cult worship, the gods had a real existence, but they were also invisible and did not usually communicate directly with mortals. Greek communities did not choose their gods on the basis of what they read in poems, but found gods in the places they inhabited. They might sometimes guess what some of those gods might be called, and how they should be worshipped. But there were also gods who could not be identified and about whom therefore stories could not be told. These are effectively gods without myths.

Some people, Herodotus among them, were interested in gods and religion and were well travelled. They might be expected to be interested in discussing such matters with the people they met in their travels and then to draw their own conclusions about the cult practices they witnessed. It is not unlikely that Herodotus noticed similarities between what he saw of the cult of the Kabeiroi and the cult on Samothrace, and himself made the connection between the Great Gods and the Kabeiroi: we need not assume that he was told this by anyone on the island.[28]

Kabeiroi, Great Gods and Dioscuri

We find other evidence for uncertainty about the identity of these nameless gods. A sanctuary on the island of Delos was identified as the Kabeireion which later became referred to as the Samothrakeion. Its priests are referred to in inscriptions by a number of titles, of which the fullest is *Theôn Megalôn Samothrakôn Dioskourôn Kabeirôn*, 'priests of the Great Gods of Samothrace, the Dioscuri, the Kabeiroi'.[29] This should not, I think, be taken as implying that the Delians considered these three

groups to be the same: the middle group, the Dioscuri, or Youths of Zeus, were always identified as Castor and Polydeuces (or Pollux in Latin literature) and featured in mythological stories. Instead I think the line of names should be understood as 'Gods of this sanctuary, whether you be the Great Gods of Samothrace, or the Dioscuri, or the Kabeiroi': in other words, the Delians are not committing themselves to a definite identification of the gods worshipped there.

We have a further example of the association of the Kabeiroi with the Dioscuri in the form of coins from the island of Syros depicting two young male figures, each with a star on their heads. This is the usual iconography for the Dioscuri, who are associated with the constellation of Gemini, with its two brightest stars, Castor and Pollux, represented as the heads of the two brothers. But on the coins from Syros, the figures are accompanied by the legend *Theôn Kabeirôn Syriôn*, 'The Divine Kabeiroi of Syros' [46]. In the absence of a separate notion of who the Kabeiroi were, the people of Syros represented them as the more familiar Dioscuri. On the other hand, this linkage was not made by ancient writers: presumably for them the Dioscuri, associated with a large body of stories and no obvious connection with mysteries, were very different from the obscure, unhomeric Kabeiroi and Samothracian gods.[30]

46 A silver tetradrachm coin from the island of Syros.

Why did People seek Initiation on Samothrace?

The Great Gods of Samothrace shared with the Dioscuri a reputation for protecting those in danger, particularly when at sea.[31] This may have been a reason why some people took the trouble to go to the island, but it is unlikely to be the only one. As noted at the beginning of this chapter, Samothrace was an important regional sanctuary, and there were those who would have sought initiation in order to demonstrate their respect for the Great Gods. This is presumably why Philip II of Macedon took part in the mysteries. Others, like Herodotus, may have been interested in deepening their understanding of the cult. In the Roman period, magistrates may have been motivated by a desire to do what was expected of them along with a tourist's interest in the unusual.

One story that combines the elements of elite tourism and concern for safety is the account given by the Roman historian Tacitus nearly a century later of Germanicus's attempt to visit Samothrace in AD 18. Germanicus, who was heir to the emperor Tiberius and very popular, died suddenly in suspicious circumstances the following year. Tacitus presents Germanicus very much as a tourist, stopping at various points on a leisurely journey to take up a military command in Asia: he attempts to visit Samothrace but is prevented by unfavourable winds; he then visits

Troy, considered to be the mother city of Rome, and then the oracle of Apollo at Clarus.[32] Tacitus informs his readers that it was said at the time that the oracle foretold Germanicus's imminent death, and his failure to gain the protection of the Great Gods can be read as a further omen pointing in the same direction. The fact that he was kept away by the weather suggests that the gods themselves were conspiring to prevent him from reaching their sanctuary because they knew he was fated to die.

What were the Mysteries About?

We have seen at Eleusis that Demeter was associated with grain. Those who honoured the Eleusinian goddesses did so in the expectation of continuing good harvests. Similarly those who honoured the Great Gods of Samothrace would expect divine help when in danger on the sea. In neither case, however, is it clear why mystery rites should be seen as the way to achieve these ends. It is partly for this reason that scholars have looked for more profound themes in mystery cults, focusing in particular on their relationship to eschatology: mystery cults must offer something beyond normal mortal life.

But we do not find eschatological themes associated with the mysteries on Samothrace or those of the Kabeiroi, either on Lemnos or in Boeotia. As we have seen, this is not entirely due to our ignorance, but also to the ignorance of the Greeks themselves about the gods they were worshipping. And since they did not know much about whom they were worshipping, and could not therefore tell stories about them, it is difficult to see how they could have developed theological explanations for their mysteries. Rather, as with Eleusis, we should consider that it was the experience of being initiated itself that was fundamental to these cults.

There are elements that may have been common to all three cults – Herodotus mentions statues with erect phalluses when making the link between the Samothracian mysteries and the Kabeiroi;[33] at Samothrace the mysteries included someone reciting incomprehensible words, assumed then and now to belong to the language of the pre-Greek inhabitants from whom the rites were inherited.[34] The presumed non-Greek origins of the Kabeiroi make it likely that this was a feature of their cult as well. These elements are more likely to have disoriented the initiates than helped them to understand what was going on. We have no equivalent of the *Homeric Hymn to Demeter* to provide any context and, as we have seen, it is not likely that equivalent poems or stories existed.

If after this discussion we find ourselves without an explanation for these mysteries, that is perhaps appropriate. Even initiates were given none.

3 *Other Mystery Sanctuaries in the Greek World*

Eleusis and Samothrace were recognized in antiquity as the most important sites of mystery cult. As we have seen, Hellenistic kings, Roman magistrates and even emperors visited the sanctuaries and underwent initiation there. We also know the most about these places: they were written about when they existed, and they have since been excavated by archaeologists. But they were not the only sanctuaries where people went to be initiated. There were smaller sanctuaries in parts of the Greek world, of interest largely to local communities, where people were initiated and mysteries were revealed to them. In this chapter we will look at some of these less well-known sites of mystery cults. Some are known only from passing comments by ancient writers or inscriptions left by priests or initiates, but their existence shows that the great sanctuaries were only part of the picture. We will also see that there are areas of the Greek world in which no evidence has been found of mystery cults based in sanctuaries, and that too tells us something about them.[1]

The Andanian Mysteries

There is one cult about which we do have some detailed information. The Mysteries of Andania are mentioned by Pausanias and also in a long and detailed inscription. Between these sources we can learn a lot about the festival that surrounded the Mysteries, and something about what the mysteries might have involved.

Andania was a small city in Messenia in the southwest Peloponnese. Its exact site has not been established, but a long inscription, dating from 91 BC, was discovered in the area in 1858, and subsequently built into the door frame of the church in the village of Konstantinoi [47]. This gives detailed instructions about aspects of the celebration of mysteries in honour of the Great Gods of Andania. It seems that the festival was revived by a local benefactor, Mnasistratos, who donated books and chests: the chests are probably those used to hold sacred objects in the ceremonies, while the books may have included instructions on how to carry out the rituals.[2]

The inscription gives detailed instructions for the clothing of the participants in the ceremony, and about a procession:

> In the procession Mnasistratos is to lead the way, then comes the priest of the gods whose mysteries are being held, together with the priestess, then the director of the games, the priests of the sacrifices, and the flute players. After them the sacred virgins, as they are assigned by lot, draw the carts bearing the chests that contain the sacred things of the mysteries; then come the mistress of the banquet for the worship of Demeter and the assistants who have begun their duties, then the priestess of Demeter of the Hippodrome, then the priestess of Demeter in Aegila. Then come the *hierai* [holy women], one by one, as assigned by lot, then the *hieroi* [holy men], as assigned by the council of ten. The supervisor of the women is to appoint by lot the *hierai* and the virgins and is to be careful that they take their places in the procession as assigned by lot. Animals for sacrifice also are to be led in the procession, and they are to be sacrificed: a pregnant pig for Demeter, a ram for Hermes, a young pig for the Great Gods, a boar for Apollo Karneios, a sheep for Hagna.[3]

The procession also included women 'dressed in the manner of the gods', and the whole occasion must have been a very grand sight. The inscription goes on to talk about tents, which were presumably put up by individuals to stay in during the period of the festival: the inscription gives instructions about the provision of water and the collection of

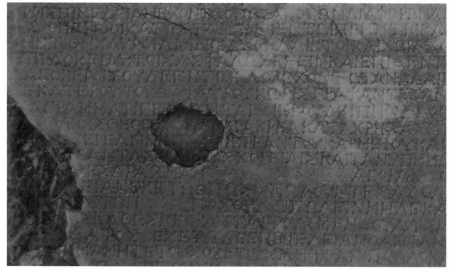

47 The Great Inscription from Andania. The text contains instructions for the administration of the festival accompanying the mysteries of the Great Gods. The writing is particularly fine and surprisingly small.

firewood. Musicians are to be hired to play for dances: 'as many capable performers on the flute and the lyre as they may find'. There are sacrifices and meals provided for the performers, and a market which presumably sold food and other goods for the general public – the supervisor of the market is given particular instructions about how much can be charged for offering people baths. The whole event has the air of an outdoor weekend music festival.

How long the festival lasted we are not told. We have a description of a similar festival, complete with tents and market, in honour of Isis in Tithorea in Phocis, in central Greece, which took place twice a year and lasted three days: the first in which the temple was prepared, the second in which market traders set up their stalls, and a final day in which a fair was held, with the sale of 'slaves, cattle of all kinds, clothes, silver and gold', and then participants gave animals to be led in procession and sacrificed, while the traders' stalls were heaped into a great pyre and set alight.[4] At some point in the festival in Andania mysteries were celebrated, which involved the initiation of men and women. Pausanias, writing later (see below), says that these took place in the 'grove of Karneios', and this place is mentioned several times in the inscription. All those present were expected to behave respectfully during the celebration of the mysteries and during the sacrifices, which suggests that, while clearly the initiated and the uninitiated were separated, everyone present was expected to know that the rites were taking place.

The Andanian Mysteries were still very much alive over two hundred years later when Pausanias visited the city. In his *Guide to Greece* Pausanias says that he considers the mysteries of Andania as second only to the Eleusinian Mysteries in sanctity, and implies that he was himself an initiate.[5] About their contents, as at Eleusis, he declines to reveal anything, but he does show that by his time the Mysteries had gained a regional status that is not hinted at in the earlier inscription.

Before 369 BC the territory of Messenia was under the control of neighbouring Sparta, and its inhabitants had been forced to turn a proportion of their produce over to their Spartan overlords. Messenians were required to live in small villages, and they had no urban centre. This situation changed in 371 BC, when the Spartans were defeated by a Theban army led by the general Epaminondas, who followed up the victory by marching into the Peloponnese and liberating the Messenians. As well as founding a new city, Messene, on the slopes of Mount Ithome, the Messenians also created a new past for themselves, developing stories about their national hero Aristomenes in a struggle against Sparta in the sixth century BC. Pausanias's description of Messenia includes detailed accounts of these stories [plate VIII].[6]

When Pausanias talks about the history of the Andanian Mysteries he makes no mention of any changes in 91 BC. As he tells the story, the mysteries were brought to Messenia from Eleusis at the time of Messenia's foundation in the mythical past. They were then refounded in the 360s BC after the restoration of Messenia, when Epaminondas was led by a dream to discover a bronze vessel, buried by Aristomenes himself, containing a scroll written on tin that gave the secrets of the mysteries.[7] Thus in Pausanias's time the mysteries were closely bound up with the history and identity of Messenia itself — a somewhat ironic development, since Messenia was by then no longer autonomous but just a region of the province of Achaea, part of the Roman empire. Pausanias probably picked up the story of the original foundation of the mysteries in Athens rather than Andania (see below). If the tin scroll found by Epaminondas in the fourth century BC had been part of the original story, one might have expected reference to it in the inscription from the first century BC, but although that refers to *biblia* — that is, books or scrolls, as provided by Mnasistratos — there is no more specific reference.

If we accept the view of some scholars, who argue that the festival was created for the first time just before 91 BC (or possibly revived after a long period, during which any memory of the rituals would have been lost), then it is an example of how a mystery cult develops over time. In 91 BC the Andanian Mysteries were a local affair. There is no mention of any sacred ambassadors being sent out to other cities to invite people to come and be initiated, as was the case with Eleusis. Special privileges are given to Mnasistratos and his family, very much as one would expect a local festival to honour its local benefactor. Two hundred years or so later, the festival is bound up with Messenian identity, and we may guess that its pretensions are much greater. But something else has happened. While the inscription shows that in 91 BC the mysteries were in honour of the Great Gods, Pausanias talks about the Great Goddesses and claims that these are the Eleusinian goddesses, Demeter and Kore (Persephone). Such a misunderstanding, if that is what it is, seems odd for one initiated into the Mysteries, although it is not difficult to see how it might happen. The priestess of Demeter occupies a prominent place in the procession at the Mysteries, and it seems that the gods are represented by two women. But Pausanias's stories about the origins of the mysteries suggest that the confusion is not his own. It seems rather that at some point during the previous two centuries the Andanians themselves had come to see their festival as honouring Demeter and Kore, a development we will also see elsewhere. Over time smaller cults seem to have been influenced by larger ones, resulting in the growing spread of a consensus about the purpose of mystery cults that is brought in from outside the local cultic community.[8]

Mysteries in Arcadia

Northeast of Messenia is Arcadia, the mountainous region of the central Peloponnese. From here we have evidence of a large number of mystery cults – mostly, but not all, said to be associated with Demeter. Most of our information about these cults comes from remarks made by Pausanias, although in a few cases we have inscriptions and even archaeological remains.[9] In several cases Pausanias suggests that they follow the practices of Eleusis although, as we have seen with Andania, Pausanias's explanations sometimes have to be treated with considerable caution.

48 A statue of Antinous from Delphi. Similar statues are found across the Roman empire, indicating the concern of the emperor Hadrian to promote his memory and his cult, which was celebrated widely.

Some of these cults invite further investigation. Pausanias mentions rites (*teletai*) in the Arcadian city of Mantineia in honour of Antinous, the lover of the emperor Hadrian, who died young (probably by drowning in the Nile) in AD 130 and was then declared a god [48].[10] Antinous's death resembled that of the Egyptian god Osiris, brother and husband of Isis (see Chapter 8); Pausanias also mentions that Antinous was born in Bithynia beyond the river Sangarius, a river associated with Attis, lover of the Mother of the Gods (see Chapter 4), who also died young. These parallels make some kind of mystery cult appropriate for Antinous, as well as adding to the religious status of Hadrian, the man whose 'consort' Antinous was.[11]

At Pheneus in northern Arcadia Pausanias talks about writings kept in some kind of stone container, and brought out to be read to the initiates at the 'Greater Mysteries' which were celebrated every other year.[12] It is possible that the books referred to in the inscription about the Andanian Mysteries served a similar purpose, but we know nothing of what the writings actually said. This is one of the cults which Pausanias claims is based on the Eleusinian Mysteries, but as we have seen, there is no suggestion that texts were read out at Eleusis.

Pausanias refers to a number of cults in honour of Demeter and Kore (Persephone), as at Eleusis, and even some rites for Kore alone, but he also mentions rites in honour of another daughter of Demeter, Despoina. Despoina means the mistress and is clearly a title like Kore (the maid). As we have seen, at Eleusis Demeter's daughter is referred to only as Kore, and her name, Persephone, is not used in public documents. The same applies to Despoina who, according to Pausanias, was the daughter of Poseidon and Demeter, and whose name was not to be spoken or written to the uninitiated.[13] It is from the cult at the village of Lycosura that we learn most about Despoina.

The Mysteries at Lycosura

Lycosura was a small community in southern Arcadia with a substantial sanctuary in honour of Despoina. Pausanias describes the sanctuary, which had a temple to Artemis Hegemone (Artemis the Leader) as well as a temple to Despoina and a portico with various statues in it. The temple of Despoina contained a cult statue with the figures of Demeter and Despoina carved from a single piece of stone, flanked by statues of Artemis and Anytus, who Pausanias explains as one of the Titans [49]. Next to the temple stood what Pausanias says was the hall (*megaron*) where the mysteries took place.[14] The site was excavated at the end of the nineteenth century and the temple of Despoina and the portico identified [50]. A further structure was identified by the excavators as the Megaron,

49 Reconstruction of the cult image from the temple of Despoina at Lycosura, created by the sculptor Damophon of Messene in the second century BC. The central figures represent Despoina, on the right, and her mother Demeter. Fragments of the sculpture were found by the excavators of the sanctuary.

50 The remains of the temple of Despoina at Lycosura, originally built in the fourth century BC. The cult statue group would have filled the rear area of the temple, to the left in the photograph.

although it was not well preserved. It has been reconstructed as a large altar with steps leading up to and around it, leading to a small portico above. It clearly has nothing in common with the Anaktoron at Eleusis and the similar buildings found on Samothrace and Lemnos.[15]

Despoina was associated with animals – in contrast to the normal association of Demeter and Persephone with grain. Pausanias describes an unusual form of sacrifice that took place at the Megaron. The Arcadians, he says:

> sacrifice to Despoina many victims unstintingly. Each of them sacrifices whatever he owns. But they do not cut the throats of the victims, as is done in other sacrifices; each person chops off a limb of the sacrifice, whichever happens to come to hand.[16]

This rather wild-sounding approach to sacrifice has been compared to the kind of slaughter associated with Dionysus (see Chapter 5); its scale and indiscriminate nature suggest that this is part of a major communal festival, perhaps not dissimilar to what took place at Andania and Tithoreia (see above). This sacrifice is distinguished from the Mysteries, which according to Pausanias are celebrated at the same place, but they may, as at Andania, have been part of the same festival. We have two sources of images for what may have been involved in the mysteries. The excavators found, in the area of the Megaron, terracotta figurines of men and women with animals' heads. Fragments of the cult statue also survive, and the veil of the figure of Despoina is decorated with a frieze that also depicts animal-headed figures, dancing and playing musical instruments [51]. The best explanation for these figures is that they depict individuals wearing animal masks, and presumably the dances were part of the celebration. At Andania the dances were part of the ceremony that was visible to all, and the same may well be true at Lycosura.[17]

51 Part of the frieze from the veil of the cult statue of Despoina.

Mystery Cults in Attica

We can complete our survey of mystery cults in mainland Greece by returning to Athens. Although they were by far the most important, the Eleusinian Mysteries were not the only mysteries celebrated in Athenian territory. There were mysteries celebrated in the village of Phlya in Attica as well. As at Eleusis, the officials at Phlya were drawn from a priestly family, in this case the Lycomidae, and some of the offices had the same titles as at Eleusis: there was a *dadoukhos* there. The cult probably dates back at least to the sixth century BC, but it may have changed over time, influenced in part by its more prestigious neighbour. The *dadoukhos* in Pausanias's time appears to have been interested in mystery cults more widely, and he is probably the person who told Pausanias about Andania (see above). Pausanias appears to assume that the mysteries were celebrated in honour of Demeter, as he did, perhaps wrongly, in Andania.[18]

Mystery Cults in Asia Minor

The Greek cities of Asia Minor were believed by their inhabitants to have been settled from the mainland. According to this tradition, which receives no clear support from archaeology, the cities of Ionia, the central part of the Asia Minor coastline from Phocaea to Miletus, were settled by Athenians. All the Greek cities were brought under the control of eastern kingdoms in the sixth century BC, first by the Lydians, then by the Persians when they conquered Lydia. Ideas of Greekness shared with the cities of the mainland grew in response to this lack of autonomy, and these were expressed in part through religion. At some point in the later sixth century BC a common sanctuary of Poseidon was set up by the Ionian cities, called the Panionion, and by the fifth century BC it was claimed that this cult dated back to the time of the Ionian settlement. By this time too a major Ionian festival was celebrated at Ephesus.[19]

One of the ways in which the Ionian cities emphasized their link with Athens was in their religious activities. The cults of the gods were similar to those in Athens, and this included an important role for Demeter. In the cities of Ionia Demeter is given a range of titles that link her to the harvest, such as *Karpotokos* (fruit-producing), *Karpotrophos* (fruit-nourishing) or *Karpophoros* (fruit-carrying), but her most common title is *Thesmophoros* (lawgiving or order-bringing). Although this last title seems to have nothing to do with the harvest, the Thesmophoria, the festival in honour of Demeter Thesmophoros that was held all over Greece, was related to agricultural fertility and associated with the story of Demeter and Persephone. These titles are not restricted to Ionia, but four of the Ionian cities – Ephesus, Erythrae, Miletus and Teos – also give

Demeter the title Eleusinia, making a direct link to the cult at Eleusis in Athens. In the cases of Miletus and Ephesus, stories are recorded claiming that the cult was introduced to these cities by descendants of the (mythical) kings of Athens. Herodotus also suggests a crucial role for the Milesian sanctuary in the defeat of Xerxes' invasion of Greece in 480–479 BC. The final naval battle of the Persian Wars was fought near Mycale, in Milesian territory, where the sanctuary of Demeter Eleusinia stood in sight of the battle. Herodotus says that the battle of Plataea, the final land battle of the campaign in mainland Greece, was fought on the same day, and also in sight of a sanctuary of Demeter Eleusinia. He emphasizes the coincidence and indicates that Demeter helped the Greeks win, precisely because the Persians burnt her sanctuary at Eleusis. Some of this story may have been improved in the retelling, but the link between Ionia and Eleusis is deliberate.[20]

Although the worship of Demeter was important in the Ionian cities, we have no certain evidence for any mystery cult in her name there in the Classical period. Asia Minor was an area where the cult of the Mother of the Gods was important (see Chapter 4), and there were festivals involving ecstatic activities associated with her. But things appear to have changed from the third century BC onwards, with the rise of rival Hellenistic monarchs. After the death of Alexander the Great, his generals fought for dominance in the eastern Mediterranean world, and one of the ways they expressed their rivalry was cultural. In Asia Minor it was the Attalids, rulers of Pergamum, who became the dominant power, and their rivalry with the Ptolemaic kings in Egypt had its effect on religion.

According to Tacitus, Ptolemy I invited Timotheus, a member of the Eumolpidae, one of the priestly families of Eleusis, to come to Alexandria in Egypt in order to introduce mysteries there.[21] There was a suburb of the city called Eleusis which supports the theory that mysteries were celebrated there as they were in Attica. The invitation to Timotheus appears to have been part of Ptolemy's aim of increasing the status of the city of Alexandria, and Athens was clearly one of the models he used.[22]

During the third century BC the rulers of Pergamum in Mysia, in northwestern Anatolia, grew increasingly powerful, and they began to expand their city along similar lines. Like the Ptolemies in Alexandria, the rulers of Pergamum established a library, and it was a sign of the long-lasting rivalry between the two cities that one of Mark Antony's gifts to Cleopatra, the last Ptolemaic ruler of Egypt, was the contents of the library of Pergamum, some 200,000 volumes: this was a symbolic, and short-lived, final victory for the library of Alexandria.[23] It is therefore unsurprising that evidence of mystery cult in Pergamum is along very similar lines to the Eleusinian Mysteries [plate VII]. The sanctuary has been excavated, and although it does not reveal where any initiations might have taken place, a number of inscriptions have been found recording dedications by individuals who held various cult titles that are also found at Eleusis, including Hierophant, *Dadoukhos* (torchbearer) and *Hierokeryx* (sacred herald). Although the inscriptions date from the time of the Roman empire, it is most likely that the cult dates back to the time of Pergamum's greatest power in the later third and second centuries BC. The title Eleusinia was not used in Pergamum, where Demeter's title was *Thesmophoros* or *Karpophoros*, but Pergamum, like Alexandria, was being built up as a city to resemble Athens.[24]

Pergamum was not the only Ionian city where mystery cults of Demeter appear in the Hellenistic or Roman periods. There are mysteries to Demeter *Karpophoros* and *Thesmophoros* at Ephesus, and inscriptions in Smyrna (modern Izmir) refer to the synod of initiates of the Great Goddess Demeter. Further north, in Cyzicus on the Propontis, there are Great Mysteries to the Saviour Maiden (Persephone) in addition to the cult of the Mother which we will look at in the next chapter. It is quite likely that some of these cults were modelled on what happened at Eleusis.[25] They were copies of older cult, rather than being themselves of any antiquity. The cities did not claim, as far as we know, that the mysteries were taught them directly by Demeter, but it was suggested that they were brought from Athens in the distant past, even if this was not quite true: as with Andania, the claim of antiquity increased the status of the cult.[26]

Mystery Cults in Sicily and Italy

Greeks started to settle in southern Italy and Sicily from the end of the eighth century BC. This is a time when the communities of mainland Greece and the Aegean were only beginning to develop into what are now called city-states, and the cities of Magna Graecia (Great Greece), as it was later described, could claim some antiquity. Places visited by Odysseus in the *Odyssey* were identified with sites in Sicily and Italy, and the hero Heracles was said to have travelled there, so it was not difficult for people to claim that other mythical events had also taken place. The cult of Demeter and Persephone was important throughout the area, with major sanctuaries set up in or outside the main cities. In some of these cults there is clear evidence of interest in the dead, and this has led scholars to assume that mystery cults were a major feature of the religious life of Magna Graecia. But while the cults were certainly important, they do not seem to have involved initiation on the model of Eleusis.[27]

52 Terracotta bust of Demeter dating from c. 510–500 BC, dedicated at her sanctuary at Predio Sola near Gela.

53 A metope (sculptural panel) of the sixth century BC from a temple in Selinus, possibly showing Malophorus and Pasicrateia.

There were a number of important cults of Demeter and Persephone in Sicily. A tradition held that Hades had risen from the earth in Sicily to capture Persephone: this was supposed to have happened either at a lake near the city of Enna or a spring near Syracuse. The Roman politician Cicero, writing in 70 BC, described Demeter and Persephone (he calls them by Roman names, Ceres and Libera) as patrons of the island of Sicily.[28] There were major sanctuaries of Demeter and Persephone in Gela, Syracuse and Acragas (modern Agrigento), all of which were established in the seventh or sixth centuries BC. Herodotus tells a story about how the first hereditary priest of Demeter and Persephone at Gela won his position by bringing the *hiera* (sacred objects) of Demeter to the city; Herodotus calls Demeter and Persephone *khthoniai theai* (underworld goddesses).[29] Excavation of one of the sanctuaries to the two goddesses at Gela has revealed the dedication there of terracotta busts of Demeter and also lamps, suggesting nocturnal rituals of some kind [52]. Another sanctuary contained a Thesmophorion, a place for celebrating the festival of the Thesmophoria.[30]

In the city of Selinus (modern Selinunte) in the west of the island was a major sanctuary dedicated to Malophorus, the Quince-bearer. Malophorus was accompanied by a younger goddess, Pasicrateia, and the two goddesses were identified with Demeter and Persephone [53]. In the fifth century BC the sanctuary began to look similar in some important ways to the sanctuary at Eleusis. There was a monumental gateway in the sanctuary wall, a well just outside, and a small temple to Hecate. Inside, however, there were some differences. There was a large altar and evidence of

large-scale animal sacrifice. A temple faced the altar and presumably held a cult statue. At some point the back of the temple was covered with mounds of sand, so that it appeared to be the entrance to the inside of a hill – a gateway to the underworld [54].[31]

Although the sanctuary at Selinus appears to have been deliberately modelled on that at Eleusis, it does not look like a place where a mystery cult took place. There is no Telesterion, and the sacrificial remains indicate that it was a place intended for public ceremonies, not exclusive initiations.

The cult of Demeter was prominent in the cities of southern Italy as well as in Sicily. There were sanctuaries in Tarentum, Metapontum, Croton, Medma, Locri and Posidonia (Paestum), and her head appears on coins in Laos, Petelia and Hipponion. Persephone is honoured alongside her mother in some cases, but as in Sicily, there is no evidence for initiation in any of these cities. Indeed, it is clear that Persephone/Kore in Italy could acquire a very different role from Kore in Eleusis.[32]

54 The sanctuary of Malophorus at Selinus. In the foreground is the monumental entrance built in the fifth century BC, with the well in front of it. Beyond the entrance, on the left of the photograph, is the temple which was made to look as if it was an entrance into the hillside behind.

55, 56 Two terracotta *pinakes* from Locri, dating to the first half of the fifth century BC. The first depicts Hades and Persephone. Persephone is holding a hen and stems of wheat, while Hades holds a *phiale* (a dish for libations) and a flowering branch of a tree. In the second a woman looks at a child within a basket. This may represent a baby being presented to Persephone.

Persephone in Locri

At first sight the cult of Persephone at Locri would appear to show links with Eleusis and mystery cults, because of the prominent position there of Hades. But in fact the evidence from Locri illustrates just how differently the story of the rape of Persephone could be treated. The city had a sanctuary dedicated specifically to Persephone, from which archaeologists have recovered a large number of terracotta plaques, referred to as *pinakes* (singular: *pinax*), with relief sculptures on them. They date from the sixth and fifth centuries BC.

Many of the *pinakes* are fragmentary, but it is possible to identify a number of different subjects. Some are scenes of women gathering fruit. Some show animals, presumably prepared for sacrifice, or items of furniture associated with cult, or scenes of people engaged in sacrifice and other rituals. Then there are scenes of abduction, usually showing a woman being carried into a chariot by a man: sometimes he is bearded, but in other cases he is a young man, without a beard. There are scenes of a woman dressing and doing her hair. There are wedding scenes, including a woman with a folded gown, processions and a young woman offering items to an older seated woman. And there are scenes showing the preparation of a bed, presumed to be part of a wedding ceremony. Other scenes show Persephone and Hades enthroned and receiving offerings from other gods [55]. There are also scenes of an older woman with a basket containing a child [56].[33]

There have been various attempts to interpret these scenes. Since some show parts of the story of the rape of Persephone, they might point to a cult similar to that at Eleusis or elsewhere, but in fact Demeter appears to play no role at all here. Instead, the seated woman who is being offered gifts by a young girl is recognized as Aphrodite – among the gifts she is given is a ball, an object associated particularly with her. It appears that Persephone's marriage to Hades is central to the images at Locri, not her abduction, and certainly not her restoration to her mother. There is no suggestion that Persephone is unhappy. There is some similarity with Eleusis in a link with fertility, shown in the scenes of fruit gathering and in scenes of Hades and Persephone together, where Hades holds a stem of wheat. Here fertility is linked with marriage. The scenes showing an older woman with a baby in a basket belong in this context, if the child is being presented to Persephone: she is nourishing the fruits of marriage. Some of the scenes are set in the human world, some in the divine, and probably they reflect rituals that took place in the sanctuary, suggesting that the cult was of particular concern to women.[34]

Despite it being dedicated to Persephone, the sanctuary at Locri appears to have had no connection with any mystery cult. Even the presence of Hades on the *pinakes* does not necessarily reveal a concern with death. The main participants in the cult were not initiates, but all the women of the community. Certainly marriage can be considered a rite of passage, marking a profound change in the life of the bride, and this is brought out by the scenes of abduction, but the evidence from Locri shows that the story of Persephone was not always understood in terms of life and death. As we will see in Chapter 7, some individuals in southern Italy and Sicily were buried with gold tablets inscribed with words addressed to Persephone as Queen of the Underworld, but these are not associated with a specific sanctuary.

Sanctuaries and Mystery Cults in the Greek World

We can now draw an overall picture of mystery cults based in sanctuaries in the Greek world. Preeminent was Eleusis. In mainland Greece, and particularly in Arcadia, there were other sanctuaries where cults required the initiation of worshippers and the revelation to them of something otherwise kept secret. We can say little about their experience, although it is likely that it was somewhat similar to what took place at Eleusis. The mysteries generally belonged to goddesses and were usually linked to Demeter, although this link may have been the result of later interpretation, influenced by the prestige of the Eleusinian Mysteries.[35] There was also a separate group of mysteries, which we considered in

Chapter 2. These originated in the northeast Aegean area, in Lemnos and Samothrace, and involved nameless gods without myths. Their rites were assumed by Greek writers to have been learned from the pre-Greek inhabitants of the area. And when their rites were introduced to mainland Greece, in Boeotia, they appear to have been adapted to fit more closely with local practices.

There is little evidence for mystery cults based in sanctuaries elsewhere in the Greek world. There is no evidence of initiation in Thessaly or Macedonia,[36] or Crete, and as we have seen, there is none in Italy and Sicily. Mystery cults in honour of Demeter were created in Asia Minor in the Hellenistic period, but these were imitations of the Eleusinian Mysteries, and there is little to suggest that they were ever of major importance.

The idea that this kind of cult could not easily be recreated in new places is not surprising. It is a feature of rituals of the imagistic mode of religiosity discussed in the Introduction that they were not easily spread. Individuals could only be initiated at these sanctuaries once in a lifetime, and when the rite took place it was presumably a profound and dramatic experience. Part of the power of the experience lay in the antiquity of the sanctuary and the prestige it gained from a long tradition of initiation. Initiates would understand that the sanctuary was the very place where the power of the divinity or divinities had been revealed in the past and that they were following a tradition, even if the meaning or purpose of the rites was not explained.

It is possible that cults like these were common in earlier periods and that only a few survived into the seventh and sixth centuries BC, when they are first identifiable in the archaeological record. In that case, the practice of initiation might be very old, predating some other ritual practices that became normal later. But this is speculation. Whatever their origins, their importance lies in the profound religious experience they gave to their initiates.

4 *The Mother of the Gods*

Initiates into the cults we have looked at so far experienced a single transformative event that changed them for ever afterwards. There were other cults, however, where participants had repeated meetings with a god or goddess. These cults developed in the Greek world but later spread west to Italy, where they were viewed with some suspicion. Two cults in particular can be examined in detail: in the next chapter we will look at the worship of Dionysus, but first we will consider the worship of the Mother of the Gods.

Herodotus records a story about a prince from Scythia, to the north of the Black Sea, who travelled into Greek lands.

> The Scythians are strongly opposed to adopting foreign customs, even those of other of their own tribes, but especially those of the Greeks, as the stories of Anacharsis and also afterwards of Scyles proved [we will meet Scyles in Chapter 5]. When Anacharsis was coming back to the Scythian country after having seen much of the world in his travels and given many examples of his wisdom, he sailed through the Hellespont and put in at Cyzicus; where, finding the Cyzicenes celebrating the feast of the Mother of the Gods with great ceremony, he vowed to this same Mother that if he returned to his own country safe and sound he would sacrifice to her as he saw the Cyzicenes doing, and establish a nightly rite of worship. So when he came to Scythia, he hid himself in the country called Woodland (which is beside the Racetrack of Achilles, and is all overgrown with all kinds of trees); hiding there, Anacharsis, carrying a drum and hanging images about himself, celebrated the whole festival for the goddess.[1]

This story gives a glimpse of a cult that spread across the Mediterranean to the city of Rome itself. For Herodotus it was particularly Greek, but for the Romans the Great Mother of the Gods, Magna Mater in Latin, was their own mother through her association with Mount Ida near the city of Troy. According to legend Aeneas, ancestor of Romulus, the founder of Rome, came to Italy after the fall of Troy. This understanding of the cult reflects historical truth, as the origins of the cult can be traced back to Anatolia, where there was a tradition of worshipping mother goddesses.

Who was the Mother of the Gods?

The iconography of the Mother of the Gods developed through the sixth century and reached a more or less fixed form by around 500 BC. She is depicted in Greek art sitting on a throne; she has a *phiale*, a shallow dish used for libations, in her right hand, and a *tympanum*, a drum like a large tambourine, in her left; she usually has a lion beside her [57].[2] This image is instantly identifiable as the Mother, but there was no comparable consistency in identifying her with a named goddess.

The title Mother of the Gods could reasonably be given to a number of mythological figures. One possibility is Ge or Gaea, that is, Earth. In a poem attributed to the early sixth-century BC poet Solon, the earth is addressed

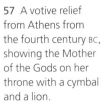

57 A votive relief from Athens from the fourth century BC, showing the Mother of the Gods on her throne with a cymbal and a lion.

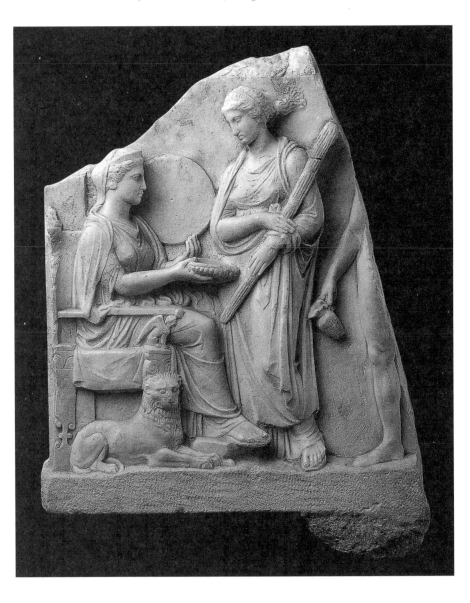

as 'Black Earth, the Great Mother of the Olympian Gods'.[3] But another candidate for Mother of the Gods was Rhea, sister and wife of Cronus, and mother of Zeus, Poseidon, Hades, Hera, Demeter and Hestia, as Hesiod presents her.[4] In a number of works of literature Rhea is named in contexts where rituals in honour of the Mother are clearly being described. Thus in Euripides' *Bacchae* Dionysus tells the chorus to 'take your drums, native instruments of the city of the Phrygians, the invention of mother Rhea and myself'.[5] A third Greek goddess associated with the Mother is Demeter, whose name contains the word Meter, mother. In another play of Euripides, *Helen*, the chorus describes 'the Mountain Mother of the Gods', riding on a chariot drawn by wild animals and followed by the sound of castanets, hunting for her stolen daughter: while the situation is clearly Demeter's loss of Persephone, the wild animals and the castanets belong only to the Mother of the Gods.[6] We also find an association between Demeter and the 'Mountain Mother' on a gold tablet found in a tomb in Thessaly (see Chapter 7). The pairing is striking as Demeter is more usually associated with plains where grain can grow.

The name most commonly associated with the Mother, however, is Cybele. The origins of the name are somewhat complex. There was a Phrygian cult of the Mother of the Mountains, *Matar Kubileya*, from which the Greek form *Meter Kybele* appears to derive [58]. There was also a separate Neo-Hittite goddess, likewise worshipped in western Anatolia, including at Sardis, capital of Lydia, called Kubaba, a name that was hellenized as Cybebe. Both these goddesses appear to lie behind the development of the Greek figure Cybele. The names occur in Greek poetry from the sixth century BC. Euripides has the chorus of *Bacchae* talk of 'great mother Cybele'.[7]

The apparent inconsistency in the identification of the Mother was not seen as problematic by poets like Euripides, who was happy to make different identifications in the same play. Philosophical or theological writers for whom such uncertainty was not acceptable could simply follow the words of the poets to their logical conclusion. Hence the author of the Derveni Papyrus (see Chapter 6), writing early in the fourth century BC, could say, 'Earth and the Mother and Rhea and Hera are the same.'[8] As we have already seen with other nameless divinities such as the Great Gods of Samothrace and Despoina, there is no reason to think that worshippers knew, or believed that they needed to know, the proper name of the object of their cult.

58 A terracotta votive for the Mother of the Gods from Gordium, in Phrygia, c. 200 BC. Although Phrygia was where the cult originated, this kind of image does not appear until after the cult had been established in the Greek world.

Cult of the Mother of the Gods

Herodotus's picture of the cult celebrated at Cyzicus is supported by one of the short Homeric Hymns, of uncertain date, addressed to the Mother of the Gods:

> Sing to me, clear-toned Muse, daughter of great Zeus, of the Mother of all gods and all human beings; she takes pleasure in the resounding of castanets and tympana and the roar of flutes, the cry of wolves and bright-eyed lions, the echoing mountains and the wooded glens. And so I salute you in song, and all the goddesses together.[9]

The Hymn describes a wild mountain setting, outside the city, just as Anacharsis held his private festival in woods, and emphasizes the role of music. This kind of ritual activity was also part of the worship of Dionysus, and we will explore it in more detail in the next chapter. There were, however, differences between the cult of the Mother of the Gods and that of Dionysus. On the one hand, the Mother was honoured as a protector of cities in a way Dionysus was not, and on the other she inspired in some of her devotees behaviour more excessive than anything historically associated with Dionysus. Before looking at these extreme acts of devotion, we will look at the way the Mother was worshipped by communities.

Cult at Cyzicus

Cyzicus, where Anacharsis witnessed the cult, was a major centre of worship of the Mother of the Gods. The city stood on a peninsula reaching into the Propontis (Sea of Marmara), on the slopes of a mountain known as Dindymon. There was another Mount Dindymon in the interior of Phrygia, in western Anatolia, the heartland of *Matar*-cult, and it is possible that Cyzicus was the first Greek city to adopt the cult.[10] In his third-century BC poem *Argonautica*, which tells the story of Jason and the Argonauts and their search for the Golden Fleece, Apollonius of Rhodes attributes the founding of the cult to Jason.[11] He was certainly following earlier traditions, and he goes on to describe the first celebration, managing to connect this Greek cult to its Phrygian origins:

> And with many prayers did Aeson's son [Jason] beseech the goddess to turn aside the stormy blasts as he poured libations on the blazing sacrifice; and at the same time by command of Orpheus the youths trod a measure dancing in full armour, and clashed with their swords on their shields, so that the ill-omened cry might be lost in the air, the wail which the people were still sending up in grief for their king. Hence from that time forward the Phrygians propitiate Rhea with the wheel and the drum.[12]

The cult in Cyzicus lasted for around a thousand years, and its importance to the city is reflected in the title *Meter Patroie* ('Ancestral Mother') given to the goddess.[13]

There has been archaeological work in the city,[14] but the principal sanctuary of the Mother of the Gods lay outside the city area, on the slopes of Mount Dindymon. Pausanias mentions that the cult statue there in his time, the second century AD, had been brought by the Cyzicenes from the nearby city of Proconessus, and was made of gold and hippopotamus ivory.[15]

The festival at Cyzicus clearly involved the community as a whole, rather than just a group of initiates. The literary accounts of the cult indicate that it took place in and around the sanctuary on Mount Dindymon. Like most city festivals, there will have been a central role for animal sacrifice. Apollonius mentions young men dancing in armour, and this was presumably a regular part of the festival: like the tambourine, this kind of dance seems particularly associated with the Mother of the Gods and her attendants. Music will have been created with flutes and drums, and this will have been loud and raucous – not the quieter music associated with the lyre. The poet Pindar, writing in the early fifth century BC but referring to his native Thebes rather than to Cyzicus, talks about girls singing at night to the Mother and to Pan.[16] Pan is himself associated with wildness and pipe music, and we may assume that women sang at Cyzicus too: they would certainly have keened during the sacrifices, as this was part of traditional Greek sacrificial ritual.[17] Major city festivals attracted visitors like Anacharsis and would have been considered an opportunity for travelling merchants to set up stalls and sell goods of all kinds. Altogether we can imagine a large and joyful celebration, full of movement and noise, with crowds spectating and joining in the activities.

59 A votive image of the Mother from Miletos, dating to the sixth century BC.

Cults in Other Cities in Asia Minor

Although we have no detailed accounts of the cults in Greek cities other than Cyzicus, it is clear that the cult of the Mother of the Gods was widespread in the Greek cities of Asia Minor. This is demonstrated by the presence of large numbers of dedications to her, sometimes in the form of *naiskoi*, small reliefs depicting a female figure in a shrine, which date from the early sixth century BC onwards.[18] The evidence of archaeology and epigraphy shows that there were city cults of the goddess in Chios, Clazomenae, Colophon, Cyme, Erythrae, Miletus and Phocaea [59].[19] In some cases, such as at Chios, the

Mother of the Gods was worshipped in a rural sanctuary, as at Cyzicus, but in Colophon, Erythrae and Smyrna temples to the Mother were built in the urban centre, and in Colophon copies of decisions of the city council were stored in the temple – as was the case at Athens, as we will see.[20]

From the third century BC the cult of the Mother became important in the cities of Ilium (on the site of Troy) and Pergamum in northwest Asia Minor. We will consider these cults later, because it was through them that the cult of the Mother came to Rome. First, however, we will consider cults elsewhere in Greece.

Cult of the Mother in Athens

The cult of the Mother of the Gods was introduced to Athens either at the end of the sixth century, or more probably in the later fifth century BC. The temple of the Mother, the Metroon, was established in the Athenian Agora, at the heart of the complex of administrative buildings there, and it became the location of the city archive [60], as it was at Colophon.[21]

The cult statue in Athens depicted the goddess seated with a lion and holding a tympanum [61], the symbols of her connections to the wild and to noisy worship. At the same time her role as guardian of the city's public records indicates that she was recognized as an ancestral figure, which, as mother of all gods, she was.

The only known Athenian festival in honour of the Mother of the Gods was called the Galaxia, named after a kind of barley porridge that was eaten in the festival. Other festivals associated with vegetarian food – as opposed to sacrificial meat – include the *Pyanopsia* in honour of Apollo, where bean stew was eaten, and the *Diasia* in honour of Zeus Meilichios (the Gracious), which involved non-meat sacrificial offerings. These appear to have been celebrated by local communities throughout Attica, rather than in the city itself.[22]

We do not know how the Galaxia was celebrated, but we do have one artwork from Athens that appears to depict small-scale ecstatic cult of the Mother. This is a vase painted in the early fifth century BC, depicting two seated divinities – or probably cult statues – surrounded by worshippers [62]. One of the two seated figures is a woman wearing a crown and holding a dish, and beside her is a small lion: she is clearly the Mother of the Gods. The male figure next to her is another god, possibly Dionysus, whom we will meet in the next chapter. He has snakes bound around his hair. In front of the gods is an altar with a fire on it. Next to the altar stands a woman carrying a covered basket on her head. She is most probably a priestess, and the basket may contain offerings to the gods to be offered on the altar. The other worshippers include three flute-players and a woman

ABOVE
60 The site of the Metroon, the temple of the Mother of the Gods in Athens.

61 A votive image of the Mother of the Gods on her throne, from Athens, fourth century BC.

62 The Mother of the Gods and a male god, possibly Dionysus, on an Athenian red-figure krater of the early fifth century BC. The gods are attended by two flute-players and a woman standing by an altar carrying a basket on her head.

BELOW
63, 64, 65 Details from the other side of the same vase showing worshippers dancing ecstatically. On the left are a man and a woman, holding snakes in their hands; in the centre two women play the flute and tambourine, while two young girls dance around them; on the right is a boy with snakes in his hair, between two women, one probably adolescent and one an adult, also holding snakes. In total there are twelve dancers and four musicians.

playing the tambourine, along with a man and a number of women and children who are dancing wildly [64, 65]. The dancers are holding snakes, and the man has snakes in his hair [63]. We have some evidence of snakes being handled in a number of ecstatic cults in Greece, and we will look at this phenomenon in more detail in the final chapter.[23]

The scene on the vase appears to depict a sanctuary of the Mother. The worshippers could be a family group or represent a larger community. Whether it represents a common scene from Athenian life or owes more to the painter's imagination is uncertain, but it does suggest that ecstatic worship of the Mother of the Gods was understood by Athenians, whether or not it was regularly practised.

Corybantic Mysteries

Another form of ecstatic worship known from Athens in this period was also associated with the Mother of the Gods. This is the cult of the Corybantes, who were attendants of the Mother.[24] In Erythrae in Asia Minor there was a formal cult of the Kyrbantes (taken to be another version of the name),[25] but they are also known in Athens.[26]

The Corybantes are mentioned quite frequently in Athenian literature from the fifth and fourth centuries BC, which suggests that the cult was well established.[27] The most specific description of what the cult involved comes from Plato, comparing the activities of two speakers in a dialogue to Corybantic ritual:

> They are doing the same things as in the *teletai* of the Corybantes, when they perform the *thronesis* [enthronement] around the person who is to be initiated. For there is dancing and playing, as you know if you have been initiated. And now these two are simply performing a choral dance around you, and as it were they are dancing in play, so that afterwards they can initiate you.[28]

The dancing presumably involved the playing of drums and flutes that we have seen was associated with the Mother of the Gods, and the initiate sitting in a throne may be in the position of the Mother herself, since she is always portrayed on a throne. In other passages the Corybantes are associated with madness: either people acting madly are compared to the Corybantes,[29] or Corybantic initiation is proposed as a cure for madness,[30] and this has led some scholars to conclude that the cult was primarily therapeutic in purpose. More often, however, the verb *korybantizo*, 'acting the Corybant', is used simply to mean wild dancing;[31] ecstatic cult in general, and indeed some kinds of music, are said to have curative powers.[32]

We do not know where in Athens Corybantic rites took place, although it would appear to be in private rather than in public, or how frequently, or among which part of the Athenian population, although some of the comments in Plato suggest that it might have been familiar to the wealthy people who generally populate his dialogues. But it clearly was another example of ecstatic worship known to Athenians.

Cult of the Mother in Hellenistic Greece

So far we have looked at the cult of the Mother of the Gods in the sixth,
fifth and fourth centuries BC. Inscriptions show cult continuing in the
cities we have already looked at, and elsewhere in mainland Greece [66],
but there were also new developments, most importantly in Asia Minor.

In the course of the third century BC, the city of Pergamum in northwest Asia Minor grew increasingly important. We have already seen that it
adopted the cult of Demeter, which imitated features of the Eleusinian
Mysteries, but it also had a number of important sanctuaries of the
Mother of the Gods, both in the city and in the surrounding countryside.
In the city she was known as Meter Megale, 'Great Mother', and her sanctuary, which has not been certainly identified, was known as the
Megalesion. There were also two sanctuaries in the surrounding hills,
where numerous terracotta dedications have been found. It seems likely
that here, as at Cyzicus, worship of the Mother generally took place in the
countryside.[33]

The third century BC also saw a new cult of the Mother of the Gods at
Ilium, the city that stood on the site of ancient Troy. There was a sanctuary in the city area and also on Mount Ida nearby, where she was
known as Meter Idaia.[34] By the later part of the century, Ilium had come
under the control of Pergamum. Meanwhile, in the course of the same
century, groups of Celts moved into central Anatolia, creating the region
of Galatia. Here, from the end of the century, the city of Pessinus developed as an important centre for the cult of the Mother of the Gods. During
the following century, as the power of Pergamum increased further,
Pessinus, like Ilium, came under its control, but this still lay in the future
when, in 205 BC, the Romans came to Pergamum in search of the Mother
of the Gods.[35]

The Mother of the Gods Comes to Rome

The story of the introduction of the cult of Magna Mater into Rome at the end of the third century BC is surrounded by considerable confusion, some of it ancient, some rather more recent. According to Livy:

> About this time [205 BC] a sudden wave of religious concern swept over the citizenry. The Sibylline Books had been consulted because it had rained stones that year more often than usual, and in the books a prophecy had been found that if ever a foreign enemy should invade Italy, he could be defeated and driven out if the Idaean Mother were brought from Pessinus to Rome.[36]

He goes on to say that a Roman delegation then came to Pergamum and enlisted the help of its ruler, Attalus, who escorted them to Pessinus, where the Romans were given the sacred stone that was the cult image of the Great Mother [67].[37] But, as we have noted, Pessinus was in Galatia, not at this time within the orbit of Pergamene power. The name of the

67 The temple of the Mother of the Gods at Pessinus. The remains of the temple visible now date from between 25 BC and c. AD 100, when the area was under Roman rule.

goddess also suggests a slightly different story. Her title in Rome is Magna Mater Deorum Idaea, or Mater Deum Magna Idaea, that is, the Great Mother of the Gods of Mount Ida, and there is no Mount Ida near Pessinus. As we have seen, at Pergamum the Mother was worshipped as Meter Megale, which in Latin is Magna Mater, and at Ilium she was Meter Idaia, or Mater Idaea in Latin. It seems most likely that the Roman poet Ovid was right, in his *Fasti*, to claim that the stone was brought from Mount Ida near Troy with Attalus's reluctant consent.[38]

Rome and Pergamum had no formal diplomatic relations at this point, but they shared a common enemy in the shape of the king of Macedon, Philip V; the transfer of a cult image from Pergamene territory to Rome may have suited Attalus for diplomatic reasons.[39] More importantly, Mount Ida, near the site of Troy, was the ancestral home of the Romans, through their descent from the Trojan Aeneas, and on that basis Magna Mater could be understood as the Romans' own mother. Livy says that her cult was introduced on the instructions of the Sibylline Books, which were recognized as the most ancient and venerable source of religious guidance for the Romans. Two stories relating to the actual arrival of the cult image in the city emphasize the honour and virtue of the goddess. One story tells how the ship carrying the stone ran aground and could not be moved until it was pulled free by the Vestal Virgin Claudia Quinta, who proved by doing this that she was a virtuous woman [68]. The other story is that the prophecies associated with bringing the goddess to Rome stated that she had to be welcomed by the best of the Romans, along with, in some versions, the matrons of Rome. Both stories emphasize the close relationship between the Mother and Roman women, and with ideas of virtue: this is a highly respectable cult.[40]

A temple was built for Magna Mater on a Palatine hill, in the heart of the city, and dedicated in 191 BC. Large quantities of terracotta votives to Magna Mater were dedicated there in the early years of the cult [70, 71]. In later centuries the dedications were grander [plate IX]. In 111 BC the temple was damaged by fire, and rebuilt [69]. At some point soon after the arrival of the cult a festival was introduced in her honour, called the Megalesia – another Pergamene term –

68 An altar dedicated to Magna Mater in the second century AD, with relief carving showing Claudia Quinta pulling free the ship on which the cult statue came to Rome.

MATRI DEVM ET NAVI SALVIAE
SALVIAE VOTO SVSCEPTO
CLAVDIA   SYNTHYCHE
        D   D

1 Magna Mater, originally dedicated in 191 BC.

2 Victoria Virgo, originally dedicated 193 BC.

3 Victory, originally dedicated 294 BC.

4 area where plays were performed during the Megalesia.

BELOW
70, 71 Terracotta images of Magna Mater (left) and of Attis (right), dedicated at the temple on the Palatine between 191 and 111 BC.

which soon lasted a week and included racing in the circus and other elements of a typically Roman festival.[41] However, the Anatolian origins of the cult were not ignored. The chief priest of the cult was known as the Sacerdos Phryx Magnus (Phrygian High Priest), and the sanctuary of the Mother of the Gods on the Vatican was known as the Phrygianum. On the other hand, the Roman Megalesia appears to have followed a typically Roman pattern and had little in common with the kind of festival we saw in Cyzicus. However, there were aspects to the cult that appear to have shocked some Roman observers and fascinated modern scholars. And it is to these that we now turn.

Eunuch Priests?

It is generally stated that Magna Mater at Rome was served by eunuch priests, known as Galli.[42] It is assumed that these eunuch priests arrived with the cult from Anatolia, and that eunuch priests were a usual feature of the cult of the Mother there [72].[43] It is assumed too that the castration of priests of the Mother lies behind myths about Attis, who is supposed to have castrated himself out of devotion for Cybele, that is, the Mother.[44]

There is no doubt that castration – in particular self-castration – was a feature of the worship of the Mother of the Gods, but most of these assumptions need to be reconsidered. To start with, there is no clear evidence that the priests of the Mother in Anatolia were ever eunuchs. It must be admitted that there is very little evidence about the organization of the cult in Phrygia in any case, but no Greek authors comment on it. Eunuchs and castration play no role in the formal cult of the Mother in the Greek world in the Classical period either. Priests of the Mother, in Anatolia and in the Greek world, were noted for their distinctive dress, which included a long loose gown hung with images.[45] This might be considered as effeminate, but it does not imply emasculation: Herodotus describes Anacharsis dressing in this way, but does not say that he castrated himself. There is a story of a priest of the Mother from Pessinus addressing the Roman senate in 102 BC. He was attacked by a tribune of the plebs, either as an imposter, or as a promoter of superstition, but not for being a eunuch, which might have been a more powerful objection to his being allowed to speak, if it were true.[46] We must look elsewhere for the origins of the tradition.

72 Silver figurine of a Phrygian priest of the Mother, c. 700 BC. The absence of a beard has led to the suggestion that he may be a eunuch.

Metragyrtai

There are various references in ancient literature to wandering devotees of the Mother of the Gods known as *metragyrtai*. An *agyrtes* was an itinerant religious figure. The term is used, pejoratively, by Plato in the *Republic* to describe travelling initiators or similar figures. In surviving literature the word *metragyrtes*, 'beggar for the Mother', first appears in the fourth century BC in fragments of comic poetry,[47] and in Aristotle's *Rhetoric*,[48] where *metragyrtai* are presented as the least honourable religious figures, in contrast with the *dadouchos*, one of the priests of the Eleusinian Mysteries, given as an example of the most honourable. The Byzantine lexicon-writer Photius tells a story set in Classical Athens about a *metragyrtes* being ultimately responsible for the introduction of the cult of the Mother of the Gods there.[49] The story is mentioned, rather more briefly, in the *Hymn to the Mother of the Gods*, a speech by the emperor Julian in the fourth century AD.[50] The word does not appear in inscriptions.

We are given a detailed, although again very negative, depiction of the activities of a *metragyrtes* in Apuleius's *Metamorphoses*, where we are introduced to a travelling priest of the so-called Syrian Goddess, also known as Atargatis, who shares some aspects of cult and myth with the Mother of the Gods. The figure in Apuleius is a eunuch, who leads a band of travelling players from village to village, performing music and dance, and collecting money from the audiences as they go. All this is done in honour of the Syrian Goddess, whose statue is carried by the troupe as they move on.[51] There is no reason to assume that all *metragytai* were eunuchs, but it does seem to be a common feature of the way they are described in literature.

Galli

More depictions of eunuchs and *metragyrtai* come in five poems collected in the Greek Anthology, an important compilation made in the tenth century AD of Greek epigrams dating back to the sixth century BC.[52] They were written in the late third or early second century BC — that is, the time when the cult of the Mother was introduced to Rome, and when it was beginning to gain importance at Pessinus — and tell the same story, of how a wandering devotee of the Mother of the Gods comes across a lion, and

73 A relief of the third century AD depicting an Archigallus making an offering of fruit in front of a statue of Magna Mater on her throne.

manages to scare it away with his tambourine and his noise and dancing. In the first and fifth of these poems, the man is called Gallus; in the second he is described as a *metragyrtes*; in the third he is called an *ithris anêr*, that is, a eunuch; in the fourth he is named Atys, and described as castrated. An additional poem doesn't mention the lion, but is a dedication by 'long-haired Gallus, newly gelded from Lydian Timolus'.[53] For these poets, then, the term *metragyrtes* was interchangeable with eunuch, or with the term Gallus.

The word Gallus is used in other literature to refer to devotees of the Mother of the Gods. The word itself probably simply means Gaul or Celt, and it was originally applied to the priests of the Mother in Pessinus and elsewhere.[54] As we have seen, there is no evidence to support the idea that these priests were eunuchs. In inscriptions from Rome from the second century AD we also find the term Archigallus used to refer to the chief priest of the cult of Magna Mater, and the names are clearly the names of citizens, who will certainly not have been eunuchs [73].[55]

However, in poetry the term is used specifically to refer to eunuchs. Galli are referred to by several Roman poets, generally with the suggestion that they were obsessed with sex, despite their condition. An example from Martial, writing in the late first century AD, gives an idea of the tone used:

> What, licking women down inside there, Gallus?
> The thing you should be sucking is a phallus.
> They cut your cock off, but not so to bed,
> Cunt-lover: what needs doctoring now's your head.
> For while your missing member can't but fail,
> Your tongue still breaks Cybele's rule: it's male.[56]

While the poem is obviously not about religion, it does refer to the Gallus's relationship with Cybele, that is, Magna Mater. Clearly even in Rome there was a connection between eunuchs and the cult of the Mother of the Gods. But this is not to say that eunuchs were a formal part of the cult.

Roman Cult Practices

The introduction of the cult of Magna Mater to Rome is one of several examples of new cults being officially adopted from abroad, and in particular from the Greek east. Roman writers nonetheless promoted a view that Roman religion remained free of contamination from outside. This tradition is reflected in some remarks of Dionysius of Halicarnassus, a Greek who wrote about Roman customs in the first century BC:

> Indeed, there is no tradition among the Romans either of Uranus being castrated by his own sons or of Cronus destroying his own offspring to secure himself from their attempts or of Zeus dethroning Cronus and confining his own father in the dungeon of Tartarus, or, indeed, of wars, wounds, or bonds of the gods, or of their servitude among men. And no festival is observed among them as a day of mourning or by the wearing of black garments and the beating of breasts and the lamentations of women because of the disappearance of deities, such as the Greeks perform in commemorating the rape of Persephone and the adventures of Dionysus and all the other things of like nature. And one will see among them, even though their manners are now corrupted, no ecstatic transports, no Corybantic frenzies, no begging under the colour of religion, no bacchanals or secret mysteries, no all-night vigils of men and women together in the temples, nor any other mummery of this kind; but alike in all their words and actions with respect to the gods a reverence is shown such as is seen among neither Greeks nor barbarians.[57]

We will see more evidence of a Roman distaste for bacchanals and nocturnal meetings in the next chapter, but it is the specific example that Dionysius goes on to give that concerns us here. Dionysius somewhat misleadingly implies that foreign cults were only introduced for the benefit of immigrants to Rome, emphasizing that the Romans never adopted such practices themselves:

> The rites of the Idaean goddess are a case in point; for the praetors perform sacrifices and celebrate games in her honour every year according to the Roman customs, but a Phrygian man and a Phrygian woman act as her priests, and it is they who carry her image in procession through the city, begging alms in her name according to their custom, and wearing figures upon their breasts and striking their timbrels while their followers play tunes upon their flutes in honour of the Mother of the Gods. But by a law and decree of the senate no native Roman walks in procession through the city arrayed in a parti-coloured robe, begging alms or escorted by flute-players, or worships the god with the Phrygian ceremonies. So cautious are they about admitting any foreign religious customs and so great is their aversion to all pompous display that is wanting in decorum.[58]

74 A funerary portrait of a priest of Magna Mater from Lanuvium near Rome, second century AD. Although there is no identifying inscription, the figure is depicted in robes decorated with cult objects associated with Magna Mater.

Here Dionysius contrasts the solemnity of the 'Roman' part of the cult with the noise, the dancing and the bright colours and strange dress of the 'foreign' element. Dionysius's contrast needs to be moderated somewhat. Despite his comments about castration just before this passage, he does not suggest that the priest was a eunuch, and by the early second century AD it is clear from inscriptions that the 'Phrygian' man and woman who were priests of Magna Mater might also be Roman citizens, and the evidence of funerary reliefs suggests that they probably did dress in robes decorated with images characteristic of the cult [74].[59] Nonetheless, Dionysius's account suggests that the cult of Magna Mater at Rome was not so different from cult elsewhere in the Mediterranean world.

Processions for the Mother of the Gods

75 A procession in Pompeii in honour of the Mother of the Gods. At the front of the procession the image of the Mother is carried on a litter.

Writing a generation or so before Dionysius, the Roman poet Lucretius describes how the image of the Mother is carried through many lands, accompanied by 'Phrygian bands', including self-castrated Galli, who dance to the accompaniment of cymbals, tambourines, pipes and horns, waving knives around.[60] A wall painting from Pompeii shows such a procession [75]. The Roman politician and philosopher Cicero in his *Laws*, written a little after Lucretius's poem, suggests that begging for alms

should be forbidden by law, but he makes an exception for 'servants of the Idaean Mother, and only on specified days'.[61] We have already seen a depiction of a travelling band begging for the Syrian Goddess in Apuleius's *Metamorphoses*; the Galli or *metragyrtai* in the Greek poems were also wandering figures, not based at a temple, and such individuals may have been the 'servants of the Idaean Mother', allowed to beg in Rome on certain days.

Therefore a distinction can be drawn between the permanent priesthood of Magna Mater at Rome and the other devotees who spent their time travelling around. We can imagine individuals and troupes of *metragyrtai* travelling from place to place through the year, begging for alms for the Mother. Their music and dancing would have made them something like a cross between a group of mendicant friars and a band of travelling players. When cities like Rome held their celebrations for the Mother of the Gods, and only then, these travelling bands would be able to enter the city and join the celebration, following the Roman image of Magna Mater through the street in the procession. It is among these itinerant devotees, not the state-organized priests, that self-castrated eunuchs would be found.

Castration for the Mother

Why did some men choose to castrate themselves as a form of devotion to the Mother of the Gods? The discussion so far has shown that it is highly unlikely that there was a requirement anywhere that priests or other formal cult officials of the Mother had to be castrated, and the emphasis in the sources is on voluntary self-castration. We cannot seek the origins of the practice in, or draw parallels with, the presence of eunuchs in royal courts, because castration there was not voluntary and served an identifiable administrative purpose.[62] The practice was certainly unacceptable for Roman citizens: we are told of a slave who castrated himself for the Mother being exiled from the city, while another eunuch devotee was denied an inheritance for the same reason.[63]

Modern psychological studies of self-castration tend to associate it with other forms of self-mutilation, interpreting the practice as a response to powerful feelings of anxiety or self-loathing. In early Christian writings self-castration is sometimes discussed, generally associated with extreme asceticism: men made themselves eunuchs so that they would not be tempted sexually — a form of reasoning which Martial for one would have questioned.[64] These approaches may help us make sense of the self-castration of devotees of the Mother, but we also have more closely related evidence, in the form of the story of Attis and Cybele.

Attis and Cybele

In Greek literature from the first century BC onwards there are a number of stories about Attis, who is presented as a devotee of the Mother of the Gods under her alternative name, Cybele. Some of these stories tell of the establishment of the cult of Cybele, but the best known, which exists in several versions, tells the story of how Attis loved Cybele, and how when he was unable to remain faithful to her alone, he castrated himself and then died. The story is usually set in Anatolia, but there is no reason to think that it is ancient. It probably developed in the Hellenistic period, to provide an explanation for self-castration in the cult of the Mother, although it contained some older elements.[65]

This is suggested by the fact that the earliest representations of Attis are found not in Anatolia, but in Greece, from the fourth century BC. There we find depictions of the Mother with an accompanying male god who is identified as Attis [76]. Attis was not the name of any Anatolian god, but it was used later as the name or title of one of the priests of the Mother at Pessinus. One explanation for his existence is that he was a personification of the ecstasy experienced by devotees of the Mother. We saw that the

76 Attis and Atargatis (a goddess who shared some features with the Mother of the Gods) on a fourth-century BC relief from Piraeus.

procession of the initiates to Eleusis was led by a representation of the Eleusinian Iacchus: 'Iacchus!' was supposed to be the ecstatic cry of the initiates, so the god was a personification of that ecstasy. In the same way we find cries of 'Attes!' associated with other ecstatic cults,[66] and thus a god Attis might be considered an appropriate companion for the Mother of the Gods.[67] The later stories about Attis maintain the link between Attis and ecstatic behaviour in honour of the Mother, but they focus on more violent expression.

The earliest surviving account of the story in which Attis castrates himself for Cybele is found in Ovid's poem *Fasti*, written at the very start of the first century AD. The story comes as part of the mythological background for the festival of the Megalesia. As Ovid tells the story, Cybele fell in love with Attis and he swore fidelity to her, but he then broke his oath by sleeping with a nymph. When she discovered this, Cybele killed the nymph, and Attis, in a fit of madness, castrated himself, claiming that his genitals were responsible for his breaking of the oath. Ovid ends his account by saying that this set a precedent for Attis's servants to castrate themselves and toss their long hair.[68] The Roman poet Catullus, writing fifty years earlier, refers to the story in a poem that depicts Attis becoming a *metragyrtes* as a result of his action (and changing at the same time from masculine to feminine gender in the Latin):

> Carried in a fast ship over profound seas
> Attis, eager and hurried, reached the Phrygian grove,
> The goddess's dark places, crowned with woodland.
> And there, exalted by amorous rage, his mind gone,
> He cut off his testicles with a sharp flint.
> While the ground was still spotted with fresh blood
> Quickly took in her snowy hands a tambourine
> Such as serves your initiates, Cybele, instead of a trumpet,
> And shaking the hollow calf-hide with delicate fingers,
> Quivering, she began to sing to the troop.[69]

Other versions of the story from the second century AD and later claim that Attis did not break his oath by choice but was forced into marriage with the daughter of the king of Pessinus, linking the story to the most famous centre of the worship of the Mother.[70] However, the story does not offer a direct explanation for the self-castration of devotees of the Mother: they are not straightforwardly following Attis's example, or trying to become Attis, because Attis's self-castration leads to his death, and that is clearly not the aim of the *metragyrtai*, even if in all likelihood many of those who did castrate themselves would have died almost immediately as a result. It is Attis's motivation that appears to provide the key.

Devotion to the Mother

Attis is presented as driven by sexual desire, but desire exclusively for
Cybele. This makes his action different from that of Christian ascetics
who attempted to escape from their own sexual urges. Insofar as *metragyrtai* were following Attis in castrating themselves, they were
demonstrating their commitment to the Mother alone, in an excessive
form of devotion. It is possible that this behaviour was stimulated by the
experience of taking part in ecstatic rites in honour of the Mother, such as
Anacharsis experienced in Cyzicus. That story emphasizes the powerful
effect that joining in a festival in her honour might have. But of course
self-mutilation is recognized as deviant or marginal behaviour, not
something that would attract most people who joined in such a festival.
Another way of understanding the phenomenon is to suggest that
becoming eunuch *metragyrtai* was a way for individuals who engaged in
self-mutilation out of anxiety, depression or other psychological
conditions to find an accepted, or at least tolerated, social role. But that
must remain a hypothesis.

Conclusion

Eunuch *metragyrtai*, or Galli, are extreme examples of the devotees of the
Mother of the Gods. Self-castration was clearly not expected of the crowds
who took part in her festivals whether in Greek cities or even at Rome.
The more universal experience of her worship was the music of pipes and
horns and the noise of drums, tambourines and castanets. While Roman
citizens might be expected to watch such celebrations unperturbed, it is
clear that for most people her cult was an opportunity for dancing and
singing. This ecstatic cult activity she shared with Dionysus, and in the
next chapter we will explore it further. Many of the aspects of cult that are
better known in association with Dionysus were also part of the cult of the
Mother, so some of what we will explore can be read back into the cult
described in this chapter.

5 *Dionysus*

The god most associated with ecstatic cult in the Greco-Roman world was Dionysus. Maenads, the wild female followers of Dionysus, are a frequent subject of ancient art, sometimes in the company of satyrs, the half-human, half-goat servants of the god, sometimes on their own, at rest, dancing or carrying wild animals they have killed or tamed [77, 78]. Bacchic frenzy, the state of those driven wild by Dionysus, is an element in a number of myths, including that of the poet and musician Orpheus, who travelled to the underworld in search of his dead wife Eurydice, failed to bring her back and was subsequently torn apart by maenads. But these myths reflect a real form of ecstatic cult, well documented by both literary works and inscriptions, in which women and men would go out into the countryside at night and engage in revels in honour of Dionysus.

ABOVE
77 Dionysus accompanied by maenads, from an Athenian amphora of the late sixth century BC.

RIGHT
78 A Roman sculptural relief showing a maenad with a knife in one hand and a young animal in the other.

79 The theatre of Dionysus in Athens. The site was in use from the middle of the sixth century BC, but most of the visible masonry dates from the Roman period. The theatre could hold between 15,000 and 20,000 spectators.

Dionysus: Theatre and Wine

Dionysus is presented in myth as a latecomer to the Greek world, arriving from the east with bands of Asian followers. In the past scholars took this as evidence that the cult of Dionysus appeared in Greece rather later than those of other Olympian gods. However, the decipherment of the Linear B tablets from Mycenaean palaces has revealed that Dionysus's name was used in Greece in the Bronze Age, so his cult is at least as old as that of the other gods.[1]

Dionysus is associated above all with wine and with drama, which in ancient Athens were brought together. The god's two major festivals in Athens were the City Dionysia and the Lenaea, at which tragedies and comedies were performed in the theatre of Dionysus on the slopes of the Acropolis. The City Dionysia also involved a procession in which the god's ancient cult statue was brought from his sanctuary at Eleutherae, near the border with Boeotia, to his temple by the theatre in the centre of Athens, as well as the presentation of armour to war orphans raised by the state and, in the fifth century BC, a time when Athens was the head of a powerful naval alliance, displays of the tribute brought to the city by its allies. Large numbers of animals were sacrificed at an altar in the centre of the theatre, giving the audience a sight of real blood before the stage blood of the tragedies they would watch in the following days. [79].[2]

Dramatic festivals represented a very public form of cult for Dionysus, and we can see a similar emphasis on display in a festival held in Alexandria in 285 BC to celebrate the accession of King Ptolemy II. We have a contemporary account of the festival, which included processions in honour of several gods: the one for Dionysus is described in much the greatest detail. A series of decorated carts included some with huge statues of Dionysus himself at various points in his career, and one carried a wine-skin made of leopard skins sewn together, holding 3,000 *metretes* of wine (over 100,000 litres) which flowed out over the processional way. Walking with the carts were men dressed as *silenoi*, satyrs (Dionysus's companions), and women wearing crowns of vine leaves or ivy, some carrying snakes. In the description, the women are called *Mimallones*, *Bassarai* and *Lydai* (Lydians), which are names associated with maenads.[3]

The importance of Dionysus to the Ptolemies reflects the fact that his cult grew in the later fourth century BC through association between the god and Alexander the Great. According to the historians who wrote about his campaigns, Alexander was constantly attempting to emulate Dionysus, who was supposed, like Alexander himself, to have travelled as far east as India. On coinage produced by Alexander and his immediate successors, Alexander was depicted wearing an elephant headdress, a symbol of Dionysus [80]. After Alexander's death his successors, including Ptolemy I in Alexandria, sponsored the cult of Dionysus, in part to advertise their links with Alexander.[4]

But alongside these state festivals Dionysus was worshipped by smaller groups with rituals similar to those we found in the cult of the Mother of the Gods: dancing, singing and revelry. After Herodotus has told the story of how the Scythian prince Anacharsis was killed by his fellow countrymen for re-enacting the rites of the Mother of the Gods (see previous chapter), he tells an almost identical story about another Scythian, a king who adopted Greek customs and went as far as building himself a house in the Greek settlement of Olbia, on the north shore of the Black Sea. He decided to join the celebration of the rites of Dionysus Bacchius in Olbia and, despite ominous signs, took part in the rituals and joined the group of worshippers wandering crazed through the streets. He was observed by some Scythians from outside the city walls, who had him killed.[5] Whether this story is true or not, archaeological evidence from the fifth century BC, in the form of bone plaques with Dionysus's name written on them, has been found in Olbia, indicating that there were groups of worshippers of Dionysus in the city at the time Herodotus was writing [81].[6] Inscriptions show that similar groups existed in other cities from at least the fifth century BC onwards. Before we look at this evidence, however, we shall turn to the most detailed

80 Alexander the Great wearing the elephant headdress of Dionysus on a coin of Ptolemy I (323–283 BC).

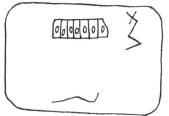

81 Bone tablet from Olbia, fifth century BC, with the words 'Peace War Truth Falsehood Dio[nysus]'.

depiction of the ecstatic cult of Dionysus, Euripides' *Bacchae*. Although the play deals with mythical characters it is set in a real city, and it provides a detailed exploration of the nature and meaning of Bacchic cult.

Euripides' *Bacchae*

Bacchae was written by the Athenian playwright Euripides at the end of the fifth century BC. The play tells how Dionysus comes in disguise to the city of Thebes, where his mother Semele had lived until she was killed by the sight of his father, Zeus. Dionysus is accompanied by maenads from Phrygia. He says that the Thebans have denied that Zeus was the father of Semele's child, thus insulting both her and himself, and he is determined to make them realize their mistake. At the start of the play the women of the city have been driven mad and are outside the city. They have no control over their actions, but the male characters do. The older, wiser men – Cadmus, the city's founder, and Teiresias the seer – have dressed themselves in appropriate costume and are preparing also to go out into the countryside. In contrast, the young king Pentheus, Cadmus's grandson, is attempting to prevent the introduction of the rites and has imprisoned as many of the women as he has been able to catch, although they miraculously escape afterwards. Pentheus also imprisons Dionysus, but the god easily escapes from captivity and then enchants Pentheus, persuading him to go out to witness what the women are doing. Pentheus is seen by the women, and his mother Agave, mistaking him for a lion cub, tears him limb from limb. The last part of the text of the play is fragmentary, but it ends with Cadmus, Agave and the other members of Semele's family being punished by Dionysus, and his rites are established in Thebes.[7]

The setting in Thebes is significant for two reasons. It is a feature of all surviving Attic tragedies set in Thebes that its rulers make disastrous decisions and suffer as a result – as well as Pentheus there is Oedipus, and Creon who is the ruler of Thebes in Sophocles' *Antigone*.[8] More significantly in this context, Thebes was widely held to be the first city where Bacchic cult was practised. Dionysus says at the beginning:

> I came first to this land of the Greeks, dancing and setting up my rites (*teletai*), so I might be revealed a god to men… This city [Thebes] must learn, whether it likes it or not, not having celebrated (*ateleston*) my Bacchic rites (*bakkheumata*), that I speak for Semele my mother, saying that I am revealed to men as a god whom Zeus bore.[9]

The chorus emphasizes the benefits available to those who celebrate the rites, in language reminiscent of that used about the Eleusinian Mysteries in the *Homeric Hymn to Demeter*:

> Blessed is he who, being fortunate and knowing the *teletai* of the gods, keeps his life pure and joins his soul to the *thiasos*, dancing in Bacchic revels over the mountains with holy purifications, and who, revering the *orgia* of great mother Cybele, brandishing the *thyrsus*, garlanded with ivy, serves Dionysus.[10]

The connection between Dionysus and Cybele in Athenian understanding may explain the figure looking like Dionysus that we saw on the vase showing ecstatic worship of the Mother in the previous chapter. Sophocles in his *Antigone* makes a link between Dionysus and Demeter at Eleusis:

> God of many names, glory of the Cadmeian bride and offspring of loud-thundering Zeus, you who watch over far-famed Italy and reign in the valleys of Eleusinian Deo where all find welcome! O Bacchus, denizen of Thebes, the mother-city of your Bacchants, dweller by the wet stream of Ismenus on the soil of the sowing of the savage dragon's teeth![11]

We find more similarities between the rites of Dionysus and those of other mysteries in a conversation between Pentheus and Dionysus:

> Pentheus: Why do you bring these *teletai* to Hellas?
> Dionysus: Dionysus, the child of Zeus, sent us.
> Pentheus: Did he compel you at night, or in your sight?
> Dionysus: Seeing me just as I saw him, he gave me the *orgia*.
> Pentheus: What appearance do your *orgia* have?
> Dionysus: They cannot be told to mortals who have not participated in Bacchic rites (*abakkheutoi*).
> Pentheus: And do they have any profit to those who sacrifice?
> Dionysus: It is not lawful for you to hear, but they are worth knowing.
> Pentheus: You have counterfeited this well, so that I desire to hear.
> Dionysus: The *orgia* are hostile to whoever practises impiety.[12]

Here we have the idea of secret elements in the rites, which those who have not joined in them are not allowed to hear. Some scholars have argued that the cult of Dionysus involved initiation similar to what initiates underwent at Eleusis and have interpreted elements of *Bacchae* to support this idea.[13] We will consider this further later, but here we can note that the chorus describes the rites as involving dancing in the mountains and joining the *thiasos*, the band of Bacchic worshippers. We should therefore start our study of historical Bacchic cult with the *thiasos*.

The Dionysiac *Thiasos*

The word *thiasos* has been used with a range of meanings in modern discussions of the cult of Dionysus. In antiquity it was frequently used to describe a group of worshippers of a divinity (not necessarily Dionysus), who engaged in ecstatic activity. The word is used by Herodotus to describe the group of men with whom Scyles dances in Olbia, and by a messenger in Euripides' *Bacchae* to describe the groups of women led by Agave and her sisters through the hills around Thebes. It is also found in inscriptions relating to cult associations in honour of Dionysus from the third century BC until the fourth century AD, across the Mediterranean world. The evidence from these inscriptions reveals not only the large number of *thiasoi*, but also their great variety [82, plate X].[14]

An inscription from the city of Magnesia on the river Meander in Asia Minor, dating from the third century BC, reveals the existence of officially recognized *thiasoi* that are very similar to the bands of women depicted in *Bacchae*. The inscription quotes an oracle instructing the city to:

> Go to the holy plain of Thebes to fetch
> maenads from the race of Cadmian Ino.
> They will bring you maenadic rites and noble customs
> and will establish troops of Bacchus in your city.

It then reports that:

> In accordance with the oracle, and through the agency of the envoys, three maenads were brought from Thebes: Kosko, Baubo and Thettale. And Kosko organized the *thiasos* named after the plane tree, Baubo the

82 Dionysus with Silenus and bacchants on an Athenian red-figure cup of the late fifth century BC. This mythical scene can be compared with a similar depiction on the same cup of women as bacchants celebrating a festival in honour of Dionysus [plate X].

thiasos outside the city, and Thettale the *thiasos* named after Kataibates. After their deaths they were buried by the Magnesians, and Kosko lies buried in the area called Hillock of Kosko, Baubo in the area called Tabarnis, and Thettale near the theatre.[15]

83 *The Women of Amphissa* as portrayed by Alma-Tadema in 1887.

The three *thiasoi* parallel the bands led by the three daughters of Cadmus in *Bacchae*. The Magnesians may have been influenced in their actions by knowledge of Euripides' play, but the inscription, which survives in a Roman copy of the original, is evidence that this kind of cult was taken seriously there.

Even earlier than this is evidence about the *thyiades* of Delphi. These were a group of women who danced in honour of Dionysus on the slopes of Mount Parnassus at night.[16] They are mentioned in the fifth century BC and Plutarch, who was a priest at Delphi in the early second century AD, tells a story from the fourth century BC. A group of Delphic *thyiades*, disoriented and exhausted after their nocturnal dances, found themselves at the neighbouring city of Amphissa at a time when Amphissa was in dispute with the city of Delphi. The women collapsed in the city's market place, and the women of Amphissa formed a guard to protect them from the men of the place [83, 84].[17] In Roman times at least the Delphic *thyiades* were joined every other year by *thyiades* from Athens, who danced at places en route to Delphi.[18]

BELOW
84 A sleeping
bacchant, a
terracotta statuette
from Locri in Italy
from the third
century BC.

We have other inscriptions that refer to Bacchic worshippers going out to the mountains beyond their cities. An epitaph from Miletus dating from the third or second century BC honours a priestess of Dionysus:

> Bacchae of the City, say 'Farewell, you holy priestess.' This is what a good woman deserves. She led you to the mountain and carried all the sacred objects and implements, marching in procession before the whole city. Should some stranger ask for her name: Alcmeonis, daughter of Rhodios, who knew her share of blessings.[19]

An inscription from Physcus in Caria, in southwest Anatolia, gives us a glimpse of the organization of Bacchic *thiasoi* in the second century AD. The inscription is a set of regulations, indicating fines for those who do not play their part in cult activity. Its concern for polite behaviour seems at odds with the idea of maenads as wild or uncontrolled, and it is not clear what these 'maenads' and 'herdsmen' did, but it does show that going to the mountains was still a necessary part of their cult practice:

> A maenad is not to attack or abuse a maenad. Similarly a herdsman is not to attack or abuse a herdsman. But if someone does this, they shall pay to the association for each utterance a fine of 4 drachmae. And for anyone in town who does not attend a meeting, the same applies. Anyone who does not assemble on the mountain owes a fine to the association of 5 drachmae.[20]

Women and Men

Inscriptions referring to *thiasoi* mention a number of activities, including meetings and dinners, as well as formal processions that led the members to the mountains. Some refer to women alone, but some also mention men. Diodorus Siculus, referring to his own time, the first century BC, specifically mentions women gathering in Bacchic celebrations and engaging in ecstatic worship in honour of Dionysus, every other year in

Women worshipping Dionysus, on a Lucanian volute crater of the late fifth century BC. The scene is taking place at night, and the woman on the right behind Dionysus is holding a torch.

II Reconstruction of the gold and ivory cult statue of Athena from the Parthenon, created in the second half of the fifth century BC. The goddess represents the success and power of the city of Athens at the time the statue was made. She holds Nike (goddess of victory) on her right hand, and her shield covers a great serpent that was said to guard the Athenian Acropolis.

BELOW
III Wooden votive plaque of c. 540 BC (from Pitsa cave, west of Sicyon), depicting the sacrifice of a sheep. The procession is led by a girl with a basket containing sacrificial implements. Behind the sheep are two musicians and women carrying garlands. The figure on the left is probably the man who paid for the sacrifice and dedicated the plaque.

OPPOSITE
IV Jupiter (Zeus) and Semele, as depicted by Gustave Moreau in 1895.

ABOVE

V Attic red-figure krater by the Hektor painter, 430 BC. On the right is Triptolemos, holding a sceptre and stalks of wheat. He is addressed by Demeter, who carries two torches, and behind her is Persephone, holding a plough.

VIII The Asclepieion, the civic centre of the city of Messene, founded in 369 BC as part of the creation of a new national identity for the inhabitants of the territory.

IX Bronze statuette of Magna Mater on her chariot drawn by lions, from Rome, second century AD.

XI A girl acting as a 'bear' for Artemis at Brauron on a fragment of an Athenian vase of the fifth century BC.

XII Bacchic worshipper on a South Italian vase of the fifth century BC. A snake is wound around her right wrist.

X Maenads celebrating a festival in honour of Dionysus on an Athenian red-figure kylix by Makron, 490–480 BC. The god is represented by a mask on a draped column. In a mythical scene from the same cup [82], Dionysus himself is present.

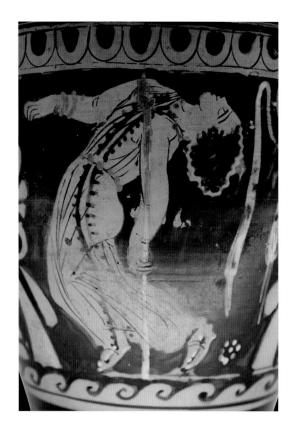

many Greek cities. He makes a distinction between the younger women who engage in frenzied activity while the older women offer sacrifices and sing hymns. Men are not mentioned.[21] Pausanias, writing in the second century AD, mentions a temple of Dionysus at Bryseae in Laconia in the Peloponnese where the statue could be seen by women only, because they alone performed his secret rites.[22]

On the other hand, we have an inscription from Miletus from 276/5 BC detailing the responsibilities of the priestess of Dionysus Bacchius there. She was responsible for leading the public *thiasos*.[23] There were also private *thiasoi* who paid her a fee every other year (suggesting that, as in Diodorus's account, they held their celebrations biannually). The inscription refers to men as well as women sacrificing privately to Dionysus, and to priests as well as priestesses leading out the procession. As we saw in *Bacchae*, the wiser men dressed in Bacchic clothes but stayed apart from the women who had been driven from the city. It seems likely that the more frenzied activities were restricted to women only – in contrast to the cult of the Mother of the Gods in which male figures are more prominent.

What did *Thiasoi* Do?

Surviving inscriptions indicate a variety of rituals associated with the cult of Dionysus. These include sacrifices and processions such as we see in the public aspects of other cults. Inscriptions mention *kistophoroi, liknophoroi* (carriers of containers and baskets) and *phallophoroi* (phallus-carriers), who presumably carried these things in processions. The containers probably concealed *hiera* (sacred objects) similar to those in the Eleusinian procession [85]. It seems likely that the normal sequence of events involved sacrifices and a procession from the city, which anyone could see and join in, followed by secret activities 'on the mountain', usually restricted to women, or perhaps with separate groups of men and women. This would parallel the pattern we found in sanctuary-based mystery cults, with a combination of public activity and activities restricted to initiates.

The inscriptions indicate that *thiasoi* would usually have a meeting place, which might be described as a cave or a temple.[24] We know of one group subscribing money for the construction of a 'temple', and in general the buildings they met in appear to have belonged to the groups, rather than being city temples.[25] In the period of the Roman empire *thiasoi* were sponsored by patrons, and although groups like the *thyiades* and the 'public *thiasos*' at Miletus acted under city control, most *thiasoi* seem to have been voluntary bodies. The variety in the titles they use shows also that there was no central authority to encourage uniformity of practice.

OPPOSITE
XIII, XIV The frieze of the Villa of the Mysteries in Pompeii: above, Dionysus reclines against a female figure, either his mother Semele or Ariadne, while Silenus, on the left, holds a mirror in which a young man sees a mask held up behind him by another. Below, an attendant reveals a phallus in a *liknos* (basket) while a young woman is whipped by a winged female figure, and a bacchant dances.

85 A basket, a cup, a *phiale*, ribbons, a torch and other objects being carried in a procession in honour of Dionysus on a South Italian bell krater of the fourth century BC.

It was the activity 'on the mountain' that was the most important part of the *teletai*. In *Bacchae* we are given two descriptions of how the women of Thebes behaved in the mountains. First of all, Dionysus says:

> Therefore I have goaded the daughters of Cadmus from the house in frenzy, and they dwell in the mountains, out of their wits; and I have compelled them to wear the outfit of my *orgia*. And all the female offspring of Thebes, as many as are women, I have driven maddened from the house, and they, mingled with the daughters of Cadmus, sit on roofless rocks beneath green pines.[26]

Later, a messenger describes the scene before the women become enraged by the presence of Pentheus:

> There was a little valley surrounded by precipices, irrigated with streams, shaded by pine trees, where the maenads were sitting, their hands busy with delightful labours. Some of them were crowning again the worn *thyrsus*, making it leafy with ivy, while some, like colts freed from the painted yoke, were singing a Bacchic melody to one another.[27]

Although Euripides may not have had any opportunity to observe the actual Bacchic rituals, restricted as they were to women, none of these things seems unlikely in real life. Other references in the play give more detail about what the women carried: fawn skins, wreaths of ivy or oak, and *thyrsoi* – sticks also twined with ivy. These are regularly found in artistic depictions of Dionysus himself and of his worshippers, and there are also references in other literature and inscriptions. The chorus also refers to the meat of a goat eaten raw, and even here we have evidence that this related to an actual ritual act. It is unlikely that the women did eat raw meat, but the inscription from Miletus outlining the responsibilities of the priestess of Dionysus Bacchius states that no one is permitted 'to throw in the *omophagion*' (literally, 'the meat eaten raw') until the priestess has done so.[28] What exactly this meant is far from clear, but raw meat is not part of normal Greek ritual [86].

All these activities – going out of the city to the uncultivated mountainside, staying in the open air, wearing animalskins and not cooking meat – form a pattern that can be understood by looking at their opposites. Living in cities, in houses, wearing woven cloth and cooking meat are all indications of civilization. They mark humans out as different from animals. We might add agriculture to this list of civilized activities, including wine-making: it is striking, given Dionysus's association with it, that wine is not mentioned in these scenes, and we will return to this point later. One way of explaining what Dionysus has forced on the women of Thebes, and what *thiasoi* do voluntarily, is that they are transported from civilization to wildness, both in location and in behaviour.[29]

This is not something unique to the worship of Dionysus. The same interpretation is used to explain a number of women's religious rituals: these can be seen as a temporary inversion of social norms after which women are reconciled with and reintegrated into male-dominated society. So, for example, in the Athenian festival of the Brauronia, held every four years, pre-pubescent girls spent a period of time in the sanctuary of Artemis at Brauron, in eastern Attica. They were referred to as 'bears', and their period of service to Artemis, the goddess associated with wild animals, can be understood as a period of wildness between childhood and marriage [plate XI].[30] At the Thesmophoria in

86 Dionysus, wearing an ivy wreath and animal skins, tearing apart a goat on an Athenian red-figure stamnos of the first half of the fifth century BC.

Athens, women gathered together for three days, sitting on the ground, living in temporary shelters and making indecent jokes (similar to the *aiskhrologia* that was part of the Eleusinian procession). Even though the Thesmophoria was celebrated within the area where the women usually lived, rather than out in the wilderness, it nonetheless represents a temporary departure from the domestic space.[31]

But there are differences between these festivals and Bacchic cult: above all, they lack the frenzy that Euripides and Diodorus both mention. Before we consider what the experience might have meant for those involved, we will turn from the Greek world to look at the cult of Dionysus in Italy. Roman reaction to Bacchic cult gives us a different perspective.

The Senatus Consultum de Bacchanalibus

In 186 BC the senate in Rome issued a decree that applied to all Romans and their allies, forbidding certain Bacchic practices unless explicitly approved by the Roman authorities, and ordering the dismantling of certain related structures. If anyone disobeyed the decision of the senate they would be tried as for a capital offence. The decree survives in a bronze copy that was originally put up in Bruttium in southern Italy [87].[32]

OPPOSITE
87 The surviving bronze copy of the *senatus consultum de Bacchanalibus*.

Precisely what was being forbidden and what was being allowed by the decree is not absolutely clear, but it does not appear to outlaw long-established religious rites in honour of Dionysus. The decree talks of *bacanals*, which are considered to be shrines of some kind. The decree allows those who considered that they needed to have a *bacanal* to take their case before a Roman magistrate (the *praetor urbanus*), who would then bring the matter to a meeting of the senate. The decree also excluded from destruction any *bacanal* that contained sacred objects (Latin *sacra* equivalent to the Greek *hiera*). Women could apparently continue to be bacchants, but men were forbidden to join them without the consent of the authorities. So *thiasoi* of the kind we find in the Greek world would not necessarily be forbidden.

The decree appears to be mainly aimed at conspiracy rather than religious activity. It forbids people from taking positions of authority, so there could be no male Bacchic priests, no *magister* (master) either male or female, and no common fund of money. It also forbids the swearing of oaths and the creation of mutual bonds of obligation, secret activities, and the gathering of mixed groups of more than five people (up to two men and three women), although even these could take place with the permission of the Roman senate.[33] In order to discover why the Romans felt it necessary to act against these cultic elements, we must turn to the account of the Roman historian Livy.

Livy's Account of the Bacchanalia

Livy was writing at the end of the first century BC, in the reign of the emperor Augustus, and his history has an explicit moral purpose, holding up the values of earlier centuries to demonstrate how far the standards of his own time have fallen. In his account of the events of 186 BC he had access to accounts now lost, and he was certainly aware of the contents of the senatorial decree. It is by no means clear, however, that the story he tells can be trusted.

In the course of his narrative Livy gives two accounts of how the Bacchanalia developed in Italy, both of which are distinctly hostile. He first says that it was introduced by a 'lowborn Greek', whom he presents as an itinerant private initiator of a sort we will consider in the next chapter. This man, according to Livy, initiated a few individuals in Etruria, but then the number of initiates, both male and female, increased, and the cult spread through Etruria to Rome. As Livy presents it, the nocturnal meetings were the occasion for debauchery and crimes of all kinds, with the noise of drums and cymbals and the shrieks of the participants drowning out the screams of murder victims, whose bodies were secretly removed.[34] The whole of this first description is hysterical, and for that reason should be treated with some suspicion.

The second account is more interesting. Livy tells a rather dramatic story about the discovery of Bacchic cult activity by one of the consuls. In this tale a prostitute called Hispala, the mistress of the hero, describes how the cult has developed. According to her, in earlier times Bacchic cult was restricted to women, with rites celebrated three times a year during the day, and with married women acting as priestesses.[35] This is similar to Diodorus's roughly contemporary description of the Bacchic practices in Greek cities.[36]

Hispala goes on to explain that the rites were changed by a woman from Campania called Paculla Annia. She began to initiate men, to perform the ceremonies at night, and to do so on five nights each month. Subsequently all kinds of wild behaviour and debauchery took place during the ceremonies:

> Whoever would not submit to defilement, or shrank from violating others, was sacrificed as a victim. To regard nothing as impious or criminal was the very sum of their religion. The men, as though seized with madness and with frenzied distortions of their bodies, shrieked out prophecies; the matrons, dressed as Bacchae, their hair dishevelled, rushed down to the Tiber with burning torches, plunged them into the water, and drew them out again, the flame undiminished, as they were made of sulphur mixed with lime. Men were fastened to a machine and hurried off to hidden caves, and they were said to have been rapt away by the gods; these were the men who refused to join their conspiracy or take a part in their crimes or submit to pollution.[37]

How such activities could take place throughout Italy without being noticed is not explained, and much of this is probably exaggeration, if not pure fantasy. The presentation of Paculla Annia herself, active with her sons in suspicious nocturnal activities, appears very similar to the hostile description of another private initiator, the mother of the Athenian orator Aeschines, provided by Demosthenes, which will be discussed in the next chapter: this suggests that it may not be entirely reliable. But the description of the innovations for which she is held responsible need to be considered in the light of the evidence from the senatorial decree. The decree forbids secret rites and mixed gatherings of men and women and is aimed at suppressing recently created shrines, while permitting women to continue to be bacchants and preserving older shrines. It would therefore be an appropriate response to precisely those changes attributed to Paculla Annia.

However, this does not guarantee that much else in Livy's story can be accepted as true. Livy describes the Bacchic initiates as 'a great crowd, almost a second state' and sees them as presenting a threat to the whole Roman republic.[38] The story of how the extent of the threat was revealed revolves around an innocent young man whose mother and stepfather almost trick him into being initiated, as well as the young man's mistress – a prostitute who truly loves him – and his aunt and also the mother-in-law of one of the consuls for the year. The whole plot reads like a piece of drama, and it has been plausibly argued that Livy did in fact take the story from a comic play.[39]

Establishing Livy's veracity is important because he goes on to relate how the events were brought to an end. He describes the consul telling the Roman people that the *Bacanals* represent a major threat to the state, and then taking measures to suppress them. According to Livy, more than 7,000 people were involved. He does not give any figure for the number of people arrested and then either imprisoned or executed, but he leaves the impression – perhaps deliberately and falsely – that it was high. He suggests that the senatorial decree, which he summarizes accurately, was introduced to prevent the situation arising again.[40] As Livy presents it, the suppression of the Bacchanalia was a huge and bloody act, and it has been perceived as a rare but significant example of Roman religious intolerance.

However, Livy's account of the suppression may be as exaggerated and hysterical as his descriptions of what happened during the initiation ceremonies. Certainly the suspicion of foreigners and women displayed in the narrative may owe more to Livy's wish to contrast the uprightness of the Roman officials with the wickedness of others. Although scholars have attempted to defend the value of Livy's account, it should probably be dismissed as largely fictitious.

Roman Attitudes to Bacchic Cult

Despite Livy's narrative, it seems unlikely that the Romans had no experience or knowledge of ecstatic worship of Dionysus in the cities of southern Italy until it was uncovered in the early second century BC. There are depictions of bacchants on south Italian vases from the fifth and fourth centuries BC [plate XII]. Although the evidence for *thiasoi* in Italy in this period is limited, they are mentioned in the comedies of Plautus, which date from the early second century BC. In two of his plays, *Miles Gloriosus* (The Braggart Soldier) of *c.* 200 BC and *Casina*, *c.* 184 BC, there are references to groups of female bacchants, with no suggestion that they represent a threat. On the other hand, in *Miles Gloriosus* one character threatens jokingly to denounce another in the forum for having a *bacchanal* in his cellar, suggesting that secret shrines were a cause of concern before 186 BC. Livy's description of the plot being revealed for the first time to one of the consuls of the year is also at odds with his earlier statement that the two consuls were assigned the task of investigating domestic conspiracy by the senate when they took up office.[41]

Livy's hostile presentation of Bacchic cult suggests the same distaste for imported religious practices as we found in Dionysius of Halicarnassus's discussion of the cult of Magna Mater in the previous chapter. But as we have seen, the *senatus consultum* was not aimed at abolishing Bacchic practices entirely. Rather it is aimed against secret meetings of men and women together, and the swearing of oaths. The terms of the decree suggest that the cult of Dionysus was suspected of being a cover for politically dangerous activities. The secrecy that was associated with the rites could be used as a cover for groups plotting against Rome. Whether there really was a serious conspiracy against Rome at this time we do not know, but the episode indicates that the Romans thought there was.

There is not much evidence for Bacchic cult in Italy in the period after 186 BC – but there is not much from earlier either. It is clear, however, that *thiasoi* did not disappear altogether. Indeed we have evidence for a very large *thiasos*, including both men and women, in an inscription from Torre Nova near Rome dating from AD 160. The inscription honours a priestess, Agrippinilla, and lists the members of the *thiasos* according to their titles. Agrippinilla's family were originally from Lesbos, in Greece, and more than three hundred of the names on the list are Greek. There are seventy Romans listed, and they tend to occupy the positions of highest status. The list shows both the detailed hierarchy of the *thiasos*, which probably reflects the complexity of the social hierarchy in Italy in this period, and the extent to which it appears to have borrowed titles from other mystery cults. The inscription refers to the following: *dadoukhos* (torchbearer, a title derived from the Eleusinian Mysteries, although here held by a woman), priests, priestesses, *hierophant* (another Eleusinian title), *theophoroi* (literally God-bearers, a male role), *hypourgos* and *silenokosmos* (a title referring to Silenus, one of the half-man, half-goat figures associated with Dionysus), *kistophorai* (basket-bearers, a female role), chief herdsmen, sacred herdsmen, chief bassarids (male and female: *bassaroi/bassarai* are words usually used in the same sense as *bakkhoi/bakkhai*, i.e. bacchants), *amphithaleis* (acolytes), *liknophorai* (another kind of basket-bearer, again a female role), *phallophorai* (phallus-carriers, another female role), fire-bearers (male), *hieromnemon* (literally, sacred remembrancer, but the title is found in other cult contexts with a fairly unspecific role), guardian of the young, herdsmen, sash-wearers (male and female), bacchants wearing the sash (male and female), sacred bacchants (male, and the largest number of individuals), bacchants (male and female), guardians of the cave (male), and silent ones (male and female).[42] Some of these titles (e.g. *dadoukhos*, *kistophoros*) clearly reflect roles, while others seem more like status levels (e.g. silent one, bacchant, bacchant wearing the sash, sash-wearer, chief bassarid – this is possibly a sequence). The status levels (apart from herdsmen, who are all male) can be achieved by both men and women, while the roles are mostly gender-specific (there are both priests and priestesses, but their functions may not have been parallel).

More than three centuries separate this inscription from the *senatus consultum de Bacchanalibus*, but they do not necessarily reflect a radical transformation in attitudes to Bacchic cult. In both cases the Greek roots of the cult are clearly visible. The main difference is that the Torre Nova *thiasos* was led by rich Romans, and its membership appears to be organized on principles of hierarchy and patronage that characterized Roman society. In contrast, the secrecy of the *bacanals* aroused suspicion, possibly correctly, that they were a cover for plots against the Roman social order. But the attempt to defend the state from conspiracy did not turn into an attack on religion: established cult centres were protected, and legitimate cult activity, which included *thiasoi*, was able to continue.

Secrecy and Initiation

Roman concern about secrecy in Bacchic cult was based on some reality. In *Bacchae*, Dionysus emphasizes that there are some things that those who do not participate in the cult are not permitted to hear. In Plautus's *Miles Gloriosus* there is a brief conversation between two slaves about a supposed secret known to one of them:

> Palaestrio: You conceal it from the profane. I am reliable and
>   trustworthy to you.
> Milphidippa: Give me the password, if you are one of our bacchants.
> Palaestrio: 'A certain woman loves a certain man.'
> Milphidippa: Well, many women do that.[43]

The implication is that bacchants identified each other by exchange of passwords. As we have seen, one of the words used to refer to Bacchic rites is *teletai*, and this is often associated with cults involving initiation. Some inscriptions relating to *thiasoi* dating from the first century BC onwards describe members as *mystai* in place of the more usual *bakkhoi*, and also sometimes refer to *arkhimystai* (chief initiates).[44] All this has led scholars to argue that individual personal initiation, perhaps in rituals similar to those experienced at Samothrace, or like the initiation into the cult of Isis that we will investigate later, was a usual feature of Bacchic cult.[45]

There may have been Mysteries of Dionysus of this sort at some sanctuaries of the god. Pausanias says that *orgia* of Dionysus were celebrated in a temple to him at Heraea in Arcadia.[46] It is difficult, however, to find much direct evidence. It has been argued that Euripides' *Bacchae* is itself a symbolic representation of initiation into the Mysteries of Dionysus, in which Pentheus represents the initiate: Pentheus's 'actual' death stands for the symbolic death of the initiate in the course of the ritual of initiation.[47] Yet there are problems with this approach. The evidence used to reconstruct the rituals tends to be drawn from a wide range of images and descriptions of initiation that are not all associated specifically with Dionysus [88–91]. And since Bacchic cult took place in a great many places, with no central authority, there is no reason to suppose that initiation in one place would necessarily resemble initiation in another.

The Frescoes of the Villa of the Mysteries

In the hope of learning about initiation in the cult of Dionysus, scholars have turned to the so-called Villa of the Mysteries at Pompeii. One room of the villa painted in the first century BC [92, 93, plates XIII, XIV] shows a series of scenes at the centre of which sits Dionysus. Near him a young woman lifts a cloth covering a basket that appears to contain fruit and a phallus, while another young woman is being whipped by a winged female figure as a bacchant dances. Very little about the frescoes is certain. Dionysus is reclining against a female figure who has been identified as either Ariadne or Semele: her identity would influence interpretation. A vast amount has been written about the images, in which two interpretations stand out. The scenes relate either to marriage or to initiation into mysteries, or perhaps to both at the same time. Interpretations that relate the scenes to initiation focus in particular on the covered basket containing the phallus. The basket is a *liknon*, and it appears frequently in Dionysiac contexts. Female *liknophoroi* are listed in the inscription from Torre Nova discussed earlier, and we find pictures of *likna* on vases containing either a phallus or a mask of Dionysus. But the *liknon* also appears in the iconography of weddings. The presence of Dionysus obviously also suggests that he is central to the events. However, the painting is not a representation of an actual initiation ceremony. The active involvement of supernatural beings (the winged figure holding the whip in particular) suggests that it is more fanciful than that. The room in which the frescoes are painted is generally identified as the *triclinium*, the main dining space of the villa, and it is unlikely that a ritual supposed to be kept secret would be displayed in a room to which uninitiated guests would have had access. The scene might still relate to

LEFT, FROM TOP
88–90 Satyrs play music to a woman and dance around her, and then she puts on an animal skin and dances with a *thyrsus*. These scenes on an Athenian red-figure cup of the mid-fifth century BC have been interpreted as a depiction of Dionysiac initiation.

RIGHT
91 A marble relief from Rome, a copy of a Greek original of the second century BC. It is not easy to make sense of the fragment, but it has been interpreted as a scene of Dionysiac initiation. The lower figures may be underground. Objects including the mask held by the woman can be associated with Dionysus.

initiation, but only in an allegorical form. And once the element of allegory is introduced, interpretation becomes more difficult — is it an allegory for Bacchic initiation, or are the elements, including Dionysus himself, representing something else altogether, such as the experience of a woman approaching marriage? The frescoes thus cannot easily be used as evidence for Dionysiac mysteries.[48]

Private Dionysiac Initiation

We do appear to find evidence for individuals undergoing individual initiation into the cult of Dionysus in Livy's account of the Bacchanalia at Rome. The young man at the centre of his story, Aebutius, is told that he must observe ten days of abstinence, followed by a banquet, a purificatory bath, and then entry to the Bacchic shrine.[49] These preparations are more or less identical to those undergone by Lucius in Apuleius's *Metamorphoses* before his initiation into the cult of Isis (see Chapter 8). The description of the ceremony itself, led by a woman assisted by her sons, as we have seen, is similar to other descriptions of initiations conducted by private initiators. Accounts of such private initiations are in any case the most likely inspiration for Livy's account. We will examine the whole phenomenon of private initiation in the next chapter. Here we can note that initiation along the lines of the Eleusinian Mysteries does not appear to have been a much-mentioned feature of Bacchic cult, and we should interpret the cult on the basis of the features for which there is abundant evidence, above all the central act of going out to the mountains.

OPPOSITE
92, 93 The *triclinium* (dining room) of the Villa of the Mysteries in Pompeii, decorated with frescoes of the first century BC which have been interpreted as showing scenes of Dionysiac initiation. Dionysus sits enthroned on the far wall, where the plaster is damaged. Below, a detail from the same wall shows a young woman lifting a cloth to reveal a *liknon* (basket) containing fruit and a phallus.

Behind the Mask

This discussion has used material from a wide chronological period to suggest that the mysteries of Dionysus took broadly the same form from the sixth century BC to the fourth century AD. It also emphasizes the activities of the *thiasos* as the key to understanding Dionysiac *teletai* throughout this period. This conclusion differs from traditional scholarly approaches, which tend to argue that ecstatic ritual activity was a feature only of the earliest period of Dionysiac cult, if it existed at all, which was superseded in the Hellenistic and Roman periods by more restrained forms of cult characterized, they suggest, by initiation. It is in part to explain why there are so many references to bacchants and initiates in documents from later periods that the idea of individual initiation is given such prominence, despite the lack of evidence for it. Ecstatic behaviour might also be seen as too 'primitive' for the intellectually sophisticated world of Hellenistic and Roman Greece.[50]

But it is difficult to doubt that through the Hellenistic period and afterwards Dionysus was worshipped in the Greek world with ecstatic dances that took place in the countryside. In this his cult clearly resembles that of the Mother of the Gods, although, as we have noted, Bacchic cult is usually associated with women rather than men, and there are none of the sexual aspects of ecstasy that appear to lie behind the practice of self-castration in the cult of the Mother.

The link between Dionysus and uncontrolled behaviour is not difficult to understand. He is the god of wine, and wine breaks down restraint, leading to wild uncontrollable actions [94]. One of Dionysus's titles in Athens was Eleutherios, 'the liberator', and this is naturally taken to refer, among other things, to the effect of wine. It is important to note, however, that drunken worship of Dionysus appears to have been an exclusively male practice in the Greek world. It was men who engaged in the *komos*, a wild procession and revel through the city streets [95]. The *komos* can also

ABOVE LEFT
95 Scene of revelry on an Athenian 'Komast cup' from the sixth century BC.

BELOW LEFT
96 A terracotta mask of Dionysus from the second or first century BC.

RIGHT
97 A mask in a *liknon* on an Athenian red-figure *chous* (jug) from the second half of the fifth century BC.

be the concluding activity of the symposium, when, after time spent inside, reclining, speaking or singing and listening, participants would go outside and dance; this generally took place within the city and was the form of worshipping Dionysus in which the Scythian Scyles took part in Olbia. But the effects of alcohol – elation, ecstasy, disorientation and so on – could be achieved by other means, and still be identified with Dionysus.

Dionysus was also associated with masks [96].[51] This is most apparent in Attic drama, performed at his festivals where all the performers wore masks. But the mask also represents the god in other contexts. On Greek vases we find depictions of cult images of Dionysus made up of a mask tied to a post or a tree. There are also images of a mask in a *liknon*, the kind of basket in which sacred objects might be carried in procession [97].

There were usually cult statues of Dionysus in his temples, but these representations suggest that the mask could be thought of in the same way as a cult statue, or perhaps as the *hiera* carried in the procession of the Eleusinian Mysteries: a sacred representation of the god.

The purpose of the mask is to hide the identity of the person wearing it, so Dionysus is normally seen in disguise. In *Bacchae* he arrives in Thebes in disguise before appearing in his real form accompanied by an earthquake, thunder and lightning. In the same way, Bacchic rites give bacchants the opportunity to see the god without his mask. To do this they abandoned the trappings of civilization, represented by hearth and house and woollen clothes, and went out into the wild landscape beyond the city and beyond the cultivated land around it, up into the uncultivated mountains and hills, dressed in animal skins. This journey would be disorienting in itself. Once there they would sing and dance wildly, actions usually associated with ecstatic cults, and seek to achieve a trance state in which they might meet Dionysus unmasked.

Of course, this is an idealized description. We might wonder whether members of the *thiasos* from Physcus in Caria, which had to threaten them with fines for not coming out to the mountain, or of the Torre Nova *thiasos* with its vast number of office-holders and status ranks, always managed to experience the heights of ecstasy – although we should beware trying to read the character of a club from its rule book. Diodorus's description suggests that ecstatic dancing was an activity for the young, not for everyone. But that does not mean it could not be achieved by many bacchants over the centuries that Bacchic cult lasted.

6 *Private Initiation*

Alongside the ritual activities of groups such as Bacchic *thiasoi* or the annual crowd of initiates at Eleusis, we find individual religious specialists offering to perform mystic rites, *orgia* and *teletai*, to anyone prepared to employ them. These 'private initiators' are generally portrayed negatively in our surviving sources, which has led modern scholars to treat them as, at best, marginal figures and, at worst, confidence tricksters, preying on the gullibility and superstition of the masses. In this chapter we will examine the world of the private religious specialist. I have followed established practice in calling them 'initiators', as the rituals they carried out, usually referred to as *teletai* and involving purification and some kind of revelation, can be considered a form of 'initiation'.

Dionysiac Initiators

Sometime between 221 and 205 BC, Ptolemy IV Philopator, the ruler of Egypt, issued an edict controlling the activities of individuals who performed rites for Dionysus:

> By decree of the king. Persons who perform *teletai* for Dionysus in the country [i.e. outside Alexandria itself] shall sail down to Alexandria... and shall register themselves before Aristoboulos at the registration office within three days from the day on which they arrive, and shall declare straightaway from whom they have learned the rites [*or: received the sacred objects*] as far as three generations back, and shall hand in a sealed copy of their sacred text (*hieron logon*), each writing his own name on it.[1]

This document reveals the existence of religious practitioners about whom we have no other information. Philopator does not appear here to be trying to prevent these Dionysiac initiators from working; he appears to be trying to monitor them and guarantee the authenticity of their rites by establishing that they have been handed down for several generations and are based on genuine texts – whatever that might mean.

We can get some idea of how these initiators might have worked by looking at a description of a similar figure from Athens. As part of his attack on his political rival Aeschines, the fourth-century BC Athenian orator Demosthenes tells how he used to assist his mother Glaucothea in her *teletai*. At night he washed and purified initiates, scouring them with clay mixed with bran; then he helped to dress them in fawn skins and read from a book while his mother performed various actions. At the height of the ceremony he called out, 'I have escaped the bad; I have found the better.' Then in the daytime he led *thiasoi* through the streets, wearing a wreath and waving snakes around.[2] We are not told for which god these rituals were held, and this is a description that was supposed to make Aeschines seem ridiculous, so it is not necessarily accurate. Glaucothea's *teletai*, however, look very similar to those performed by Paculla Annia in Livy's description of the Bacchanalia in Italy (see Chapter 5). There a woman, assisted by her sons, oversaw rituals involving purification and initiation, and although Livy prefers to imagine depraved activity following on from this, Demosthenes' picture of the newly initiated dancing through the streets is probably a more accurate indication of what happened after such ceremonies.

Itinerant Initiators and Seers

98 Orpheus entertaining a satyr and a Thracian with his lyre, on an Athenian vase from the early fifth century BC.

Dionysus was not the only name associated with private initiation. The most influential depiction of private initiators comes from Plato's *Republic*, where one of the characters in the dialogue, Adeimantus, describes them in these terms:

Itinerant priests (*argyrtai*) and seers (*manteis*) go to rich men's doors and make them believe that they by means of sacrifices and incantations have accumulated a treasure of power from the gods that can expiate and cure with pleasurable festivals any misdeed of a man or his ancestors, and that if a man wishes to harm an enemy, at slight cost he will be enabled to injure just and unjust alike, since they are masters of spells and enchantments that constrain the gods to serve their end...

And they produce a babble of books of Musaeus and Orpheus, the offspring of the Moon and of the Muses, as they affirm, and these books they use in their ritual, and make not only ordinary men but states believe that there really are remissions of sins and purifications for deeds of injustice, by means of sacrifice and pleasant sport for the living, and that there are also special initiations, which they call *teletai*, that deliver us from evils in that other world, while terrible things await those who have neglected to sacrifice.[3]

99 Orpheus, Eurydice and Hermes on a Roman copy of a fifth-century BC relief sculpture from the surrounding wall of the Altar of the Twelve Gods in Athens, now in Naples. The names were not on the original sculpture, and it is debated whether it depicts Orpheus's reunion with Eurydice or his final farewell.

Musaeus was a legendary author of oracular verses, cryptic texts which, rather like the prophecies of Nostradamus in the sixteenth century AD, were claimed to have correctly predicted important events, with other verses still to be fulfilled. Orpheus was a better-known figure, the legendary singer and lyre-player, whose music had the power to soothe wild animals and who had even travelled to the underworld and charmed Persephone and Hades into restoring his wife Eurydice to him [98, 99, plate XV]. (The story that he then lost her again on his way back to the world of the living, of which the earliest surviving version is Virgil's written in the first century BC, may not have developed until well after the time of Plato.) From early on, Orpheus was associated with mystery cults – by the fourth century BC Athenians could think that he was involved in the foundation of the Eleusinian Mysteries. So it is no surprise that private initiators claimed his authority for their work. In the past scholars have suggested that there was a whole religious movement based on his teachings which they called 'Orphism'. That is probably incorrect, but nonetheless Orpheus is a dominant presence in the world of the mysteries.[4]

In his collection of satirical *Characters*, written late in the fourth century BC, Theophrastus describes the Superstitious Man regularly visiting the *orpheotelestai*, that is 'Orphic initiators', who are presumably similar to the figures depicted by Plato.[5] It is possibly a sign of his excessive religious timidity that the Superstitious Man chooses to visit the *orpheotelestai*, rather than waiting for them to come knocking on his door. Both Plato and Theophrastus are writing in and about Athens, where initiators of this sort must have been recognizable.

Books

The passage from the *Republic* emphasizes the importance of books (*biblia*) in the activities of the initiators in Athens, and Aeschines was supposed to have read from books during his mother's initiations. The decree of Ptolemy Philopator also refers to texts that were to be copied and deposited. In one play Euripides has a character refer to followers of Orpheus with their 'books full of smoke'.[6] The use of books therefore appears to be a mark of the religious specialist. What did such books contain?

Adeimantus, in Plato's *Republic*, links initiators with seers, or perhaps more precisely with *chresmologoi*, collectors and interpreters of written oracles. *Chresmologoi* are also given generally hostile treatment in written sources, and it is clear that some were important figures in Athenian politics. We get a picture of such an individual from Herodotus, who describes the activities of one Onomacritus in the late sixth century BC. Onomacritus was a friend of the rulers of Athens and advised them on religious matters, but was exiled after he was caught interpolating a text into the collection of the oracles of Musaeus that he was editing.[7] In 'editing' his oracles, he was probably adding a commentary to the verses, perhaps indicating where events predicted in the oracles had already happened and suggesting to what obscure descriptions might refer.[8]

Onomacritus used his religious expertise when he was advising his political patrons. That the kind of book he dealt with could have a practical application is also clear from a story told by the fourth-century BC Athenian orator Isocrates. He describes how a poor man, Thrasyllus, had inherited a collection of books on divination from a seer who had become his friend. Thrasyllus used the books to develop a career of his own as an itinerant diviner, behaving, as Isocrates describes it, in a thoroughly disreputable way.[9]

This was presumably what Plato was referring to when he talks about books of Musaeus, and books of Orpheus must have been similar: a text, or a collection of texts, attributed to Orpheus, accompanied by commentary, and with some practical guidance. And one example of such a book has survived from antiquity. It is known as the Derveni Papyrus.

The Derveni Papyrus

The Derveni Papyrus is the only surviving text on papyrus from Greece. It was discovered in 1962, partially burned, in a cremation burial in Derveni near Thessaloniki in northern Greece, and formally published in 2006, although its contents had been known and discussed by scholars for a while. It is now in the Archaeological Museum in Thessaloniki [100]. The single papyrus roll had been put in the funeral pyre of a rich man around 300 BC, although the text probably dates from about a generation earlier. It was most likely a prized possession of the man with whom it was buried, who chose to have it cremated with him. Exactly what sort of a text it is, and who wrote it, are questions that have fascinated scholars since its discovery was announced.[10]

It is clear that much of the text is a commentary on a poem attributed to Orpheus, but in the early, very fragmentary, part of the text it also appears to include instructions for some kind of ritual concerned with the dead, and the names *Erinyes* and *Eumenides* (that is, the Furies) appear in the text.[11] There is also some discussion of mystery cults, with an emphasis on how they are, and should be, understood. In one passage the author comments first on the fact that those who experience mysteries 'together with other people in the cities' — by which he presumably means at festivals like the Eleusinian Mysteries — do not understand what they are experiencing. But this, he says, is not surprising, as 'it is not possible to hear and simultaneously comprehend what is being said' — although what exactly he means by this is not clear. He goes on to say:

> But those who believe that they learned from someone who makes a profession of the rites deserve to be wondered at and pitied: wondered at because, although they believe before they perform the rites that they will learn, they go away after performing them before having learned, without even asking further questions, as if they knew something of what they saw or heard or were taught; and pitied because it is not enough for them that they paid the fee in advance — they also go away devoid even of their belief.[12]

This author seems to be describing people who pay supposed experts ('someone who makes a profession of the rites') to take them through rites, but learn nothing from the experience. This is presumably to be contrasted with those who go to genuine experts, who will be able to explain fully what the rituals are all about. And it is difficult to doubt that the author included himself among those who really understood these rites. Since the passage comes in the middle of a commentary on a poem by Orpheus, and includes reference to what must be city-based mystery cults, the author must be describing here initiation into rites associated with

100 Part of the Derveni Papyrus. The fragment illustrated here is commentating on lines of an Orphic poem describing the sexual union of Zeus and Aphrodite.

BELOW

101 The contents of the tomb where the Derveni Papyrus was found. The papyrus had been burnt in the funeral pyre, and the remains had been deposited on the stone slabs covering the tomb.

Orpheus. And since the author appears to be claiming expertise on this subject, it makes sense to see him as an Orphic initiator, an *orpheotelestes*. It is unlikely that the owner of the papyrus was himself the author, especially if, as most scholars think, the ideas fit more naturally into a later fifth-century BC context, rather than the world of around 300 BC when the owner died.

The tomb in which the papyrus was found was 'suffocatingly full of bronze and clay pots, vessels, jewelry and various small objects' [101].[13] The papyrus was found in the scattered ashes of the funeral pyre along

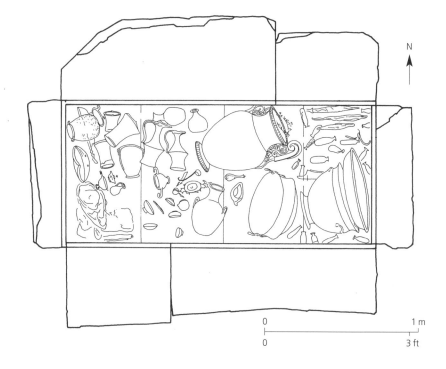

N

0   1 m

0   3 ft

with the remains of weapons and armour and a horse's harness. The neighbouring tomb contained a spectacular gold-coloured bronze burial urn with Dionysiac scenes on it [plate XVI]. The excavators conclude:

> It might be assumed that the Orphic papyrus accompanied the dead man on the pyre either because of its general religious-eschatalogical content, similar to that of the 'Dionysiac' krater B1, or because the owner liked to read such texts, or was indeed the commentator.[14]

Their last suggestion, as we have seen, is unlikely, but the text clearly ended up in the hands of a rich man. If this tells us something about the social world of the papyrus, and possibly therefore of its author, the text itself can give us valuable, and possibly surprising, information about the intellectual world of the *orpheotelestai*.

Initiators and Philosophers

Most of the surviving part of the Derveni Papyrus is concerned with the precise meaning of the words of the Orphic poem on which it is commenting. Here scholars have seen strong influence from Presocratic philosophy, and in particular two philosophers who wrote in the middle of the fifth century BC, Anaxagoras of Clazomenae and Diogenes of Apollonia. We have relatively little information about Diogenes, but Anaxagoras was a fairly prominent figure in Athens and a friend of the statesman Pericles. He was supposedly tried for denying the divinity of the sun and moon, preferring natural explanations for the phases of the moon and eclipses.[15] This preference for 'scientific' natural explanations for phenomena rather than 'irrational' religious ones is usually taken to characterize the Presocratic philosophers in general, so to find a writer who uses the ideas of Anaxagoras to interpret the poetry of Orpheus, and who also appears to be an *orpheotelestes* himself, is interesting. In his *Meno*, Plato has Socrates talk about 'certain priests and priestesses who have studied so as to be able to give a reasoned account of their activities', who understand what happens to the soul after death:

> They say that the soul of man is immortal, and at one time comes to an end, which is called dying, and at another is born again, but never perishes. Consequently one ought to live all one's life in the utmost holiness. For from whomsoever 'Persephone shall accept requital for ancient wrong, the souls of these she restores in the ninth year to the upper sun again; from them arise glorious kings and men of splendid might and surpassing wisdom, and for all remaining time are they called holy heroes amongst mankind.'[16]

The quotation is assumed to be from Pindar, a poet writing in the first half of the fifth century BC, who is generally treated respectfully by later prose authors. Religious practitioners who understand what they are doing, and are knowledgeable about what happens to the souls of the dead, sound very much like the author of the Derveni Papyrus.[17]

In fact, it would be wrong to draw too firm a line between Presocratic philosophers and religious practitioners. Herodotus, a historian who was very interested in religious subjects and was, as we have seen, an initiate of the Great Gods of Samothrace and probably of other cults too, was very much part of the intellectual world in which Presocratic philosophers and other 'scientific' writers worked. In his account of Egypt in particular, his discussion moves from geology to theology and back again, referring to the evidence for both equally. The Sicilian philosopher Empedocles, also writing in the middle of the fifth century BC, could promise his followers the power to prevent disease and old age, to control the winds and to raise the dead. Empedocles' work was known in antiquity by the title *Purifications*, and his claims appear rather similar to those of the *agyrtai* attacked in the passage from Plato's *Republic* quoted above.[18] Pythagoras, considered in more detail below, is another philosopher associated with initiation.

Orpheotelestai and other private initiators, therefore, although they might include among their number individuals more interested in making money than in transmitting ancient wisdom, were at least as often serious thinkers who saw no difficulty combining an interest in religion with science.

Explaining Ritual

Even if we accept, as we should, that most *orpheotelestai* and other initiators were not frauds, the fact remains that they were probably not associated with public cults in Greek cities and that they therefore had to persuade potential adherents of the benefits of initiation. They had to explain what was involved and why it mattered. This is what Plato says, and indeed it is suggested by the Derveni Papyrus. This aspect of their work turns out to be their most significant legacy.

As we have seen, Socrates in Plato's *Meno* claims to have learned about the experience of the soul after death from religious experts, and he associates these figures with poets, including Pindar. In Plato's *Protagoras*, Protagoras mentions Orpheus and Musaeus favourably, alongside Homer, Hesiod and Simonides, as ancient *sophistai* (wise men, but also, less positively, sophists).[19] In Plato's *Timaeus*, Socrates says, albeit with some possible scepticism:

It is beyond our powers to know or tell about the birth of the other gods; we must rely on those who have told the story before, who claimed to be the children of the gods, even if they give no probable or necessary proof of what they say: we must conform to custom and believe their own family history...[20]

He is probably referring again to Orpheus and Musaeus. In the intellectual circles of the fifth and fourth centuries BC in which philosophers like Socrates and Plato moved, poetry was analyzed as an authoritative source for understanding divine matters, and these circles also included *orpheotelestai*.

Much of what we are told about the content and apparent meaning of mystery cults comes from the writings of Christian apologists from the third and fourth centuries AD. It is often taken for granted that their information comes, directly or indirectly, from sanctuaries like Eleusis where cult activities took place. This is despite the fact that often these accounts do not specifically refer to a particular cult. As we saw in earlier chapters, it is unlikely that any doctrines were transmitted as part of the process of initiation in these cults: experience, not information, was central to their functioning. It is rather more plausible to see Christian writers basing their accounts on literary sources, and in particular the philosophical tradition that goes back to Plato and his predecessors. And the ultimate origin of the tradition will have been the *orpheotelestai* and others who needed to explain what they were doing. The Derveni Papyrus, whose author compares his own activities to what takes place in city cults, is evidence from this earlier part of the tradition: writers such as the Neoplatonist philosopher Iamblichus, whom we will meet in Chapter 10, represent its later form.

102 Pythagoras, as imagined by a German sculptor in the fifteenth century.

Pythagoras and Pythagoreans

One figure who has been seen to belong to the world of both philosophy and mystery cult is Pythagoras, who was active in the sixth century BC. He was born on the island of Samos but spent much of his life in southern Italy, where his influence appears to have been quite widespread [102].[21]

Herodotus mentions him several times and tells the story of how a former slave of Pythagoras who moved to Thrace tricked the members of his new community into believing that Pythagoras had returned from the dead. Herodotus elsewhere comments on the Egyptian habit of not using woollen garments when burying the dead, saying:

> This practice agrees with the rites which are called Orphic and Bacchic, but are actually Egyptian and Pythagorean: for it is impious, too, for one partaking of these rites to be buried in woollen wrappings. There is a sacred story (*hieros logos*) about this.[22]

The link between Pythagoras and Orpheus was also made by the philosopher Ion of Chios, writing in the later part of the fifth century BC, who claimed that Pythagoras wrote poems in the name of Orpheus.[23]

Pythagoras wrote nothing in his own name, although fragments of some of the works of his followers have survived. A great deal was written about him in antiquity, mostly many centuries after his death, and trying to establish facts about the man himself or his views is very difficult. One philosophical doctrine particularly associated with Pythagoras is *metempsychosis*, the idea that the soul survives death and is reborn into the body of another person or an animal. It is this concern with what happens after death that particularly links Pythagoras's ideas with the interests of the *orpheotelestai*. Pythagoras is also associated with vegetarianism, although here the evidence is much more inconsistent.

It is not clear whether these ideas actually influenced the behaviour of Pythagoras and his followers. It is true that by the middle of the fifth century BC, 'Pythagoreans' had gained a dominant position in a number of cities in southern Italy, which led to an organized attack on the meeting house of the Pythagoreans by their opponents followed by a period of political turmoil.[24] Some scholars have followed writers such as Iamblichus in creating a picture of individuals seeking initiation into Pythagorean groups, giving their possessions to the community and listening in silence for years to Pythagoras's teaching. Even if this were a reliable picture of how individuals were admitted into Pythagorean groups, it is not initiation in the sense that we have used it elsewhere in this book: it is more like a monastic novitiate. In any case, it is difficult to see how the kind of lifestyle implied by these activities could fit with the situation mentioned above, when Pythagoreans dominated the politics of the towns of southern Italy: the secluded contemplative philosophical life was not compatible with the active political one. Pythagoras's followers may have adopted some restrictions on what they wore, or what they ate, but even these would have had to be compatible with public life, which included, for example, sacrificing animals and eating the meat.

Pythagoras's importance for us lies less in what he and his followers did than in his significance to later philosophers. Plato only mentions Pythagoras once, and there is modern scholarly debate about how much

influence Pythagorean ideas had on Plato's philosophy. But Plato's followers were certainly interested in Pythagoras and wrote about his ideas,
although their works do not survive. By the third century AD some philosophers can be described almost interchangeably as Neo-Platonist or Neo-
Pythagorean. At this point Pythagoras became the subject of long works
on leading the ideal philosophical life, of which Iamblichus's *On the
Pythagorean Life* is the most substantial. The descriptions of mystery cults
in Christian and non-Christian writings in the fourth century AD were
influenced by these Neo-Pythagorean writings.

How Important were Private Initiators?

The negative portrayal of private initiators in Plato's *Republic*, along with
negative depictions of *chresmologoi* and *manteis* in the plays of Aristophanes, could easily lead us to think that Greek cities were crowded with
religious fraudsters. This picture is certainly false. Greek cities relied on
religious experts to advise them, and they were were sometimes citizens
and sometimes not. Cities and individuals acquired copies of ritual texts
and other sacred writings, and these were treated with respect. The implication of the edict of Ptolemy Philopator is that there were many
'initiators of Dionysus' in Egypt who could trace their professional lineage
back three generations.

Plutarch, in his biography of the Athenian statesman Pericles, tells a
story that possibly links *orpheotelestai* to the very heart of Classical Athens.
He reports a debate between Lampon, a leading Athenian religious expert
who was honoured by the city of Athens, and Anaxagoras the philosopher,
about a lamb with a single central horn which is found among Pericles'
flocks. Lampon interprets it as meaning that soon a single individual
would gain a dominant position in Athens, whereas until that point two
statesmen had been fighting for political dominance; Anaxagoras has the
skull split open and shows how the central cavity was misformed. Plutarch
goes on to say that at first Anaxagoras received the praise, but soon after,
when Pericles' last opponent lost his influence and Pericles became the
dominant figure in Athens, Lampon was praised in his turn.[25] Plutarch
sees this story as illustrating that both scientist (*physikos*) and seer (*mantis*)
could be right about these things. But the two debaters are linked in
another way. As we have seen, Anaxagoras was an important influence on
the author of the Derveni Papyrus, whom we can consider to be an
orpheotelestes. It has been argued that Lampon, who had an interest in
mystery cult according to Aristotle,[26] was buried in a tumulus in Thurii in
Italy where a number of the gold tablets associated with the work of
orpheotelestai have been found,[27] which are discussed in the next chapter.

7 *Words Written on Gold*

In a number of tombs in Thessaly in northern Greece, in Crete, Sicily and southern Italy, small, very thin sheets of gold foil have been found with writing inscribed upon them. These are usually referred to as gold tablets or gold leaves, and some actually in the shape of leaves, although most are roughly rectangular. Examples with very similar texts have been found in widely separated locations. The texts themselves are clearly concerned with the fate of the deceased, but what exactly this indicates about the individuals buried with gold leaves is the subject of much debate. It is generally accepted that the presence of gold tablets in tombs indicates that the dead person had been initiated into a cult of some kind. References in some of the texts to *bakkhoi* and *mystai* indicate that they bear some relationship to the cults examined in this book.[1]

The areas where gold leaves have been found are generally not the places where sanctuaries offered initiation. Apart from two tablets whose origins are unknown, one apparently from Lesbos and another currently in a Turkish museum (which is probably a rather different sort of text),[2] there are no examples from Asia Minor, Attica or Boeotia. There are examples from the Peloponnese and the North Aegean, but these generally provide little more information than a name.

The Hipponion Text

The oldest example found so far is also one of the clearest and longest texts. It comes from the burial of a woman in Hipponion in southern Italy and is dated to around 400 BC. The piece of gold foil is 59 mm wide at the top, narrowing to 49 mm at the bottom, and 32 mm high. It has sixteen lines of text, and the letters are less than 2 mm high [plate XVII]. The text reads:

> This is sacred to Memory: when you are about to die you will find your-self at the House of Hades; on the right there is a spring, by which stands a white cypress. Descending there, the souls of the dead seek refreshment. Do not even approach this spring; beyond you will find from the Pool of Memory cool water flowing; there are guards before it, who will ask you with clear penetration what you seek from the shades of murky Hades. Say: 'I am a son of earth and star-filled Heaven, I am dry with thirst and dying; but give me swiftly cool water flowing from

the Pool of Memory.' And they will take pity on you by the will of the Queen of the Underworld; and they will give you water to drink from the Pool of Memory; and moreover you will go on the great Sacred Way along which the other famed *mystai* and *bakkhoi* make their way.[3]

The text is in hexameter verse, the metre of Homer and Hesiod and the Homeric Hymns, and its meaning is straightforward. The soul of the dead person is told to avoid drinking from the first spring they come to: this is presumably what elsewhere is called the waters of Lethe, which bring forgetfulness to those who drink it. Instead the soul is advised to drink from the waters of Memory (*Mnemosyne*). To reach the pool, the soul has to indicate to the guards that he or she is under the protection of Persephone, the Queen of the Underworld, and this is done using a *symbolon*, a password indicating that the owner is an initiate of some kind. The reward for such souls is that they will go on, presumably to a better part of the underworld, and also, implicitly, that they will retain their identity, in contrast to the rest of the dead, who will forget their previous life entirely.

The picture of the world of the dead suggested by the text was well established in Greek literature. In the *Odyssey*, Odysseus goes down to the edge of the underworld, where he is able to summon dead souls to him by sacrificing sheep and letting the blood gather in a trench: the thirsty dead gather around the blood, desperate to drink it [103].[4] Elsewhere in the poem Menelaus says that he has been told that, because he is married to Zeus's daughter Helen, when he dies he will not join the rest of the nameless dead but will go to the Elysian Fields, where life is always pleasant.[5] The power of Persephone to intervene on behalf of certain individuals is described by Pindar, in a fragment quoted by Plato, which we saw in the previous chapter.[6] That passage ends with the words 'and for all remaining time are they called holy heroes among mankind'; a gold tablet from Petelia, also in southern Italy, with a text similar to the one from Hipponion, promises the soul: 'they will give you water to drink from the divine spring, and then you will reign with the

103 Odysseus summons the ghost of Tiresias in the underworld, as depicted on a south Italian red-figure calyx krater of c. 380 BC.

other heroes'.[7] In one of his odes, Pindar describes the fate of the virtuous dead like this:

> Those who have persevered three times, on either side, to keep their souls free from all wrongdoing, follow Zeus's road to the end, to the tower of Cronus, where ocean breezes blow around the island of the blessed, and flowers of gold are blazing, some from splendid trees on land, while water nurtures others. With these wreaths and garlands of flowers they entwine their hands according to the righteous counsels of Rhadamanthys.[8]

This is very close to the fate awaiting Menelaus in the *Odyssey*,[9] while the road of Zeus is like the 'sacred way' in the Hipponion text. The poet or poets who produced the texts on the tablets were apparently writing within the central tradition of Greek poetry.[10]

The crucial part of the instructions would appear to be the conversation with the guardians of the Pool of Memory. A series of five gold tablets from near Eleutherna in Crete, dating from the third century BC, all bear the following inscription:

> – 'I am burning with thirst and am dying, but give me to drink water from the ever-flowing spring, on the right where the cypress is.'
>
> – 'Who are you? Where do you come from?'
>
> – 'I am the son of earth and starry heaven.'[11]

Another example, from Thessaly, has the same text but with an additional line that reads 'but my race is heavenly'.[12]

Texts from Thurii

Another group of texts consists of words written as if addressed to the powers of the underworld. For example, three from a tumulus in Thurii in southern Italy bear very similar texts [plate XVIII]. The longest one reads:

> – 'I come from the pure, Pure Queen of the Underworld, Eucles, Eubouleus, and you other Immortal Gods! I too claim to be of your blessed house, but Fate and other Immortal Gods conquered me, […] the star-smiting thunder. And I flew out from the hard and deeply-grievous circle, and stepped onto the crown with my swift feet, and slipped into the bosom of the Mistress, the Queen of the Underworld. And I stepped out from the crown with my swift feet.'
>
> – 'Happy and blessed one! You shall be a god instead of a mortal.'
>
> – 'A kid I have fallen into milk.'[13]

The other two start with the same words, before continuing:

'I have paid the penalty for unjust deeds, whether Fate conquered me
[...] with the thunderbolt and the lightning flash. Now I come as a sup-
pliant to noble Persephone, that she may be kind and send me to the
seats of the undefiled.'[14]

These are less easy to understand than the Hipponion text, but they can be
partly explained. Eucles and Eubouleus, the main gods addressed, are
probably Hades and Dionysus.[15] When the speaker describes himself or
herself as 'pure', this is taken to indicate that they have undergone a ritual
of purification, and when they claim to have 'paid the penalty for unjust
deeds', this once again is close to Pindar's words, 'from whomsoever Persephone shall accept requital for ancient wrong, the souls of these she
restores in the ninth year to the upper sun again'.[16]

A further text from Thurii combines the ideas in the Hipponion text
with the ones we have just been considering, taking the form of an address
to the dead soul:

But whenever a soul leaves the light of the sun, enter on the right,
where one must, if one has kept all well and truly. Rejoice enduring
what is to be endured! This you have never before experienced. You
have become a god instead of a man. You have fallen as a kid into milk.
Hail, hail, as you travel on the right, through the Holy Meadow and
Groves of Persephone!'[17]

The Origins of the Tablets

The texts we have been considering come from three areas: southern
Italy (along with one from Sicily and one from Rome), Crete and Thessaly.
As we have seen, similar texts have been found in more than one area. A
text similar to those from Hipponion and Petelia in Italy has been found
in Pharsalus in Thessaly, and the related shorter texts are found both in
Crete and in Thessaly. The words 'you have fallen as a kid into milk',
found on the examples from Thurii, also appear on tablets from Pelinna
in Thessaly.[18]

There are other examples with texts apparently unrelated to these.
From Pherae in Thessaly comes a tablet which reads, 'Send me to the
thiasoi of the initiates (*mystai*), for I have seen rites, the initiations of
Demeter Chthonia and Mountain Mother'.[19] Another tablet from Thurii,
which was wrapped around one of those discussed above, appears to
be largely made up of random letters, embedded in which are what appear
to be various divine names.[20] In Aegium in Achaea, in the northwest

Peloponnese, three Hellenistic tombs have been found containing leaf-shaped tablets with the word *mystas* or *mystes* on them, in two of the cases accompanied by the name of the deceased.[21] In a grave of roughly the same time from Elis, slightly to the south, a similar leaf-shaped tablet with just the name Philemena was apparently put on the mouth of the deceased.[22] Similar examples are found in Macedonia, and in two cases the name is accompanied by a greeting to Persephone.[23]

In a number of cases little or nothing is known about the graves in which the tablets were found. Where more is known, it seems that there is considerable variation between the graves. Examples are found in burials of both men and women. In some cases they are from inhumations, while in others they are found in urns containing cremations. The tablet from Pharsalus was found in a fine bronze jug, along with the ashes of its owner [plate XIX, 104]. In some cases several graves containing tablets are located in close proximity, while others are isolated. On the whole the tablets come from graves which show some evidence of wealth, but beyond that there is no easily discernible pattern in the burials where gold tablets have been found. Most belong to the fourth or third centuries BC, although the latest one, from Rome, dates to the second or third century AD.[24]

104 The bronze vase in which the Pharsalus gold tablet was found, mid-fourth century BC. The relief decoration depicts Boreas, the North Wind, abducting the nymph Oreithyia.

The Texts

Most of the longer tablets are partly or wholly written in hexameter verse, and from early on it was assumed that behind the tablets lay one or more poems attributed to Orpheus. We have seen in the previous chapter that he was believed to have written poems, and later hymns and other poetical works were attributed to him. Furthermore, as Orpheus had himself been to Hades, spoken with Persephone, and returned, so he had the understanding to describe the underworld. Ancient commentators give the titles of poems attributed to Orpheus, and modern writers have attempted to identify from which of these our texts have come, although this does not necessarily add to our understanding of the text.

The question of whether the texts found on the tablets are all drawn from a single poem has also been raised.[25] It is not clear that this is the case. The Hipponion and closely related texts appear to take the soul from its arrival at the house of Hades to its onward journey to the sacred meadow: once the soul has got past the guardians of the Pool of Memory, it is safe. The texts addressing Eucles and Eubouleus suggest an alternative rather than additional conversation. The tablet that mentions the Mountain Mother also seems difficult to link into the other passages. It therefore seems likely that a number of separate poems provided the sources for the tablets, although the shared themes suggest that the poems originated from a common source, which is most likely to have been poems attributed to Orpheus, similar to the poem commentated on in the Derveni Papyrus. We will return to the question of how the texts reached the form they have in the gold tablets once we have considered who owned them.

Bakkhoi and Mystai

As we have seen, the Hipponion tablet refers to 'the other famed *mystai* and *bakkhoi*', and the word *mystes* is found on several; most of the longer texts assert that the dead person belongs to a privileged category. Since the discovery of the first of the tablets in the nineteenth century, they have been described as 'Orphic' and associated with initiation of some kind. More recently it has been recognized that features of the texts link them to Dionysus and they have been associated with Bacchic initiation, and it is now widely believed that all the texts relate to an Orphic 'religious movement' which was particularly concerned with initiatory rites associated with Dionysus.[26]

However, this view can be challenged. We saw in the last chapter that there were private initiators who associated themselves with Orpheus and with Dionysus, but the notion that they were associated with a coherent 'movement' is not well supported by evidence.[27] The recently published tablet from Pherae, which refers to Demeter Chthonia and the Mountain Mother but not to Dionysus, suggests that the tablets were associated with a wide range of gods (although the proponents of a 'Bacchic' interpretation have proposed fitting a reference to Dionysus into a short gap in the text).[28]

If the owners of the tablets belonged to a religious movement, we might expect evidence of their associating with each other. In particular we might expect them to be buried together. An inscription of the fifth century BC in a cemetery in Cumae in Italy excludes those who have not taken part in Bacchic rites from burial in one area.[29] But it does not seem that burials with gold tablets were grouped together in cemeteries.

It seems more likely that the tablets came from a wider range of sources and were acquired individually by their owners for a variety of reasons. It is possible indeed that they were acquired by the relatives of the dead specifically for the burial. Some were carefully placed in specific positions: either open in the hand of the deceased (in which case it could presumably be shown to the guardians of the underworld by the dead soul), or over the lips or folded in the mouth (to represent the spoken word), or on the chest.[30] This post-mortem placement may reflect the main function of the tablets. Although it has been suggested that they might have been used as part of an initiation ritual by the owners, the size of the lettering and the irregular way they were inscribed, particularly on non-rectangular tablets, makes this doubtful.[31] Indeed, the assumption that these tablets were used in initiation at all, and that their owners must have been initiates of some kind, is open to question.

Who Made the Tablets?

One of the most striking features of the tablets, and particularly the ones with longer texts, is the quality of the writing. As we have seen, the letters on the Hipponion tablet are less than 2 mm high, and on most of the rectangular tablets the writing is neat and regular. The leaf-shaped examples clearly posed more of a challenge. The letters are impressed on the foil, which is very fine and easily torn, so practice would have been needed to make sure the pressure on the stylus was right. The task would have been made more difficult in the absence of powerful sources of artificial light: the tablets would have had to be made in natural daylight.

The letters are in some cases skilfully formed, although less so in others. The texts themselves are a mess: there are spelling errors, which is not surprising – like other texts from the fourth and third centuries BC, spaces between words and punctuation marks are omitted. But the texts from which the tablets are copied are odd. Although the Hipponion tablet and those closely related to it are based on an original verse text, the text as we have it is metrically wrong, and some of the tablets have non-metrical sections inserted into the middle. Even more worryingly – at least for its owner – is the fact that the long tablet from Petelia tells the dead soul that the white cypress by the spring of forgetfulness is on the left, while all the other tablets giving directions place it on the right. It is possible that this mixture of prose and incorrect verse was used by private initiators in their ceremonies, and then repeated on the tablets.[32] But if this was the case, it suggests a sharp contrast between these ('the people who wrote, or rather scribbled these tablets were obviously not highly literate')[33] and the kind of initiator discussed in the previous chapter, who were concerned with the precise meaning of their particular texts.

It would be useful at this stage to consider where we might find the combination of ability to form the letters with carelessness in the creation of the text. It is a combination more easily associated with craftsmen than with literary experts. The individuals who could most easily manufacture the gold tablets would not be initiators, but goldsmiths, who would have access to supplies of gold foil and the tools and skill required to write on them. It is possible that goldsmiths would be working to order for initiators, or initiates, but this is not the only possible explanation.

In those cases where the tablet contained a name, it is safe to assume that it was made to order – but that could easily be an order to a goldsmith from the person before he died or from his family, with no initiator involved. In other cases, it is possible that tablets were produced by goldsmiths copying texts that they had acquired themselves – possibly copied from texts owned by other craftsmen rather than by initiators. This would explain the corrupt nature of the texts.

What was the Purpose of the Gold Tablets?

The suggestions we have just considered offer a different perspective from the prevalent scholarly view that the gold tablets are evidence of the activities of *orpheotelestai* engaged in initiating individuals into the mysteries of Dionysus. A further question can be asked: if someone had been initiated, whether into a state cult or a *thiasos*, or by an individual *orpheotelestes*, would they need a copy of a ritual text when they entered the afterlife? If initiation into the Eleusinian Mysteries or participation in Bacchic *teletai* meant actually meeting the gods face to face, then the people who experienced them would not need documents to prove who they were: they would already have been known to the gods. Is it possible then that the gold tablets, in some cases at least, might belong to those who had *not* been initiated, but had instead bought a gold 'ticket to heaven' as an alternative way in? In the previous chapter we saw that the criticisms of *orpheotelestai* as charlatans were unfair and misrepresented what private initiators might do. That does not rule out the possibility that 'Orphic' material was circulating in the hands of tradesmen as well as religious experts, and that the two were appealing to somewhat different markets. While the services of private initiators may have been in demand in Greek communities, especially from those interested in knowledge about rites as well as practical benefits, the gold tablets may be evidence for a much more pragmatic approach to religion and the afterlife.

8 *Isis*

I am Isis, the mistress of every land, and I was taught by Hermes, and
with Hermes I devised letters, both sacred [hieroglyphic] and
demotic, so that not everything would be written with the same
letters.
I established laws for mankind, and ordinances that none can change.
I am the eldest daughter of Cronus.
I am wife and sister of King Osiris.
I am she who finds crops for men.
I am mother of King Horus.

I am she that is called goddess by women.

I revealed mysteries (myeseis) to men.
I taught them to honour images of the gods.

I am the Queen of seamanship.
I make the navigable unnavigable when it pleases me.
I created walls of cities.
I am called *Thesmophoros* [Lawgiver].

Hail, Egypt, that nourished me!

These words come from an inscription of the second century AD from
the city of Cyme in Asia Minor, which claims to be copied from
another inscription erected in front of the temple of Hephaestus in
Memphis. It is an example of an aretalogy, a text extolling the powers and
achievements of a god or goddess.[1]

Although this claims to be copied from an original Egyptian document
and mentions some specifically Egyptian things, such as the invention of
hieroglyphics and Isis' relationship with Osiris and Horus, it also has some
features that could be considered more Greek. When Isis calls herself
Thesmophoros she appears to be equating herself with Demeter with
whom, as we will see, she shared a concern for crops. Other Isis aretalogies
also show Greek influence, and in particular similarities with Demeter,
with whom Isis was frequently identified.[2]

This book began with a quotation from a description of initiation into
the mysteries of Isis, an Egyptian goddess, set in Greece and written in
Latin. There is plentiful evidence for the cult of Isis from all over the

Mediterranean world, but surprisingly little clear evidence for the nature of her cult.³ In this chapter we will consider the influence of Egypt, Greece and Rome on the cult of Isis and try to establish what the mysteries of Isis were, and what their purposes might have been.

Isis in Egypt

Isis was an important goddess in pharaonic Egypt. Stories about her appear in texts from the Old Kingdom (*c.* 3100–*c.* 2181 BC) onwards, and she received cult worship in several temples in association with Osiris and Horus, although there do not appear to have been any temples devoted

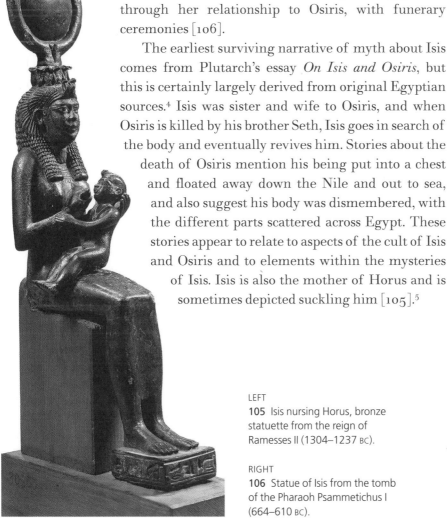

exclusively or primarily to Isis until the thirtieth dynasty, the brief period of Egyptian independence from the Persian empire in the fourth century BC. Isis was closely associated with the kings of Egypt and, through her relationship to Osiris, with funerary ceremonies [106].

The earliest surviving narrative of myth about Isis comes from Plutarch's essay *On Isis and Osiris*, but this is certainly largely derived from original Egyptian sources.⁴ Isis was sister and wife to Osiris, and when Osiris is killed by his brother Seth, Isis goes in search of the body and eventually revives him. Stories about the death of Osiris mention his being put into a chest and floated away down the Nile and out to sea, and also suggest his body was dismembered, with the different parts scattered across Egypt. These stories appear to relate to aspects of the cult of Isis and Osiris and to elements within the mysteries of Isis. Isis is also the mother of Horus and is sometimes depicted suckling him [105].⁵

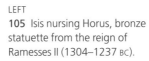

LEFT
105 Isis nursing Horus, bronze statuette from the reign of Ramesses II (1304–1237 BC).

RIGHT
106 Statue of Isis from the tomb of the Pharaoh Psammetichus I (664–610 BC).

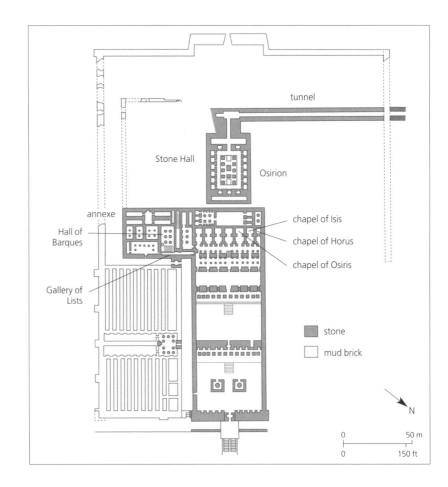

107 Plan of the temple of Sethos at Abydos.

BELOW
108 A scene from the temple of Sethos at Abydos. Osiris is lying on a bier with Horus on the left and Isis on the right.

Labels in plan: tunnel, Stone Hall, Osirion, annexe, Hall of Barques, Gallery of Lists, chapel of Isis, chapel of Horus, chapel of Osiris, stone, mud brick, N, 0 50 m, 0 150 ft

In Egypt the story of Isis's role as protector of Osiris was related to her role as protector of the pharaoh. On his accession a new pharaoh was identified with Horus and when he died he was identified with Osiris, so Isis was represented as mourning for him and overseeing his funerary ceremonies.

Osiris in Abydos

Osiris, but not Isis, had a major cult centre in the city of Abydos in Upper Egypt. An inscription from the twelfth dynasty (1991–1802 BC) describes how an official called Ikhernofret took part in an annual festival in honour of Osiris, held in the last month of the Nile's inundation. The festival lasted for several days and included a sequence of ritual performances and processions in which events from the life of Osiris were re-enacted. These included defeating his enemies in battle, his funeral, the debate between Horus and Seth in which Horus was victorious, and finally the restoration of Osiris to life. Most of these events woud have been seen by the crowds who came to Abydos for the festival and to witness the return of Osiris. However, the rituals of purification that preceded the resurrection of Osiris took place away from the public gaze and involved only the senior cult officials. The rituals probably took place in and around a building of uncertain date known as the Osirion. The pharaohs of the nineteenth dynasty (1295–1187 BC) built a major temple at Abydos in honour of earlier kings of Egypt, and this was attached to the Osirion [107]. Paintings on the walls of some rooms at the rear of this temple, aligned with the Osirion, depict ritual acts involving Osiris and probably illustrate some of the rituals that took place in private [108, plate XX]. As we will see, this pattern of ritual purification and secret ritual, carried out by a few in the context of a more public festival, has parallels to what we know of the mysteries of Isis in the Greek world.[6]

Isis and the Greek World

From at least the fifth century BC onwards, Greek writers showed an interest in Egypt. This is most visible in the writings of Herodotus, who devoted one of the nine books of his history entirely to Egypt and was particularly interested in Egyptian religion, which he considered the source of Greek religious understanding. Herodotus identifies Isis with Demeter and Osiris with Dionysus, and he mentions sacred stories about Osiris/Dionysus that he declines to tell.[7] Diodorus, writing in the first century BC, makes the same identification and also claims an Egyptian origin for the Eleusinian Mysteries and Bacchic cult.[8]

The earliest evidence for the cult of Isis in the Greek world comes from Athens, where sometime in the fourth century BC some Egyptians were given permission to acquire land and build a temple to Isis on it. As we have seen, this is also when the earliest temple of Isis in Egypt itself was built, and it may reflect a renewed Egyptian concern with the cult of Isis coinciding with regained Egyptian independence. This connection, along with the well-established association of Isis with the rulers of Egypt, may help to explain why the cult of Isis spread so rapidly outside Egypt in the following century.

The Spread of the Cult of Isis

After the death of Alexander the Great in 323 BC, Egypt was ruled by the Macedonian dynasty of the Ptolemies. Their court was in Alexandria, and for most of the third century BC they controlled significant territories outside Egypt, including islands in the Aegean. It was during this period that the cult of Isis spread most rapidly in the eastern Mediterranean, and temples appeared in Asia Minor as well as the Greek islands [109]. Isis was

109 The temple of Isis on Delos, built in the second century BC.

at this time accompanied not by Osiris but by the god Sarapis. Scholars debate the origins of Sarapis, whose name is derived from Apis, a god who took the form of a bull and was worshipped in Memphis from early in Egyptian history. Under Ptolemy I (323–283 BC) increased prominence was given to a human representation of Apis, who may already have been receiving cult worship in Memphis as Sar-Apis, or who may have been a newly developed linkage of Osiris and Apis. Sarapis is associated with several gods connected with the boundary between life and death, including Hades and Asclepius, but there is little clear evidence of mystery cult devoted to him [110].

It is possible that this was when the first mystery cult of Isis began. As we will see, initiation possibly involved time spent in some kind of underground chamber, which has been understood as a representation of the chest in which Osiris was locked. A 'crypt' of this kind has been found in the temple of Isis in Gortyn, on Crete, dating to the third or second century BC, and this may well represent early archaeological evidence for initiation into her cult [plate XXI].[9] On the other hand, it is not until centuries later that we have unambiguous references to mysteries in literary texts.[10]

110 Roman copy of a Greek statue of Sarapis from c. 300 BC.

Isis in Rome

The cult of Isis reached Italy by the end of the second century BC. The earliest temples were set up in Puteoli in 105 BC and in Pompeii in 80 BC [111, 112]. According to Apuleius, it was also in 80 BC that the college of *pastophoroi* of Isis was set up in Rome.[11] Because the cult of Isis was associated with the Ptolemaic rulers of Egypt, its development in Rome was strongly affected by politics. Although nominally independent, Egypt-ian rulers in this period looked to Rome for support, mainly against rival members of their own families. At the same time Egypt supplied Rome with large quantities of grain every year, so a cult devoted to Isis, the goddess most associated with the Egyptian harvest, had its practical purposes.[12]

There is no evidence for public cults of Egyptian gods in Rome before 43 BC, although private cult activity came under scrutiny similar to that which led to the controls on Bacchic cult in 186 BC.[13] In 43 BC there was a political reunion between Mark Antony and Octavian, who had quarrelled after the assassination of Julius Caesar the year before. Octavian, Antony and Marcus Lepidus made a pact to control the empire and vowed to establish a temple to Isis and Sarapis.[14] The choice of Egyptian gods reflected in part Julius Caesar's links with Egypt. Two ancient authors tell the story of how in that same year a political opponent of Antony and Octavian was able to escape from Rome by disguising himself as a priest of Isis.[15] This

ABOVE
111 The temple of Isis at Pompeii. The temple, buried in the eruption of Vesuvius in AD 79, had been rebuilt after its destruction in an earthquake in AD 62.

RIGHT
112 A painting of Isis from Pompeii. She holds a cornucopia in her left hand and a ship's rudder in her right, to emphasize her association with both fertility and sailing.

113 A detail from the frieze on the tomb of the Haterii in Rome, first century AD, which depicts a number of Roman buildings. Here a triumphal arch is labelled as by (the temple of) Isis.

BELOW
114 A statue of Isis from Rome, first century AD. The image is entirely in the style of Greek and Roman sculpture, rather than Egyptian.

suggests that a proper cult had been set up at once, although since the same story is told about the future emperor Domitian in another period of political chaos,[16] it may be a tale applied to lucky escapes that should not be accepted as true. In his description of the battle of Actium in 31 BC, when Octavian defeated Antony, the historian Dio Cassius put a speech into Octavian's mouth accusing Antony of styling Cleopatra as Isis and himself as Osiris.[17] This reflects a period of public distancing from Egyptian gods, and three years later Octavian forbade the performance of Egyptian rites in the city of Rome.[18] However, this did not mean that Octavian showed any resistance to the cult of Isis outside Rome and its immediate surrounding area.

An unreliable story claims that a temple of Isis existed in Rome in the reign of Tiberius (AD 14–37) until he destroyed it after a scandal,[19] but there certainly was a temple of Isis in Rome by AD 65, when it is mentioned in a poem [113, 114].[20] It was in the Campus Martius, and the emperor Vespasian (AD 69–79) and his son Titus spent a night in the temple in AD 70 before celebrating a Triumph to mark their victory in the Jewish War.[21] One of Vespasian's immediate predecessors, Otho (AD 69), is also said to have paid cult to Isis and worn a linen robe.[22] The temple was burned down in a fire in AD 80 and rebuilt by the emperor Domitian (AD 81–97). It was restored again at the end of the second century under Septimius Severus (AD 193–211).[23]

The interest Roman emperors showed in the cult of Isis would have increased interest in it more generally.[24] The two most informative literary works about the mysteries of Isis, Plutarch's *On Isis and Osiris* and Apuleius's *Metamorphoses* (or The Golden Ass), were written in the period of the cult's greatest popularity.

What Form did the Cult Take?

Not all of the cult of Isis was mystery cult. Pausanias, in his description of Greece (which again dates to the second century AD), mentions a number of temples of Isis, particularly in and around Corinth.[25] In one instance he refers to a cult image seen only by the priests of Isis, but he does not mention mysteries, even when referring to Cenchreae in Corinth, where Apuleius sets his description of the mysteries. He does describe an unusual festival in honour of Isis in Tithoreia in Phocis. The festival took place twice a year and included a fair and also the offering of animals to Isis, but these were not burned: instead they were killed, wrapped in linen and then left in a sunken chamber in the sanctuary, presumably to rot. The remains were then removed on the day before the next festival.[26] Leaving animals to rot as part of a festival is not unparalleled: at the Athenian Thesmophoria, a festival in honour of Demeter, piglets were thrown into pits and left to rot, after which the remains were brought up again to be mixed with the new grain at sowing time.[27] It has also been argued that the initiates at the Eleusinian Mysteries took to Eleusis the piglets they had earlier slaughtered and deposited them in pits in front of the Telesterion there.[28] Nonetheless the ritual at Tithoreia, which involved larger sacrificial animals and linen wrapping, is somewhat different and may well have had Egyptian roots. In his *Georgics*, written in the first century BC, the Roman poet Virgil describes an Egyptian ritual in which bullocks are beaten to death and their orifices are blocked, after which their bodies are left in a narrow chamber to rot.[29] Virgil claims that bees are miraculously generated from the rotting animals, but if he is describing a genuine ritual it may have had other purposes, perhaps associated with Isis.

Since the spread of Egyptian cults was closely linked to the political and military activities of the Ptolemaic kings, it would generally have been city councils rather than individuals who were responsible for the introduction of the Isis cult. The evidence we have for how the cult was organized comes largely from inscriptions.[30]

From the third century BC there is evidence of priests being brought to Greece from Egypt to serve in temples of Sarapis and Isis,[31] but a little later we also find Greeks holding priesthoods. In Athens, where some priesthoods were appointed each year from the citizen body, we find annually appointed Athenian priests of Sarapis and Isis.[32] In Apuleius's description of Isiac initiation, part of the ritual involved the priest reading from hieroglyphic texts. It is unlikely that many Athenian citizens knew the Egyptian language, so this kind of activity was unlikely to have been their responsibility. Annually appointed priests of Sarapis and Isis are also found elsewhere in the Greek world: in the cities Egyptian cult appears to have been set up along the lines of existing Greek cults. Later we find Roman citizens (of Greek origin) holding priesthoods.[33]

Since at first Isis was usually worshipped with Sarapis, their priesthood was shared and held by men. Priestesses of Isis only appear under the Roman empire, as Isis became more dominant than Sarapis, although earlier there are women with formal cultic roles, in particular *kanephoroi* (basket-bearers) which are found in a number of other cults including Dionysiac *thiasoi*, as we have seen, and only ever held by women.[34] As with priests, priestesses might hold their office for a year or for life.[35]

As with the Dionysiac *thiasoi*, there was much variation in cult practice in honour of Isis between different places and, like the *thiasoi*, the religious hierarchy of the cult of Isis appears to have grown more complex over time. We do not know how common initiation into the mysteries of Isis was. As far as we can tell there was not normally an equivalent of the Eleusinian Mysteries, an annual festival in the course of which all initiation took place. However, regular festivals were held in honour of Isis in places where her cult was well established, including in particular the Ploiaphesia, the ship-launching ceremony, called in Latin the Navigium Isidis. This festival took place in the spring in a number of seaports and involved a grand procession carrying a ceremonial ship to the harbour, where it would be launched to indicate the start of the sailing season. It is in the course of this festival that the hero of Apuleius's *Metamorphoses* first comes in contact with Isis, and it is his account that provides most of our information about initiation.

Apuleius's *Metamorphoses*

Apuleius's *Metamorphoses* was probably written in the AD 170s or 180s. It is a prose novel in Latin, telling the story of a rather foolish man, Lucius, who in the course of his travels finds himself transformed into a donkey. In his translated state Lucius suffers all kinds of indignity until he has a dream in which a goddess, who turns out to be Isis, appears to him. She promises to return him to human form the next day, and when this duly happens, Lucius pledges himself to the service of Isis and undergoes a series of initiations into her cult, ending up living at her temple in Rome. The whole story is narrated by Lucius and presented as if it is the testimony of a convert to Isis. It is also intentionally comic, and a significant part of the humour lies in Lucius's lack of understanding of the events he is describing.[36]

For our purposes the final book of the *Metamorphoses*, book 11, is of particular interest. This starts in the Greek city of Corinth on the night of the full moon, with Lucius, still in the form of a donkey, deciding to purify himself by bathing in the sea, and then praying to the Moon Goddess. When he falls asleep the goddess appears, telling him that she is the queen of all the gods and is worshipped under many names, including the Mother of the Gods, Proserpina (i.e. Persephone) and Demeter, but that her true name is Isis. She then tells Lucius to attend the procession the next day and to eat the garland of roses carried by the priest – this, as Lucius already knows, will be the cure for his condition. The procession is described in considerable detail and Lucius follows the instructions – although here, as throughout the novel, he does not appear entirely to trust what he has been told. Lucius is duly cured and follows the procession to the temple of Isis. He then rents a home in the temple precinct and works as a temple servant until the goddess indicates that the time has come for him to be initiated. He is instructed by the priest, who reads from a hiero-glyphic text. The process of initiation involves spending quite a lot of money, attending the local baths, and then fasting for ten days. Afterwards Lucius is dressed in a new linen robe and taken to the inner chamber of the temple for a nocturnal ritual. He claims that he will not describe what happened there but then goes on with the words quoted at the beginning of the Introduction to this book:

> I reached the boundary of death, and set foot on the threshold of Proserpina, and then I returned, carried through all the elements; in the middle of the night I saw the sun blazing with bright light; I approached the gods below and the gods above face to face, and worshipped them from nearby.[37]

In the morning he emerges dressed as the sun, holding a torch, and wearing twelve ornate robes and a crown of radiating palm leaves. The initiation is followed by days of feasting. A few days after this Lucius returns home but is almost immediately summoned by the goddess to Rome, to her temple on the Campus Martius. After a year in Rome he is told by the goddess that he must be initiated a second time, this time in the mysteries of Osiris. Lucius is puzzled and also short of money, but nonetheless he goes through the rituals. These include carrying a *thyrsos* and ivy as well as other objects that cannot be named. These are all elements that could be associated with Dionysus. Soon after this second initiation Lucius is shocked to discover that he is expected to undergo a third. He claims that he began to doubt the sincerity of the cult, but he was making money as a successful lawyer and so could afford the costs, and indeed he claims to have fasted on this occasion for longer than the required ten days. After this third ceremony he finds himself appointed to the college of *pastophoroi* and is made a decurion, both presumably high-status posts within the cult. And here the narrative ends.

How Serious is Apuleius?

The solemnity of much of book 11, compared to the crudity and comedy of the earlier books of the *Metamorphoses*, appears puzzling. Some scholars have argued that it should be taken at face value as a serious account of the worship of Isis, written by an initiate in order to honour the goddess. Other scholars have taken the view that it must be satirical, in order to fit with the rest of the work. They point to Lucius's bewilderment at the repeated initiations and claim that he is clearly being duped by the priesthood of the temples. Far from being written to honour the goddess, they say it is intended to mock her cult.[38]

It is, however, possible to see the book as comic without it being a satire on the cult of Isis. As we have noted in earlier chapters, religious professionals were often the subject of scorn in works of literature, and indeed Lucius is very hostile to the followers of the Syrian Goddess depicted earlier in the *Metamorphoses*.[39] But in book 11 Lucius is told by Isis and Osiris themselves that he needs to be initiated more than once. What is more, far from being cheated of his money through this process, Lucius finds himself, much to his own surprise, a wealthy and successful lawyer and near the top of the Isiac order. It is Lucius himself who is the butt of the humour: as in the rest of the novel, he completely fails to understand what is happening to him. What is presented in the form of testimony from someone at the heart of a cult turns out to prove that the speaker cannot even begin to explain how he ended up where he is.

One reason for taking this view of the work is that there is evidence to suggest that the rituals described, including the sequence of initiations, give a fairly accurate account of what was involved in the mysteries of Isis. Some of these elements are common to other mystery cults, but some are rather different.

Initiates and Priests

The word *mystes*, initiate, is never used in inscriptions to describe anyone associated with the cult of Isis, and this indicates an important difference between the cult of Isis, on the one hand, and Bacchic cult or sanctuary-based mystery cults on the other. Men and women who were initiated into the sanctuary-based cults examined earlier in this book were not expected to maintain a continuing relationship with the sanctuary. In contrast, those initiated into the cult of Isis appear to have been expected to carry on serving the goddess. At least in the second century AD, the period of most of our evidence, initiation appears to be a series of steps that lead to higher levels of service within the cult. It is possible that the chief priesthoods were actually only accessible to privileged individuals, but there does not seem to be the notion of initiation as simply an end in itself.

A description of Egyptian priesthood is given by the Egyptian writer Chaeremon, who wrote in the first century BC. It is probably rather idealized, but it states that priests lived near their temples and that they went through periods of fasting and purification ranging from seven to forty-two days before taking part in ritual activities. It also claims that they took no outside work and had few dealings with anyone outside the cult. These rules were strictly observed by the highest priests and to a lesser extent by 'the rest of the priests, the *pastophoroi*, the *neokoroi* [temple wardens] and assistants'. Much of Chaeremon's description could apply to Lucius's experience as an initiate of Isis. At the very least, this indicates that Isiac initiation was modelled on an idea of Egyptian priesthood.[40]

In *On Isis and Osiris*, Plutarch says that Isis 'reveals the divine things to those who are truly and rightly called "carriers of sacred things" and "wearers [or keepers] of sacred robes"', implying that initiates were expected to be active in subsequent rituals. Plutarch also discusses 'the reason why the priests shave off their hair and wear linen garments'.[41] Apuleius, in his description of the procession in Corinth in honour of Isis, talks about:

> The crowds initiated into the sacred rites, men and women of every status and age, shining with the pure brightness of their linen robes: the women with their hair anointed and wrapped in a transparent veil, the men shaven-headed with the skulls gleaming – the earthly stars of the great cult – making a noise together with sistrums of bronze and silver, and even of gold.[42]

These are distinct from the high priests (*antistites*) who follow them and from the priest (*sacerdos*) of Isis (also referred to as the *summus sacerdos*), but they are also distinct from the other people in the procession. In the temple of Isis the inner chamber is reserved for the chief priest, those who

XX Scene from the wall of a chapel in the temple of Sethos at Abydos, showing the raising of the Djed pillar. This was the climax of the Khoiak festival performed in honour of Osiris at Abydos.

BELOW
XXI The sanctuary of Isis at Gortyn. Steps in the double wall at the left lead down to a small sunken chamber which may have been a place of initiation.

XXII, XXIII, XXIV Details from a series of frescoes inside the Mithraeum at S. Maria Capua Vetere: (top) the tauroctony, in which Mithras, shown wearing brightly coloured 'Persian' clothes, kills the bull; (above left) one of a sequence of initiation scenes, showing an initiate lying on the ground; (above right) another initiation scene, in which the initiate is apparently being shown a crown.

had carried divine images (in Greek these would be *hierophoroi* or *theophoroi*) and those who had been initiated into the inner sanctuary. There is also a special role for the *pastophoroi*, whose company Lucius joins after his third initiation.[43] Initiates of Isis are expected to act as cult officials once they have been initiated, and although presumably they, like Lucius, engaged in activities outside the temple, they were more closely identified with the cult after initiation than were initiates of the Eleusinian or Samothracian mysteries. There may be some similarity in organization between the the cult of Isis and Dionysiac *thiasoi*, at least in the period of the Roman empire when they develop more complicated hierarchies. One mystery cult may have influenced the other, although it is not obvious in which direction. But while clearly there might have been an obligation to attend the meetings of the *thiasos*, it seems unlikely that the bacchants or *mystai* who made up the lowest level of Bacchic initiates were required to do more than that.

Levels of Initiation

Lucius, as he presents it, is initiated into the mysteries first of Isis, then of Osiris, and then, probably, of Isis again. One of the reasons given for the third initiation is that the robes of the goddess which he had worn before were left in storage in the temple in Corinth, and he will need robes to wear on holy days.[44] Plutarch, in a passage that is not absolutely clear, talks about the robes of Isis and Osiris. Those of Isis are multicoloured and are worn many times, while the robe of Osiris is plain and worn only once, then put away unseen and untouched. He may be referring to the robes worn during initiation – with the implication that the robe worn by initiates at their second initiation is then locked away, while they continue to wear the robes of their first (Isiac) initiation at subsequent festivals.

Before his second initiation Lucius has a dream in which he sees an initiate with a twisted heel, whom he then meets the next day. This man is a *pastophoros*, and after his own third initiation Lucius is made a member of the college of *pastophoroi*.[45] The position of the *pastophoroi* within the cult is not clear, but it is certainly possible that a third initiation was a necessary prerequisite for holding the post. This would indicate a process whereby a series of initiations led some individuals up to higher ranks within the hierarchy of the cult. Lucius himself moved from Corinth to Rome as part of his progress within the cult, and it is not clear whether there was a central hierarchy or if each temple was independent. The latter seems more likely, as there is no evidence for a centralized Isiac authority, and we can see the same arrangement, with a sequence of levels of initiation for those involved in the cult, in the mysteries of Mithras (see Chapter 9).

OPPOSITE
XXVIII The lion monument from Nemrut Dag (see previous page). The three stars above its back are named as the planets Mars, Mercury and Jupiter. The lion represents the constellation Leo, with its principal star, Regulus, on the lion's chest, cupped in the crescent moon. The monument has been understood to represent the coming together of the three planets, the moon and the sun in the constellation Leo in July 62 BC.

Who was Initiated?

Apuleius's novel can tell us little about what kind of people were generally initiated into the cult of Isis. Lucius, the narrator, despite his wayward career, claims to have been a successful lawyer while he was serving Isis. Apuleius, the author, was also a successful lawyer, but we do not know whether he was himself initiated into the cult of Isis.

As we have seen, those who went through Isiac rituals did not use the normal word for an initiate, *mystes*, to describe themselves. One inscription has been found in Italy, indicating a burial ground reserved for a priest of Isis and his *telestini* (the Latin equivalent of *telestai*, meaning someone who has experienced mystery rites) and their descendants.[46] The inclusion of descendants, who need not have been initiated themselves, suggests that the priest and the *telestini* are being honoured for their actual service to Isis – this is not a burial plot reserved for the initiated.

As we have also noted, not all cults of Isis involved initiation, and priests were appointed in many cities whose duties would have been indistinguishable from those of the priests of other gods. Indeed, in some cities the same men over the course of their adult lives may have held a long series of annual priesthoods for different gods, and they would have been expected to oversee the rituals and the finances of the different cults as a service to the city as well as to the particular gods. At the other end of the scale we have an inscription from Megalopolis in Arcadia honouring a certain Dionysia, who served Isis for forty-five years from the age of fifteen, performing the same role throughout that time.

But there were some places, by the first century BC at least, where the cult of Isis involved a large body of priests and cult officials [115, 116]. This is what Apuleius describes in Corinth and Rome, and it is illustrated by

115 A procession in honour of Isis in Rome, first century AD. Cult officials carry sacred objects including a snake, a scroll, a water jug, a sistrum (rattle) and a ladle.

116 A wall painting from Herculaneum depicting the worship of Isis, first century AD. In the foreground is an altar and worshippers, and at the back, at the top of a flight of steps, is a male figure dancing.

BELOW
117 The tombstone of a priestess of Isis from Athens, Roman Imperial period. She holds a sistrum in her right hand and a vessel, possibly containing Nile water, in her right.

paintings in Herculaneum; this must also have been the case in those places where the ship-launching festival was held, which included Byzantium[47] and Eretria in Euboea.[48]

We know many names of people involved in the cult of Isis from these places, but we can say little about them. There are a number of funerary monuments from Rome of women who had been priestesses of Isis, and these depict a woman holding a sistrum [117].[49] The names on the monuments indicate that they are often wives of freedmen, generally from the Greek world (which included most of the eastern Mediterranean area). In *Metamorphoses* Lucius came to Rome from Greece, and this may reflect reality.

Making Sense of Isiac Initiation

It is important not to forget that Apuleius's *Metamorphoses* is a work of fiction. We do not know whether Apuleius himself had personal experience of the cult of Isis, although in another work, his *Apologia*, he claims to have been initiated into several cults in Greece, including that of Dionysus.[50] It is possible that the account of initiation he puts into the mouth of Lucius is constructed from an amalgam of details from other cults and the author's own imagination.

The ten days of abstinence that Lucius undergoes before the ritual itself are very similar to the preparations Aebutius was expected to make before initiation into the cult of Dionysus in Livy's account of the Bacchanalia;[51] when Isis appears to Lucius in a dream she claims that she is worshipped by the Phrygians as the Pessinuntine Mother of the Gods, and at Eleusis as Demeter,[52] and that her high priest is called Mithras,[53] names which imply that her cult should be understood as combining features of other mystery cults. However, we have also seen that archaeological evidence exists for chambers in Isiac temples similar to the one described by Lucius; robes like those he is described as wearing are discussed by Plutarch; and his account of his activities suggests that he is acting as an Egyptian priest.

What we appear to have in Apuleius's novel is a description of initiation that is generic rather than specific to the cult of Isis. It has similarities with Plutarch's generic account of the initiate's experience that we considered in the context of the Eleusinian Mysteries in Chapter 1. And this is combined with an account of progression through the ranks of the priesthood of Isis. This progression involves direct intervention by the goddess, who directs Lucius's every move once she has appeared to him at the beginning of book 11 of the novel, and this may reflect a genuine tradition within the cult of Isis, but the result is a different kind of relationship with the goddess from that experienced by initiates into Greek cults.

Most noticeable about this account is that, although it is set in Greece and Rome five hundred years after Egypt had been conquered by Alexander the Great and brought into the Greek world (and two hundred years after Egypt had become part of the Roman empire), it depicts a cult with a clear Egyptian identity. The sacred books are written in hieroglyphics and the priests and initiates dress in Egyptian clothing. Although the aretalogy with which we began this chapter describes Isis as mistress of every land, she remained an Egyptian goddess. Becoming involved in her cult meant acquiring an Egyptian identity. It is possible that for some this may have been another example of the religious tourism we saw in the case of visitors to Samothrace under the Roman empire, but it is also possible that this represented an important step towards a new understanding of the gods and a new relationship with them.

9 *Mithras*

The Roman empire saw the emergence of a new mystery cult. The cult of Mithras emerged in the first century AD and lasted until the fourth century, and Mithraea, shrines to Mithras where the mysteries took place, have been found all over the territory of the empire. It had some similarities with the other cults that spread to Italy from the Greek world, in particular those of Dionysus and Isis, but it was in many ways very different from the cults we have discussed so far. There are no surviving accounts of myths associated with the god or his cult, and no clear accounts of what it was about. On the other hand, there is a huge quantity of archaeological evidence for Mithraism, and the iconography that this provides has enabled scholars to make some sense of the cult [118].[1]

Mithras was the name of a Persian god, and there was once a tendency to interpret the cult using parallels from Persian material. It is clear, however, that even if it borrows some Persian imagery, Mithraism was a cult that developed in the Roman empire, for the inhabitants of that empire. We will start by exploring how initiates experienced the cult before considering its place in the wider Roman religious world.

118 Map showing the extent of Mithraic cult.

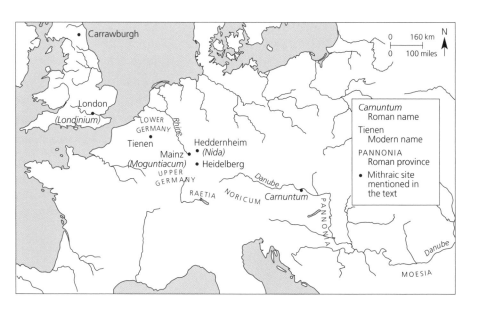

The Mithraeum

119 The Mithraeum at Carrawburgh (Roman Brocolita), near Hadrian's Wall. It was built in the early third century AD and contained altars dedicated by prefects of the first Batavian cohort, then stationed in the nearby fort.

In order to understand Mithraism, it is best to look at the place where the cult was practised, the Mithraeum. The rituals associated with Mithras that we know about took place indoors, in purpose-built chambers. Examples have been found as far north as Hadrian's Wall in Britain and as far east as Dura Europos on the river Euphrates; there are many on the northern edge of the Roman empire in Germany, and many too in the centre, in Rome and Ostia, not to mention the Greek world, including even Eleusis [119]. Mithraea all follow the same basic pattern. They are roughly rectangular, with space for seating along the long sides, and display a central cult image, the tauroctony (bull-killing), at the end opposite the entrance. They are sometimes actual caves, and even the man-made structures were clearly intended to resemble caves: there are no windows, so the interiors would have been illuminated only by lamps and torches, and they were often built partly underground with a barrel-vaulted ceiling [120, 121].[2]

Mithraea vary in size but are never very large. They are clearly designed for small groups meeting together; in cities such as Rome and Ostia large numbers of Mithraea operated simultaneously, emphasizing the point that initiates kept each individual group fairly small.

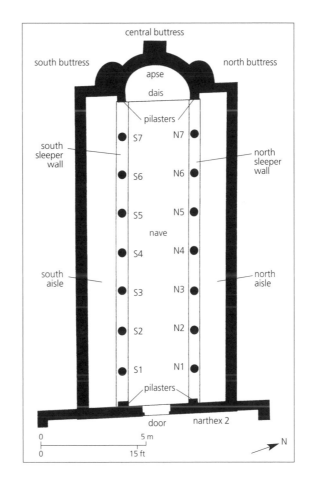

120 A plan of the Walbrook Mithraeum in London, built in the mid-third century AD.

BELOW
121 A reconstruction of what the Walbrook Mithraeum might have looked like from the outside.

The Iconography of the Mithraeum

Many Mithraea have been excavated, and although there is some variation and little of their contents has survived, it is possible to identify a number of elements that were usually present in a Mithraeum.[3] In addition to the archaeological material, much valuable information can be found in an essay by the third-century AD philosopher Porphyry, entitled *On the Cave of the Nymphs*. Although this is ostensibly a detailed discussion of a passage from Homer, describing the cave on Ithaca where Odysseus was left by the Phaiacians,[4] it makes many references to other symbolic caves, in particular the Mithraeum.

The most important element within the Mithraeum was the tauroctony, usually a relief sculpture showing Mithras killing a bull; we will discuss this further below. But generally there were also two statues of young men, one holding a raised torch, the other holding a lowered torch; the figures they represent are called Cautes and Cautopates. Their normal position is near the entrance: Cautopates, with lowered torch, on the left, and Cautes on the right [122, 123]. The planets (that is, Mercury, Venus, Sun, Moon, Mars, Jupiter and Saturn) were also represented, as often were the signs of the zodiac.

122, 123 Cautopates, on the left, wearing a 'Persian' cap and with his torch pointing down, in a statue from Palermo in Sicily, from the third century AD. On the right is Cautes, holding a raised torch, also from Palermo.

Generally found in the set order assigned to them in astrology, these show that the Mithraeum can be understood as an astrologically inspired representation of the universe. The centre of the ceiling represents the celestial north pole, the site of the pole star, with the southern pole imagined beneath the floor. The two great circles important in astronomy and astrology run around the room. These are the celestial equator and the ecliptic, the band of the sky through which the sun, moon and planets appear to move, which is subdivided into the twelve constellations that make up the zodiac. In the sky, these two circles cross at two points, called the equinoxes, and the sun is only seen at those points in the sky at the spring and autumn equinoxes. In the northern hemisphere, the point where the ecliptic is at its highest over the celestial equator is at the summer solstice, and the point where it is lowest below the equator is at the winter solstice. In the Mithraeum, the solstices are understood to be located at the sides, while the equinoxes are at the ends.[5]

The Tauroctony

The central cult image in all Mithraea is the tauroctony, a representation of the god Mithras killing a bull, and it takes a very similar form in all surviving examples [124, 125]. In the centre is Mithras, wearing a cloak and a 'Persian' hat. He is kneeling on the back of a bull, pulling back its head with his left hand and using his right hand to stab it in the neck with a sword. The end of the bull's tail is depicted as an ear of wheat. A scorpion attacks the bull's testicles, while a dog and a snake are stretching up to drink

the blood dripping from the wound. A raven flies above the scene. Above and to the right is the sun, and the moon is on the left: these are usually represented by the heads of the sun and moon gods or by the chariots in which they ride. Cautes usually appears to the right of the scene and Cautopates to the left, although sometimes their positions are reversed. In the provinces along the Rhine-Danube frontier a lion and a cup are also depicted below the bull [126].[6] Several tauroctonies also include a circle (or sometimes a different shape) with the signs of the zodiac [127],[7] and an example from Rome also includes seven stars and seven altars, representing the seven planets.[8]

124 Tauroctony from Nersae in central Italy, set up in AD 172. On either side of the central image, above the figures of Cautes and Cautopates, are other narrative scenes.

Astrology and the Tauroctony

All the elements in the tauroctony correspond to constellations in a specific region of the night sky. This is the section of the zodiac running from Taurus to Scorpio (Taurus, Gemini, Cancer, Leo, Virgo, Libra, Scorpio), including also the constellations between that band and the horizon (Crater, Corvus, Hydra, Canis Major and Canis Minor). Not all the zodiac constellations are clearly present – Cancer and Libra are not directly represented, and Virgo is represented only by the ear of wheat on the bull's tail, since Spica (which means ear of corn) is the principal star in Virgo. There are simple equivalents for the other constellations: the bull is Taurus, while Cautes and Cautopates represent Gemini; the scorpion and snake are Scorpio and Hydra, and the dog is both Canis Major and Canis Minor; the raven is Corvus; where they are present the lion is Leo and the cup is Crater, although the cup can also be thought of as representing Aquarius (the water-carrier), the constellation opposite Leo in the circle of the zodiac.

On this simple set of equivalences Mithras himself is not a mere constellation but the sun itself: the god's title is *Deus Sol Invictus Mithras*, 'The Unconquered Sun God Mithras'. And because the constellation at the centre of this section of the ecliptic is Leo, and Mithras is at the centre of the tauroctony, it follows that the tauroctony shows events when the sun is in the constellation Leo, that is, from late July to late August. In other words, the heavens in daytime in the hottest time of year show Mithras killing the bull: when the sun is at its height, the constellation Taurus is sinking below the western horizon. All this would be invisible to ordinary mortals, since the brightness of the daytime sun makes the stars invisible, but the initiate of Mithras, looking at the tauroctony in his Mithraic cave, can see the event made comprehensible.[9]

OPPOSITE
ABOVE
125 A painted tauroctony from the Mithraeum at Marino, southeast of Rome, dated to the second century AD. There are other examples of painted images, and some carved in the round, but relief carvings are most common.

BELOW
126 Tauroctony from Heddernheim (Roman Nida) in the province of Germania Superior. The lion and cup below the bull are usually found on tauroctonies from Germany.

ABOVE
127 The tauroctony from the Walbrook Mithraeum in London, with the zodiac in a circle around the central scene.

This is a considerable oversimplification of what can be read from the tauroctony: ancient astronomy was complex, and many of the elements in the image represent more than one thing. Not all initiates would have understood all the elements of the tauroctony, or indeed the Mithraeum as a whole, but they were potentially readable to anyone who understood the principles of astronomy.

Mythology and the Tauroctony

Although the tauroctony seems to be the only narrative image found in all Mithraea, it is generally recognized as one episode in a longer narrative telling the story of Mithras. No literary account of this story survives, but depictions of other events involving Mithras appear in some Mithraea, and scholars have attempted to use these to reconstruct the whole narrative.[10] Since scenes appear in different combinations in different places, any reconstruction is very uncertain. Some scholars, assuming Persian roots for the cult, have tried to use literary evidence about Persian mythology to interpret the Mithraic scenes, but it is not clear whether this provides much help. Only the very simplest narrative can be reliably reconstructed [128].

A number of images show the birth of Mithras: he rises, fully formed, out of a rock or sometimes an egg, holding a sword and a torch [129]. He chases the bull, which is associated with the moon, and eventually catches and kills it. Either as a result of this or earlier, he sets the seasons moving, promoting the growth of crops. Finally, after killing the bull, he shares a meal with the sun god, seated on the carcass of the bull. This last scene adds some complexity to the understanding of Mithras's identity: he is a companion of the sun god, but he is himself also the sun. This scene provides in addition an image of what initiates would do, because eating together was part of Mithraic religious activity.

128 Tauroctony from Neuenheim, near Heidelberg in Germany, second century AD. The central scene is surrounded by twelve small panels showing scenes involving Mithras. His birth from the rocks is depicted on the left side, fourth from the bottom. The scenes on the right side show him with the bull.

What Happened in a Mithraeum?

The archaeological evidence from Mithraea shows clearly that initiates met inside to eat and drink. In this they probably resemble the caves or meeting places of Bacchic *thiasoi*, although we know less about what was eaten by Bacchic groups. In Mithraea, finds of animal bones indicate that meat-eating was normal, along with wine-drinking.[11]

Presumably, however, rather more went on. It is generally assumed that rites of initiation must have taken place within the Mithraeum. Some Mithraea held images of other gods, and these gods, as well as Mithras himself, might have received dedications and ritual offerings.

Possibly, too, some kind of teaching took place. It has been suggested that Mithraic Fathers might explain aspects of the Mithraeum itself to the other initiates. As we have seen, Mithraea were constructed so as to represent the universe (with the earth at the centre), but this arrangement would not necessarily be obvious to the newly arrived initiate, especially given that Mithraea are likely to have been gloomy even when lit by lamps and torches. To point out how the planets and constellations are arranged around the Mithraeum, and therefore how different parts of the chamber correspond to different parts of the heavens at different times of the year, would have helped the initiates to understand their position in the universe – both in the microcosm of the Mithraeum and in the macrocosm of the world. Such teaching would not necessarily be arcane lore known only to Mithraists, since it was largely based on established astrological principles. Mithraic 'doctrine' was probably not taught. The fact that no literary account survives of any Mithraic myth or any other developed Mithraic teaching suggests that this was not central to Mithraic cult.

129 The birth of Mithras from the rocks, as depicted in a carving from Bingen in Germany.

Mithraic Feasting

Although this might count as normal Mithraic practice, we do have some evidence for rather different practices on at least one occasion. Excavations at a small Mithraeum near Tienen in Belgium, dating from the third century AD, revealed a pit dug next to the Mithraeum itself which contained animal remains and pottery. The animal remains included 285 cockerels, 14 lambs, 10 piglets, a hare, a jackdaw and eels. All these were male, except the eels (female eels are larger, but it would not have been easy for the participants to identify their sex), and they were all slaughtered on one occasion, in late June or early July. There were also remains of 79 drinking vessels, 80 cooking jars, 85 dishes, over 100 incense burners and other cult vessels. This evidence points clearly to a major feast, involving from around 100 to 300 diners, probably all men, celebrating the summer solstice. The feast was followed by the deliberate

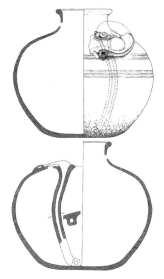

smashing of all the vessels used. The cult vessels included one particularly interesting object, a wine-jar made with a snake wreathed around it. When the jar was sealed and heated on the fire, the snake would spit wine from its mouth [130]. Whether this had a special ritual purpose is not clear, but it does show the importance attached to visual elements in Mithraic cult.[12]

The reconstruction of the feast at Tienen was made possible only by the use of modern archaeological techniques. The feast may have been a unique occurrence: certainly it seems only ever to have happened once at Tienen. But similar large-scale meetings may have taken place at other Mithraea in northern Europe, and perhaps even further afield. It indicates that Mithraic practice may have been more varied than it has so far appeared.

130 'Snake-vessel' from the Mithraic feast at Tienen in Belgium, third century AD. A pipe led from the interior of the vessel to the mouth of the snake on the outside.

OPPOSITE
The mosaic of grades in the Mithraeum of Felicissimus in Ostia, third century AD.

131 Corax, illustrated by a Raven, with a cup and the caduceus representing Mercury.

132 Nymphus, with a lamp and a diadem representing Venus.

133 Miles, with a soldier's bag and spear and the helmet representing Mars.

134 Leo, with a fire shovel (Leo was associated with fire) and sistrum and the thunderbolt representing Jupiter.

135 Perses, with a scythe and hooked blade and the crescent of the Moon.

136 Heliodromos, with torch and whip to drive the sun's chariot and a radiate headdress representing the Sun.

137 Pater, with a mixing bowl, the Persian cap of Mithras and the sickle representing Saturn.

Mithraic Grades

The organization of Mithraism included a series of seven grades, each corresponding to one of the seven planets. These were, in ascending order, Corax (Raven), Nymphus (Bridegroom), Miles (Soldier), Leo (Lion), Perses (Persian), Heliodromos (Sun-runner) and Pater (Father). The corresponding planets were, in order, Mercury, Venus, Mars, Jupiter, Moon, Sun and Saturn. The grades are mentioned in a letter of Jerome (AD 340–419)[13] and are depicted, with texts identifying their tutelary planets, on frescoes in the Mithraeum of S. Prisca in Rome. They are also illustrated with their relevant symbols, including planetary signs, in a mosaic pavement in the Mithraeum of Felicissimus in Ostia [131–138]. No detailed account survives of what the different grades meant, or what was expected of their holders. The apparently random selection of titles (two animals, one ethnic description, three human roles and one apparently astrological notion) was based on contemporary ideas: modern scholars have shown how ancient understanding of the animal world, for example, reflected in stories and sometimes relating to the position of constellations in the sky, linked ravens and lions closely to the human world. The same would have been true of the other grade titles.[14]

131

132

133

134

135

136

137

138

BELOW
138 At the head of
the ladder of grades,
the donor Felicissimus
has his own name and
a mixing bowl. He is
presumably a *Pater*.

The hierarchy of grades bears some similarities to the variety of titles in some Bacchic groups (see Chapter 4). There titles included both ritual offices (priests, basket-bearers, etc.) and also what are best understood as grades (bacchants, herdsmen, etc.). Titles varied somewhat between *thiasoi*, reflecting the lack of central control. As far as we know there was no central authority in Mithraism, but the process by which Mithraic groups spawned new ones directly, and the fact that so much of Mithraic cult was informed by the established principles of astrology helped to maintain the consistency of its organization.

Grades and Initiation

Some scholars have argued that the system of grades referred to levels of priesthood within Mithraism, since most Mithraic inscriptions do not indicate the grade of the initiate. If this were so it would be similar to what we have seen in the cult of Isis (see Chapter 8), where initiation seems to have been limited to those who served in the temple. But the cult of Isis combined rituals for the minority with major public festivals which were visible to all. In contrast, Mithraic groups appear usually to have been quite small, and there were no well-known major public festivals of Mithras. Where words like *sacerdos* (priest) appear on inscriptions, they are usually used to refer to *Patres*, suggesting that it was only the Pater who was considered to have a priestly role.[15]

There is evidence for separate ceremonies for initiation into each grade. So, for example, the Christian writer Tertullian can make this reference, apparently to the initiation of the Miles (Soldier):

> Do you blush, fellow soldiers of His, who are to be judged not by Him, but by some soldier (Miles) of Mithras? When he is initiated in the cave, in the very camp of darkness, a crown is offered to him at sword-point, as if in imitation of martyrdom, and then when the crown has been placed on his head, he is urged to raise his hands and dash it from his head on to his shoulder, if he can, saying that Mithras is his crown.[16]

It is possible that Tertullian here uses the term 'soldier of Mithras' to mean any Mithraic initiate, rather than one of a specific grade, but Porphyry describes part of the initiation of the Leo (Lion) which is more obviously specific:

> So when instead of water honey is poured to wash the hands of those being initiated in the Leontika, they are urged to keep their hands clean from all that is distressing and harmful and hateful; since he is an initiate of fire, which purifies, they apply a liquid that is appropriate, rejecting water as inimical to fire.[17]

We do not have such information about initiation into any of the other grades, and on inscriptions there are far more individuals identified as Leontes than any other grade other than Pater (which is much more common). In the well-preserved Mithraeum at Dura Europos on the Euphrates, graffiti mention all the grades except Heliodromos, and there are also references to 'Lion-to-be', 'New Lion' and 'Companion Lion'. One ancient author stated that in Mithraism those who had a share in the mysteries (i.e. those fully initiated) were called Lions, while subordinates were called Ravens,[18] and this suggests a basic division into three groups, with priests at the top (who were drawn from the Patres), full initiates (of the grade Leo and above), and subordinate initiates (Corax, Nymphus and Miles). Passing between the intermediate steps may not have involved major ceremonies.[19]

Initiation Rituals

Two visual sources suggest what initiation into the mysteries of Mithras may have involved. A sequence of frescoes on the walls of the Mithraeum at S. Maria Capua Vetere in Campania, just north of Naples [plates XXII, XXIII, XXIV], although very damaged, shows what looks like a ritual of initiation, and a cup from Mainz in Germany has relief decoration that can also be read as showing scenes of initiation.

The frescoes show a naked and initially blindfolded man, taken to be an initiate. He is accompanied by two other figures, who are taking him through the ritual. The initiate is made to kneel, with his hands tied behind him; a sword is pointed at him, then possibly thrown down in front of him; a crown is placed on his head; he is then held down, and is finally shown lying on the ground. These images bring to mind Tertullian's description, which mentions the sword and the crown. This may mean that the images relate specifically to the initiation of the Miles, or, as seems more likely, that Tertullian is describing the initial rite of initiation into the mysteries of Mithras.[20]

The Mainz cup, dating from the second century AD, shows two scenes. In the first, a man dressed as a Mithraic Pater [139] pretends to shoot at a naked figure, again assumed to be an initiate, with a third figure looking on [plate XXV]. In the other scene a procession involves a Heliodromos, accompanied by a figure who may be a Miles, and two others who may represent Cautes and Cautopates [140, plate XXVI]. It is impossible to connect these scenes to any known description of initiation into a particular grade. The first scene, 'the archery of the father', has been seen as representing an episode in the life of Mithras, when he shot an arrow into a rock and water gushed out, but also as a depiction of an actual ritual.

LEFT AND RIGHT
139 Details of 'the archery of the father' [plate xxv], a scene of initiation on a Mithraic cup from Mainz in Germany, AD 100–125.

BELOW
140 Details of 'the procession of the Sun-Runner' [plate xxvi], also from the Mainz cup.

Similarly the second scene, 'the procession of the Sun-Runner', represents the sun midway between the equinoxes as it is ritually expressed by a procession within the Mithraeum. The cup therefore combines elements from the mythology and the astrological content of Mithraism, and while the first scene looks like one of initiation, the second may have been another kind of regular ritual performed in Mithraea. Those involved in these rituals would have experienced them from different perspectives at different times and created their own understandings.[21]

When and Where did the Mysteries of Mithras Begin?

Mithraism, as we have seen, was an amalgam of astrological understanding and Persian religious imagery. While elements of Mithraic iconography can be linked back to much older Persian religious imagery, it is no longer widely accepted that Mithraism was simply an eastern cult. The earliest ancient author who offers evidence about the origins of the cult is Plutarch, writing about the Cilicians of southwest Anatolia, who were conquered by the Roman general Pompey in 67 BC. According to Plutarch the Cilicians had no respect for Greek sanctuaries, but offered non-Greek sacrifices and 'celebrated certain *teletai* that cannot be spoken of; those of Mithras have continued to the present day [i.e. around AD 100], having been received from them'.[22] While the Cilicians may have influenced the emergence of the mysteries of Mithras, Pompey's conquest does not mark the most likely moment for this to have happened.[23]

The earliest evidence for the cult of Mithras in a recognizable form comes from the end of the first and the start of the second century AD, about the time that Plutarch was writing. It appears more or less at the same time in the provinces of Upper Germany, Upper Pannonia, Noricum and Lower Moesia — that is, along most of the length of the Rhine-Danube frontier of the empire — as well as in Phrygia and Judaea. The Roman poet Statius, writing around AD 90, describes a Mithraic scene in one of his works, indicating that the cult was known of in Rome at that time. However, we have no evidence for initiation, or grades, at this stage. The distribution of evidence suggests that Italy, and specifically Rome itself, was the origin of Mithraism, and that soldiers recruited there took the cult with them to the frontiers.[24]

Commagene

Nevertheless it is not obvious why the elements of Mithraism would have come together in Rome. An alternative suggestion is that the cult developed on the edge of the Roman empire, in the kingdom of Commagene in eastern Anatolia. The kingdom emerged in the second century BC: most of Anatolia had been part of the Hellenistic Seleucid kingdom, established after the death of Alexander the Great in 323 BC. Following the example of Alexander, the Seleucid rulers adopted local practices in the administration of their territories, including the continuing use of cuneiform script in administrative documents and support for the Babylonian astrologers, who had important functions in the royal court.[25] By the second century BC Seleucid power was collapsing, with the Romans attacking from the west and the Parthians from the east. The rulers of Commagene, who were connected by marriage to the Seleucid royal family, also claimed descent from the Achaemenid kings of Persia and from Alexander the Great.[26]

In the first century BC, King Antiochus I (70–38 BC) encouraged a form of ruler cult that brought together elements of Greek and Persian religious practice and gave a prominent role to Mithras under the name Apollo Mithras Helios Hermes. Antiochus built a huge monument on the mountain of Nemrut Dag, the remains of which can still be seen today [plate XXVII]. One of the monuments erected there, a relief of a lion, has stars carved on it, three planets above it, and a crescent moon hanging from its neck. This has been shown to be a representation of a horoscope [plate XXVIII]. It depicts the heavens on 7 June 62 BC and represents the climax of a sequence of events around then, when five planets (all but Venus and Saturn) passed through the constellation of Leo, and the moon passed the sun without eclipsing it. This followed two lunar eclipses in the previous year and represented the triumph of the sun over the moon. The astrological and religious imagery found in this monument had its roots in Babylon, filtered through Seleucid iconography. This combination of astrological, religious and royal imagery was to characterize Mithraism.[27]

In AD 72 King Antiochus IV (AD 38–72) was deposed by the Romans and allowed to live in retirement in Rome. During his reign Antiochus had campaigned in Cilicia and may have been in contact with the cult of Mithras as it was practised there, but he inherited from his predecessors the religious system illustrated by the monuments on Nemrut Dag. Antiochus's son was married to the daughter of the leading Roman astrologer of the period, Tiberius Claudius Balbillus, so astrology was of serious interest in his court. It seems highly likely that Mithraism developed in and around the court-in-exile of Antiochus IV and was spread by its members, and presumably also by the soldiers in his entourage. Since Antiochus was no longer a king, the cult was no longer concerned with the fortunes of the kingdom of Commagene. The central elements of the mysteries of Mithras, including the Mithraeum, the tauroctony, initiation and the system of grades, are not found in Commagenian cult. In that sense Mithraism is a new cult, not an imported eastern one. But the basic building blocks, the imagery and the importance of astrology are best explained as coming from Commagene.[28]

Who were the Mithraic Initiates?

Mithraism was exclusively male. The passage referred to above, which says that Mithraists identified full initiates as Lions and subordinate members as Ravens, adds that women were identified as Hyenas, which, if true, seems to show a strongly negative attitude to women. The cost of constructing Mithraea and having tauroctonies carved, as well as the cost of supplying food, wine and other materials for rituals, would have been significant, so there must have been Mithraists with money to support the cult. Inscriptions show that Mithraic groups included members from the upper orders of the Roman empire, but most of the evidence that we have for membership from before the fourth century AD concerns slaves and freedmen, soldiers and minor officials. This is not to imply that the cult was frowned upon: slaves are likely to have needed their masters' permission to take part in the cult, and freedmen and minor officials played a major role in the cult of the Roman emperors. Mithraic groups are known in some cases to have been made up of both citizens and non-citizens, and it seems likely that the cult was attractive to non-citizens who wanted a closer connection with Rome: despite its Persian imagery, the mysteries were seen in the provinces of the Roman empire as a particularly Roman form of cult.[29]

Why did Men join Mithraic Groups?

Social advancement may have been one motive for seeking initiation into the mysteries of Mithras, but it was not the only possible route into a closer relationship with the Roman state. It is also true that the cult of the sun and the cult of the Roman emperors were increasingly bound together. In the third century AD the emperor Aurelian (270–75) associated himself closely with the cult of Sol Invictus (The Unconquered Sun) [141], and this close connection continued through the reign of Constantine (AD 306–37). Although it was not a formal cult of the empire, Mithraism was seen as honouring the same god acknowledged by the emperors. But the cult's success was largely due to what it offered.

141 Coin of the emperor Aurelian, showing him wearing a radiate crown similar to the crown of the Mithraic Heliodromos [136].

As we have seen, Mithraism contained elements found in other mystery cults. There was the transforming experience of the rite of initiation, which was probably frightening and possibly painful. There was the sense of belonging to a privileged group, even if that privilege did not lead to any obvious benefits outside the Mithraeum itself. But what Mithraism also appears to have offered its initiates is some kind of sense of their place in the universe. This was communicated through the design of the Mithraeum as a representation of the universe and the ritual processions which acted out cosmic movements. As has already been said, this understanding did not amount to a doctrine, and there is no strong evidence that Mithraism promised a particularly privileged afterlife to the initiate. Because it is expressed in astrological terms, it is easier to identify what this involved than it is to understand the central experience of Bacchic cult or the Eleusinian Mysteries. Astrology, with its earth-centred view of the universe, is no longer generally recognized as having scientific validity. But for Mithraists it offered one of the most powerful ways available of making sense of the universe, explaining the position not only of humans, but also of the gods themselves.

10 *The End of the Mysteries*

In AD 376 the Christian Prefect of the city of Rome destroyed a Mithraeum there. In AD 395 the sanctuary of Demeter and Kore at Eleusis was destroyed by the Goths, and it was not rebuilt. In a series of decrees from AD 391 to 399 the Roman emperor Theodosius and his successors forbade pagan worship, took away the privileges of pagan priests and ordered the destruction of temples and altars. These decrees were reiterated in the fifth century AD. In AD 410 Rome itself was sacked by the Goths. This series of events brought an end to mystery cults in the Greco-Roman world, but it does not mean that mystery cults had ceased to matter in the fourth century AD. 'Pagan' religious practices (the derogatory word used by Christians of the period) flourished and indeed might have continued to do so, had not the Roman authorities forced them to end.

Religion in Fourth-Century Rome

In AD 313 the emperors Licinius and Constantine, in the city of Milan, issued an edict announcing religious toleration throughout the Roman empire and requiring that any buildings or other property that had been confiscated from Christians should be returned to them. Although there had been periods of toleration of Christianity before, and the persecution of Christians by the Roman authorities was occasionally renewed in subsequent years, the so-called 'Edict of Milan' is generally taken to mark a great turning point in the history of Christianity. It brought an end to the 'Great Persecution' started by Diocletian a decade earlier, in AD 303, and it marked the beginning of the period when Christianity grew under the patronage of Constantine, the first Christian emperor.

In the same year, a leading Roman senator had the following inscription put up:

> In the year of the third consulships of our lords Constantine and Maximinus, Augusti, I, C. Magius Donatus Severianus, *vir clarissimus* [i.e. a Senator], Father of the rites of Unconquered Mithras, Hierophant of Liber Pater [i.e. Dionysus] and the Hecates, carried out the *taurobolium* on 15 April.[1]

Later in the century, in AD 376, the following was inscribed on an altar which is now lost:

> To the Great Gods
> Ulpius Egnatius Faventinus, *vir clarissimus*, public augur of the
> Roman people of the Quirites, Father and *hierokeryx* [sacred herald]
> of the Unconquered Sun God Mithras, Chief herdsman of the god
> Liber, Hierophant of Hecate, priest of Isis, having carried out the
> *taurobolium* and the *criobolium* on 13 August, in the consulship of our
> lords Valens Augustus, consul for the fifth time, and Valentinian
> Augustus, with good fortune.
> Faventinus vows that after twice ten years, he will sacrifice again the
> two horns on the gilded forehead.[2]

A third inscription, this time from AD 384, again now lost, read:

> For Fabia Aconia Paulina, *clarissima femina*, daughter of Aconius Cat-
> ullinus, *vir clarrisimus*, former prefect and ordinary consul [one of the
> first consuls of the year, as opposed to the less grand suffect consuls],
> wife of Vettius Praetextatus, *vir clarissimus*, prefect and consul desig-
> nate, initiated at Eleusis [into the rites of] the god Iacchus, Demeter
> and Kore, initiated at Lerna [into the rites of] the god Liber and
> Demeter and Kore, initiated on Aegina [into the rites of] the goddesses,
> *tauroboliata*, worshipper of Isis [*Isiaca*], hierophant of the goddess
> Hecate, *Graecosacranea* of the goddess Demeter.[3]

All three of these inscriptions come from Rome, and there are a number of other similar documents from the latter part of the fourth century AD. Together they provide a very interesting picture of the place of mystery cults in Roman society in the period when Christianity was becoming the dominant religion of the empire. The inscriptions advertise the fact that leading Romans had been initiated into (and held high office in) multiple mystery cults. They also show an interest in one particular ritual, the *taurobolium*, which is associated in particular with the Mother of the Gods, and we will examine that first.

Taurobolium

It is universally accepted that the *taurobolium* involved the sacrifice of a bull. Beyond that there is virtually no scholarly agreement, either about what else it involved or what its purpose was. At one end of the scale it is considered to be a form of sacrifice particularly used to pray for the well-being of the emperor. At the other, it is believed to be an elaborate ritual of initiation in which a person stood in a pit and was showered with the blood of a bull slaughtered above them. There is evidence to support both views, but it is not easy to decipher.

There are inscriptions in Greek including the words *taurobolion* and *kriobolion* (referring to a ram rather than a bull) from Asia Minor in the second and first centuries BC, where they refer either to sacrifices in the course of festivals or to bullfights (which presumably ended with the slaughter and sacrifice of the bull).[4] In the second century AD there are a number of inscriptions recording individuals carrying out the *taurobolium*, either for their own well-being or that of the emperor. Where these mention the divinity to whom the offering is being made, it is almost always the Mother of the Gods under her Roman title, Mater Deum Magna Idaea (the Great Idaean Mother of the Gods) [142]. Some of the inscriptions indicate that the bull's genitals are cut off as part of the rite and then dedicated separately from the remainder of the animal, which is presumably cooked and eaten. This is taken to distinguish the *taurobolium* from other types of sacrifice.[5]

In the fourth century AD the Christian writer Prudentius gives a very different description of the *taurobolium*. He describes how a pit was dug and covered with a lattice of planks. A bull was led on to this wooden floor and stabbed with a spear. He goes on:

> Then by the many paths of the thousand openings in the lattice the falling shower rains down a foul dew, which the priest buried within catches, putting his shameful head under all the drops, defiled both in his clothing and in all his body...
>
> Afterwards, as the corpse stiffens now that the blood has flowed out, the flamens draw it off the lattice, and the pontifex, horrible in appearance, comes forth, and shows his wet head, his heavy beard, his dripping fillets and soaking garments.[6]

This description has been taken as broadly accurate by most scholars, who have then generally explained it in terms of a ritual of purification, hence associated with initiation. There is evidence that the purifying power of blood is associated with the cult of the Mother of the Gods in other contexts, although, as we have seen, the Mother of the Gods was not directly associated with private initiation, and particularly not in Rome. But it has been more recently argued

142 A relief from the side of a taurobolic altar dedicated on 19 July AD 374 by a Roman senator, Alfenius Ceionius Iulianus Kamenius. It depicts a ram in front of a pine tree, from which hang castanets and a Phrygian hat associated with Magna Mater and Attis. The dedicatory inscription refers to the sacrifice of a ram (*criobolium*) as well as a *taurobolium*.

that Prudentius's account is fiction: it is not supported by any other evidence and appears to be an attempt to produce as distasteful as possible an image of non-Christian cult practice. If that is the case, then the fourth-century AD *taurobolium* inscriptions refer to the same ritual as the earlier ones: the sacrifice of a bull and the dedication of its genitals.[7]

It still needs to be explained why the performance of this particular sacrifice should be commemorated on altars and included along with the list of initiations in the fourth-century inscriptions. The main location of the altars commemorating performances of the *taurobolium* is the Phrygianum, a sanctuary of Magna Mater on the Vatican hill, and even though the altars do not mention her, the ritual is related to the cult of the Mother of the Gods. Faventinus ends his dedication, quoted above, with a vow to repeat the ritual after twenty years, and it seems most likely that the *taurobolium* was understood to guarantee the ritual purity of the dedicator for that period. An anonymous Christian poem from the late fourth century AD says that this is what those who performed the *taurobolium* expected from it.[8] The benefits of this purity were not indicated, but the fact that the word *tauroboliatus* ('having performed the *taurobolium*') is listed on inscriptions alongside priesthoods and initiations suggests that it was intended somehow to bring the person who did it into a closer relationship with the Mother of the Gods. Whatever its form, it was not an initiation ritual, but it shared some features of initiation.

Fourth-Century Mithraism

In AD 308, when at least six men were all claiming the title of Augustus, one of them, Galerius, called a council at Carnuntum in Upper Pannonia, in what is now Austria, where a degree of order was established. It was agreed that Galerius, Licinius, Maximinus and Constantine should share imperial power. This agreement was commemorated by the building of a shrine to Deus Sol Invictus Mithras, The Unconquered Sun God Mithras, who was named patron of the emperors' rule.[9] This is a sign that Mithras was recognized as an important figure by the rulers of the empire, perhaps in this case partly because Carnuntum was an important military settlement. Later in the century we can see further evidence of the increased status of Mithras not only in the fact that the dedicators of the altars were often Mithraic Patres, but also in the existence of Mithraea in the houses of Roman senators [143].

There were Mithraea in Roman houses in previous centuries, although it is not clear who used them. Probably initiates would have included household slaves, with freedmen in the senior roles: their masters would permit the practices, but not join in. In the fourth century it was

143 A Mithraeum in a Roman house, now under the Basilica of S. Clemente in Rome.

clearly the heads of the households who were responsible for them, acting as Pater and initiating others into the cult. A series of inscriptions, now lost, from AD 357–76, records two senators, Nonius Victor Olympius and his son Aurelius Victor Augentius, presiding over entry into the grades of Leo, Heliodromos, Pater, Cryfios (i.e. Nymphus) and Hierocorax (i.e. Corax).[10] Senators were taking the role of Mithraic Pater seriously. The inscriptions from the Phrygianum, whose dedicators are frequently Mithraic Patres, emphasize that this was one among many cults in which they held significant roles, and since those altars commemorated active religious participation in the cult of Magna Mater, it is likely that the other priesthoods mentioned were more than merely honorary postions.[11]

Senators and Mystery Cults

The inscriptions we have been examining are generally interpreted as evidence of a late revival of 'paganism' in the fourth century AD, in response to the growing power of Christianity from the time of Constantine onwards. This 'revival' is often associated with particular individuals, among whom Vettius Agorius Praetextatus is the most frequently mentioned [144]. He and his family were responsible for several of the dedications discussed above, including that of his wife Fabia, quoted near the beginning of this chapter. Praetextatus is know for his opposition to attempts by Christian bishops to have the altar of Victory removed from the Senate House in Rome in the late fourth century AD.[12]

But revival implies a previous decline, and this is less easy to identify. It was once believed that the third century AD represented a period of internal crisis and collapse within the Roman empire, and indeed since the time of Gibbon the third century has been taken to mark the beginning of the 'Decline and Fall' of the empire. However, that picture is no longer generally accepted. It is certainly the case that there were significant changes to the administration and social structure of the empire in this period, mainly in response to increased pressure on the frontiers. Emperors became more visibly associated with the army than before, and the link between the emperor and the city of Rome had been broken by the time of the reign of Diocletian. Few new public buildings were constructed in the middle and latter part of the century, and there are relatively few inscriptions from this period. At least part of the explanation for this is that the emperor, who was often responsible for encouraging public building, was usually at the frontier, so there was less incentive for such buildings. What is not so easy to argue is that the lack of building reflected a 'crisis of faith': once the dangers on the frontiers reduced, investment in public works returned.[13]

As we have seen, mystery cults were part of Roman religion from the period of the republic, and the notion that they were usually treated with suspicion and hostility is not easy to maintain. In the second century AD Roman emperors were initiated at Eleusis and showed interest in Egyptian cults. There is no evidence for their

144 Altar of Vettius Agorius Praetextatus (died AD 384) in Rome, listing his priesthoods and other religious titles.

acting differently in Rome. Worship of Magna Mater in Rome always took a Roman form, and Mithraism was essentially a Roman cult. Thus the evidence does not support the view that 'oriental cults' were accorded a new respect in the fourth century that they had not received before.[14]

In the fourth century AD, a more stable period than the third, we have evidence not of a rebirth of 'paganism' in opposition to Christianity, stimulated by a new interest in 'oriental cults'. Rather we have evidence of the continuing strength of traditional religion in Rome, which included cults of gods who were associated with mystery cults, and continuing interest among the Roman elite in the mystery cults of the Greek world. The three Greek mystery cults mentioned in the inscription of Fabia Aconia Paulina quoted above – at Eleusis, at Lerna and on Aegina – are mentioned by Pausanias, writing two centuries earlier.[15]

The continuing strength of traditional religious practices in Rome was not necessarily reflected throughout the empire. The impression given by the career of the last non-Christian emperor, Julian (AD 361–63), is that traditional religious practices were falling into disfavour as Christianity became more popular [145]. Julian was not well received by the population of the city of Antioch, who were unimpressed by the large numbers of sacrifices he performed, at least partly because of the behaviour of the soldiers who were eating and drinking too much in consequence.[16] Julian himself complained about the behaviour of local priests and their lack of dignity.[17] By this stage the Christian clergy would have benefited considerably from the privileges accorded them by the emperors. At Antioch, which was an early centre of Christianity with a large Christian population who met regularly for services, clergy would have been able to organize demonstrations against Julian's activities. Since traditional cult had no churches or congregations, it would have been impossible to organize counter-demonstrations. At the same time Julian's own writings, which are the main source for the idea that his actions were unpopular, may give an excessively pessimistic picture of the state of traditional religion. Even if Julian disapproved of the behaviour of cult officials, generally they were still being appointed.[18]

This book is not the place to examine how and why Christianity had become the dominant religion of the Roman empire by the end of the fourth century AD, but it is clear that this cannot be explained simply by the decline in traditional religious practices at this time.

Philosophy and Mystery Cult

At the end of the third century AD, the Neoplatonist philosopher Iamblichus wrote a work entitled *On the Mysteries*. Despite its title, it is not primarily about mystery cult, but more generally about the relationship between gods and mortals. It is particularly valuable here because Iamblichus is concerned to relate his arguments to religious practice rather than philosophical theory. Iamblichus presents his essay in the form of a response to another Neoplatonist, Porphyry, by an Egyptian called Abamon: in doing this, he is recalling the tradition that goes back at least to Herodotus of making Egypt the source of Greek religious ideas.[19]

Iamblichus is interested in divine possession and engages in a substantial discussion of oracles and prophecy,[20] which also includes brief allusions to the ecstatic cults of the Corybantes, Sabazius and the Mother of the Gods.[21] In a discussion of why ritual purity is a necessary prerequisite of initiation, he mentions mysteries of Isis and of Osiris at Abydos (see Chapter 8).[22] But the most general explanation of the aim of religion is given at the end. Here the focus is on what he calls theurgy, by which he means the invocation of divine presence, and initiation into mystery cults as a form of theurgy:

> But the sacred and theurgic gift of well-being (*eudaimonia*) [sometimes translated as happiness] is called the gateway to the creator of all things, or the place or courtyard of the good. In the first place, it has the power to purify the soul, far more perfect than [the power] to purify the body; afterwards, it prepares the mind for the participation in and vision of the Good, and for a release from everything which opposes it; and, at the last, for a union with the gods who are the givers of all things good.[23]

This description owes a great deal to the end of Plato's *Phaedo*, where Socrates describes what will happen to the soul of the philosopher after death.[24] However, the rest of Iamblichus's work indicates that it is not simply a development of Plato's ideas but is concerned with actual practice. It rather seems to suggest that the purpose of the mysteries, as Iamblichus understood it, was purification and direct contact with the gods. This is similar to the way Apuleius describes Lucius's experience of initiation into the cult of Isis a century earlier.[25] Although it is always difficult to know how far written sources reflect a general understanding, rather than the author's own views, Iamblichus's work does illustrate two things. Philosophers in the third century AD were interested in actual religious practice, and their interpretation appears to have been similar to that of earlier periods.

OPPOSITE
145 A statue bought by the Louvre in Paris in 1803 as an ancient portrait of the emperor Julian. It is now identified as a copy made c. 1790 of a portrait of a priest of Sarapis dating from AD 120–30. Hailed as emperor in Paris in AD 360, Julian provided a model for Napoleon, who crowned himself emperor in the year following the purchase of the sculpture.

This interest in actual practice is also visible in the work of Iamblichus's older contemporary, Porphyry, to whom *On the Mysteries* was addressed. As we have seen in Chapter 9, his essay *On the Cave of the Nymphs* provides valuable information about the form of the Mithraic cave, suggesting that Porphyry must have seen the interior of a Mithraeum and therefore may have been an initiate into its mysteries. Porphyry was educated in Athens, and it is likely that he was also an initiate of the Eleusinian Mysteries: he mentions Demeter and Kore in the essay, using the Eleusinian title Kore rather than the name Persephone, although this alone is not proof. Iamblichus's essay *On the Mysteries* is written in response to Porphyry, and while this shows that their interpretations of religion could differ, it does appear that this debate was taking place between two men for both of whom mystery cult was a significant part of life.

Christian Writing about Mystery Cults

While writers like Iamblichus and Porphyry wrote about mystery cults from the perspective of initiates, Christian writers inevitably wrote as outsiders. We cannot tell how much they actually knew about the rituals, but we know they were not really interested in making sense of them. The most sustained Christian discussions of mystery cults, those of Clement of Alexandria and Firmicus Maternus, are clearly written for a Christian audience. They show knowledge of the myths associated with mystery cults and perhaps some of the passwords (*symbola*) used in some cults. It is possible that information was provided by initiates who had subsequently become Christians, but, as we have seen throughout this book, initiates were not given any explanation of what they had experienced, so it is unlikely that they could have supplied much useful information to writers who wanted to reveal their secrets. However, this did not stop Christian apologists claiming to know about the cults.

Clement of Alexandria, writing early in the third century AD, devotes the second chapter of his *Protrepticus* (Exhortation) to mocking 'the absurdity and impiety of the mysteries and pagan myths'. Although this chapter has been picked over by scholars for evidence about actual practices in mystery cults, it is not clear whether it shows any real knowledge of what they involved. Rather it allows Clement to engage in word-play and make clever connections. For example, he takes the cry '*euan euoi!*',[26] which is associated with dancing in general, and claims that '*euan*' is a Bacchic cry, and also that snakes played a major role in Bacchic cult. This leads him then to interpret '*euan*' as a reference to Eve, and so prove that initiates of Dionysus are honouring the woman who brought error into the world.[27] While Clement's account resembles Demosthenes' description of Aeschines' *thiasos*[28] (see Chapter 6), on which it may have been based, his explanation is designed only for Christian readers.

A similar approach is taken in the fourth century AD by Firmicus Maternus, whose essay *On the Error of Profane Religion* is mostly concerned with mystery cults. It discusses the cults of Isis, Mithras, the Mother of the Gods, Dionysus, Demeter and several others, ending with chapters discussing specific *symbola*. These include the supposed Bacchic phrase, 'The bull is father of the snake and the snake is father of the bull'. The same link between snakes in Bacchic cult and the serpent in the Hebrew Bible is made here as was made earlier by Clement,[29] but at greater length. Firmicus has little to say about religious practices that are not connected with mystery cults, and this may be taken as further evidence that mystery cults were recognized as an important element in non-Christian religious practice.

Christianity and Mystery Cults

The evidence we have been examining suggests that there was little contact between Christianity and mystery cults at any time. This contrasts with a long-established scholarly tradition that tried to find considerable influence of mystery cult on Christianity. Often the debate was as much to do with contemporary concerns as with the distant past. So, for example, it suited Protestant polemicists to argue that the 'primitive Christianity' of the early church was corrupted by the incorporation of rites and doctrines drawn from non-Christian mystery cults, as part of an attempt to make the new religion palatable to potential intellectual converts. And it suited critics of Christianity as a whole to claim that many elements of Christianity, including the sacramental rituals of baptism and holy communion, were taken over directly from Mithraism.[30]

An obvious reason for seeking links between mystery cults and Christianity is their shared vocabulary. But this is misleading. The word *mysteria* and its singular form *mysterion* are used a number of times in the Letters of Paul, four times in the Revelation of John, and in one episode in the Gospels, which is told in more or less similar words by Matthew, Mark and Luke.[31] In all of these cases the term has the same meaning. It does not refer to any religious rite such as the Eleusinian Mysteries, but to secret knowledge. In the Gospels, after he recounts the parable of the sower and the seed, Jesus explains its meaning to his disciples, prefacing his remarks with the comment that to them it is given to know the *mysteria* (or *mysterion*) of the Kingdom of Heaven, whereas he speaks to the masses in parables so that 'seeing they may see but not perceive, and hearing they may hear but not understand'. In Paul's letters (and in Ephesians and 1 Timothy, which are probably by other authors), the *mysterion* or *mysteria* generally refer to God's plan for the world, previously kept hidden but now revealed in Christ.

The use of the words *mysteria* and *mysterion* in the New Testament developed from their use in the Septuagint, the Greek version of the Old Testament that would have been familiar to Paul and the Gospel writers. Here again it generally means something secret and is often used without any religious implications at all.[32] There is, however, one point in the Septuagint where the word is used to refer to a religious rite. In the Wisdom of Solomon there is a diatribe against worshipping idols, which includes an account of how the worship of cult statues might have begun. Starting with a grief-stricken man setting up an image of his dead child and making offerings to it, the writer suggests that his actions were copied and developed until they became 'ritual killings of children or secret mysteries' (*teknophonous teletas e kryphia mysteria*).[33] This probably indicates a Hellenistic Jewish distaste for mystery cult which Christian writers then continued.

The works that made up the Septuagint were translated or written from the third century BC onwards. Most of the texts that refer to *mysteria* do not exist in Hebrew versions and are assumed to have been written in Greek. In using the words *mysterion* and *mysteria* simply to refer to things kept secret, their authors are following in the philosophical tradition of which Plato is the clearest example. When Paul used the word *mysterion*, even when he was writing to the Christian community in Corinth, where there were major festivals in honour of Isis, he was not trying to evoke these rival cults. He was using a word that might still have had some general religious overtones but was hallowed more by its use in philosophy than its origins in Greek cult practices.

From the time of the emperor Constantine in the early fourth century AD – that is, from the time when Christianity came to be favoured by Roman emperors – the word *mysterion* begins to be used to refer to Christian rituals, most particularly the Eucharist, but also baptism or Christian liturgy more generally.[34] Other related terms are used in similar contexts, with Christians occasionally referred to as *mystai* (initiates) and biblical prophets as *mystagogoi* (guides to the mysteries).[35] It might seem that this is an attempt by Christians to take over the vocabulary of rival cults, but that is probably not the case. Christian rituals are referred to as *mysteria* because, like everything to do with Christianity, they were once secret, known only to God and hinted at by the prophets in the Hebrew Bible, but later revealed to all through Jesus. Indeed, by revealing God's mysteries to all, Christ is doing the opposite of what would be expected from those involved in mystery cults.

Even if the shared vocabulary does not indicate a common religious understanding, it may be the case that ritual practices were much more similar. Here we have the problem that there are no reliable descriptions, since the accounts of non-Christian practices frequently come from Christian writers. Writers such as Plutarch in the second century AD and Iamblichus and Porphyry in the third are more interested in interpreting than in describing cult practices. Another problem is that some elements of ritual are found so widely that they cannot be taken to indicate specific influences or shared meanings. For instance, shared meals were an important part of the life of early Christian communities, as they were in Mithraea and in Dionysiac *thiasoi*. But shared meals are so universal a feature of the ancient world that this is not really surprising. The challenge is to identify features that cults have in common with each other that were not simply parts of everyday life.

Baptism and Initiation

One ritual that at first sight appears to be distinctively Christian and at the same time closely parallels rituals in mystery cults is the sequence of baptism and communion which marked the entry of converts into Christianity. Baptisms were held once a year at Easter, and until the early fourth century these would have involved small numbers of candidates on any one occasion [146]. While Christians still faced the possibility of persecution, not all those who took part in Christian services sought baptism. The ritual was preceded by a long period of preparation, and candidates would fast through Lent, the forty days preceding Easter. On the night before Easter they would take part in a vigil and then, dressed in white, would be baptized by total immersion, either in a river or lake or in a cistern inside a house. Baptism would be followed immediately by communion, after which the candidates would become full members of their Christian community.[36]

This description bears a remarkable resemblance to the depiction of Isiac initiation in Apuleius's *Metamorphoses*, discussed in Chapter 8. Closer examination, however, reveals the similarities as less surprising. Christian baptism was established as an imitation of the baptism of Jesus described in the Gospels. Jesus' baptism was a Jewish ritual of purification, similar in form and purpose to the ritual purification widely found in

146 Baptism, depicted in a painting from the Catacombs of Saints Marcellinus and Peter, third century AD.

Mediterranean religion. The differences between Christian baptism, practised either in private or out of doors, and Lucius's visits to the public baths on the days of his initiations, are as significant as the similarities. The period of abstinence before baptism is also a common practice associated with purification.[37] The climactic experiences in both cases – Lucius's vision of the gods and Christian communion – could be understood as involving intimate contact with the divine, but they were not, as far as we can tell, similar in form.

The experience of baptism and communion might not have been as overwhelming as Lucius's initiation, or the experience of initiates at Eleusis or Samothrace. We can consider early Christian baptism as a ritual belonging to the imagistic mode of religiosity even while acknowledging that much of Christian practice belonged to the doctrinal mode from the beginning. But this was because Christianity and mystery cults drew on a common religious heritage, and even more on universal human responses to certain kinds of ritual. It is not evidence of borrowing between the two.

After AD 313, when the persecution of Christians came to an end and Christianity received the active support of the emperor Constantine, the number of converts rapidly increased. In response to this, baptism came to be treated as a preliminary ritual, to be followed by a period of education into the meaning of Christianity, rather than as the conclusion of a long period of preparation. In particular the fourth century saw the growth of the practice of infant baptism, which became normal in the mainstream Christian churches. As a result the character of baptism changed, losing its imagistic features. This coincided with the suppression of mystery cults, and thus the 'triumph' of Christianity took place at precisely the time when it was losing whatever similarities it had once had to mystery cults.

This reading is, of course, an oversimplification and, as we have seen, the evidence is limited for what happened to religion, Christian and non-Christian, in the third and fourth centuries AD. What is not in doubt, however, is that by the fifth century AD mystery cults were no longer a feature of the Mediterranean world. Sanctuaries such as Eleusis were not rebuilt after they were destroyed; Mithraea were destroyed – possibly by the last Mithraic worshippers; inscriptions indicating the activities of *thiasoi* are no longer found. With them the religious experiences they offered also faded from view.

Christianity did not completely extinguish ecstatic religious experience. Later 'mystics' such as Julian of Norwich (*c.* 1342–*c.* 1420) and Theresa of Avila (1515–82) wrote about their personal experiences of divine love [147, 148] in ecstatic terms. But although the Catholic Church recognized

the sanctity of these women, they did not become models for imitation. 'Enthusiasm', that is, religious frenzy experienced by large groups, was generally discouraged. Before Christianity, mystery cults were a recognized element of the religious and social life of many communities in the Greco-Roman world. After the fourth century AD, ecstatic religion was driven to the margins of society.

11 *Encountering the Sacred*

There are differences between the cults we have been examining in this book. A basic distinction is between cults based at sanctuaries, those that were made up of groups of worshippers, and those organized by often itinerant individuals. Another distinction is between those that took the form of a one-off ritual of initiation, those that involved regularly repeated ecstatic activities, and those that led to full incorporation into a temple cult. Despite these differences, there were also similarities between cults which were recognized by those who participated in them. In this final chapter we will examine the common features of mystery cults in order to understand their role in the religion of ancient Greece and Rome.

Some aspects of mystery cult are not considered here. For those cults which involved regular meetings, membership of a worshipping community could offer social benefits including mutual support, both practical and emotional. Mithraic Patres and patrons of *thiasoi* might also be in a position to assist fellow members. Clearly this was not the case with cults whose initiates might never meet again. In this book, however, we are concerned with the more directly 'religious' aspects of the mystery cults.

Borrowed Language and Shared Expectations

Although the cults we have discussed were distinct from each other, it is clear that they influenced each other. Most obviously, the titles of officials of the Eleusinian Mysteries – hierophant, *dadoukhos* and others – are used not only in other cults of Demeter but also in Bacchic *thiasoi*. The attributes of Dionysus, including the *thyrsos* and ivy wreaths, are associated with Osiris in Isiac cult. The very term 'the Mysteries' (*ta mysteria*) originally belonged specifically to Eleusis and was then used by analogy to refer to similar cults.[1] This indicates a recognition that the different mysteries had common features.

The word *mystes* is often used without any qualification, most clearly in the gold tablets (see Chapter 7) but also in other inscriptions. To be an initiate in some cult seems to be enough: there is no need to specify into whose mysteries one has been initiated. There were individuals such as Herodotus, Pausanias and Apuleius who apparently experienced initiation into a number of different mysteries, but they were probably unusual –

not least because of the travelling this involved. The self-advertisement of elite Romans in the fourth century AD, who also sought multiple initiations (see Chapter 10), is not typical of earlier periods, but it does not necessarily represent a different understanding of the mysteries. The crucial difference is between the initiate and the non-initiate, and not, say, between the initiate at Samothrace and the Bacchic initiate.

This lack of qualification of the term *mystes* should discourage us from looking for distinctively different intentions on the part of those who went to be initiated: for example, the idea that the mysteries of Samothrace were mainly about safety at sea, while Eleusis was mainly concerned with the afterlife. It may well be that the different divinities involved in the various cults were associated with different spheres of influence, but the reason for seeking initiation was in order to become an initiate – to gain a new status and to establish a closer relationship with the divine. All kinds of good things might then flow from the gods because of this new status.

Secrecy and Fantasy

One feature shared by mystery cults was a stress on secrecy. There are words, objects or rituals that must not be heard or seen by non-initiates. This secrecy has generated many false ideas of what mystery cults might have involved, often reflecting the preoccupations of those writing about the cults, who project their own fears or desires on to the mysterious unknown. We can take as an example Livy's technological fantasy:

> Matrons, dressed as bacchants with their hair dishevelled, would run to the Tiber with burning torches, and plunge the torches into the water, then bring them up again still alight – as live sulphur was mixed with calcium. Men were said to be abducted by the gods, when they were tied to machines and carried out of sight into hidden caves.[2]

Or there is Prudentius's gruesome vision of the taurobolium (see Chapter 10), with 50 litres or so of hot bull's blood pouring over a pontifex standing in a pit.

As well as mechanical terror, Livy imagines Bacchic gatherings to be occasions for every kind of illicit sexual practice. Other writers used the formulations of mystery cults as a way of introducing erotic material. In his *Satyricon*, written in the first century AD, Petronius presents a priapic orgy as a secret mystery rite. The text is fragmentary but sexually explicit, and at one point the narrator parodies the secrecy of mysteries with the claim that 'we each swore in the most solemn terms that so dreadful a secret would die with us'.[3]

149 A man dancing with glow-sticks in a club in Washington, D.C. Use of the drug ecstasy makes the eyes more sensitive to light, so the glow-sticks may resemble the torches used in the Eleusinian Mysteries [150].

Modern enthusiasts have sometimes turned from sex to drugs in the search for the secrets of the mysteries. This is most effectively depicted in fiction. For instance, in Donna Tartt's 1992 novel, *The Secret History*, a group of students manage to recreate a state of Bacchic ecstasy through a combination of ritual actions and ingestion of mind-altering plants. Apparently more seriously, there have been claims that the hallucinogenic effects of ergot or other fungi had a central role in both the Eleusinian Mysteries and the mysteries of Mithras. Similarities have been identified, with more or less plausibility, between ancient mystery cults and modern rave culture [149], although here the focus has been on the use of intoxicants, which is questionable in ancient contexts, rather than the role of loud, rhythmic and repetitive music, which certainly was common to both.[4]

But the desire to identify a lost secret – something that, once it is correctly identified, will explain what a mystery cult was all about – is bound to fail. As we have seen repeatedly through this book, it is unlikely that any such lost secret ever existed. There were certainly objects and actions that were only meant to be seen by initiates, but knowing what these were would not necessarily help us to understand the mysteries. It is quite possible that within the surviving contradictory descriptions of the mysteries we actually have all the information there ever was. Rather than searching for lost secrets, we should examine what we do know.

Common Experience and Different Settings

In the course of this book we have come across a number of descriptions of what the mysteries were like. Plato gives one version in his *Phaedrus*, describing the condition of the soul when freed from the body, but using the vocabulary of the Eleusinian Mysteries:

> They could see beauty shining, when with the divine chorus they beheld the blessed sight and vision – we following after Zeus and others after other gods – and we went through the initiations which it is right to call the most blessed, which we celebrated in complete whole-ness and without any touch of the ills which followed us in later time, seeing, as *mystai* and *epoptai*, entire and whole and calm and happy visions in pure light.[5]

Dio Chrysostom, writing in AD 97, describes the experience of someone:

> brought to be initiated in some mystic chamber extraordinary in beauty and size, where he would see many mystic sights and hear many such sounds, with darkness and light appearing to him in alternation, and thousands of other things taking place.[6]

This too probably reflects what happened at Eleusis, although neither author mentions a specific cult. Nor does Plutarch, who uses very similar language in a passage quoted in Chapter 1.[7]

These extracts all mention the contrast of light and darkness, and the same idea can be found in Lucius's account of Isiac initiation in Apuleius (Chapter 8), which, with its reference to Proserpina, need not be taken as specific to Egyptian cult. Sudden light played a role in initiation at Eleusis and almost certainly elsewhere [150]. Given the importance of the sun in Mithraism and the fact that rituals took place in a cave, we can assume that the contrast between light and dark was part of those mysteries, too (see Chapter 9). The depiction of Mithraic initiation on the frescoes of a Roman Mithraeum shows an initiate blindfolded, and this may also have been a feature of other initiation rites. Dio's description of mystic sounds can be paralleled in the cult of the Mother of the Gods and of Dionysus, and devotees of Isis have their sistrums to shake.

This indicates that rituals designed to disorientate the initiate by over-whelming their sight and hearing, and possibly other senses, were common to most if not all initiation rites. Where the various cults differed was in the context of this disorientation. We have seen that at Eleusis the initiates probably came to think of themselves as reliving the experience of Demeter searching for, and eventually finding, her daughter Kore. Isiac initiates may have shared the experience of Osiris sealed into a chest (Chapter 8). The experience of Mithraic initiates was related to their

150 Marble relief from Eleusis, c. 450 BC. Hecate, on the right, holding two torches, stands before Demeter. Torches are shown in many Eleusinian images [13, 17, 25, 26, 27] and must have played an important part in the nocturnal rituals of the Mysteries.

position within the Mithraic cave, which was a model of the universe, and that of bacchants will have been heightened by the wildness of their mountain setting.

But mystery cults were about more than disorientation. Participants understood themselves to be meeting the gods – the same gods who were the recipients of other forms of religious cult. Mystery cults were not isolated from the rest of the religious practices of the Mediterranean world, and worshippers brought to them an understanding of the nature of the gods no different from the one they brought to public festivals and private devotions. If we are to understand more fully the experience of those who took part in these cults, we have to start from this point.

In the Introduction to this book, it was suggested that Pentecostalist Christianity offered an experience similar in some ways to that of Bacchic *thiasoi*, or worship of the Mother of the Gods. In this concluding chapter we can look in greater detail at a type of Pentecostalism that offers striking parallels with some mystery cults. Personal accounts of involvement in this form of worship provide support for the approach to religious experience adopted throughout this book.

Serpent-Handling Sects

The phenomenon of snake-handling in Pentecostalist religious services is thought to have started in 1910 with George Went Hensley in Tennessee. A century later there are snake-handling churches scattered through the southern Appalachian mountains, in rural communities of West Virginia, eastern Kentucky, Tennessee and Alabama [151]. In the mid-1990s they were estimated to have around 2,500 members, generally white and poor. As well as handling poisonous snakes, members also speak in tongues, handle fire, drink strychnine and engage in acts of spiritual healing.[8]

Hensley justified his practices by referring to words of Jesus from the Gospel of Mark (16.17–20):

> 'And these signs shall follow them that believe; in my name shall they cast out devils; they shall speak with new tongues; they shall take up serpents; and if they drink any deadly thing, it shall not hurt them; they shall lay hands on the sick, and they shall recover.' So then after the Lord had spoken unto them, he was received up into heaven, and sat on the right hand of God. And they went forth, and preached everywhere, the Lord working with them, and confirming the word with signs following.

Jesus' words are taken as a command in snake-handling churches, and these practices are said to be signs of the presence of the Holy Spirit. Although snake-handling preachers frequently visit each other's churches, each one is autonomous, and there are doctrinal divisions between snake-handlers in different areas, including a fundamental division between Unitarian and Trinitarian groups. On the other hand, their codes of dress and behaviour are largely the same, including a disapproval of short hair for women and long hair for men, and an expectation that women should wear long skirts.[9]

Snake-handling services are accompanied by very loud music from a range of instruments [152]. One observer mentions at a service 'acoustic and electric guitars, fiddles, steel guitars, bass guitars, pianos, harmonicas, drums, banjos and cymbals... The sound was deafening.'[10] These accompany the singing and dancing:

> As the singing becomes stronger and stronger and the rhythm of the guitars and tambourines quickens, the devotees feel the power of the Lord begin to move upon them. They shout, cry, dance, tremble, prance about, sway, strut, jump up and down, and whirl rapidly in place. Several women, their heads and bodies jerking convulsively, shriek loudly and speak in 'unknown' tongues.[11]

Although music is an important part of the services, there are also periods of quiet, and individuals also speak, either preaching or testifying.

It would be possible to depict snake-handling services as almost indistinguishable from ancient Bacchic cult. Meetings often take place in the open air in the mountains, around 'brush arbors', temporary shelters made from tree branches.[12] In some communities men and women are segregated for worship. The loud rhythmic music, the dancing and the snakes are all features of Bacchic cult; so too is the autonomy of each worshipping group. But this would be misleading. Although open-air meetings do take place, groups usually prefer to meet in their own churches; segregation, where it does exist, does not require meeting in separate places or at separate times, but simply occupying different parts of the same room. And certainly the handlers themselves would deny that their practices are derived from anything except the Bible.[13] It is not the superficial similarities that make these churches worth examining, but their religious understanding and the emotions that underlie this.

The actual handling of snakes happens in various ways. In an account of a service in Jolo, West Virginia, an old woman is described in this way:

> She seemed the least likely person in the world to pick up a rattlesnake, but in the midst of her dancing, she suddenly veered toward one of the serpent boxes. Unclasping its lid, she took out a two-and-a-half-foot-long canebrake rattlesnake and held it up with both hands. Then she turned a slow circle with the snake outstretched, her face transfigured by something like pain or remorse.[14]

151 A snake-handling service at the Church of Lord Jesus in Jolo, West Virginia.

A different tone is suggested by this description of snake-handling in a service in Kentucky:

> One young man jumped up from his seat and ran to the front of the church. He reached into one of the snake boxes, removed a large rattlesnake, and shouted, 'Glory, thank you, Lord.' An elderly gentleman clad in bib overalls opened a box and handled five rattlesnakes simultaneously.[15]

Another account, of a service in an unspecified church, says this:

> A young man about twenty-five, sitting on the edge of the platform and holding a pair of copperheads in his cupped palms, allows two older men to drape eight or ten rattlesnakes and copperheads about his head and shoulders. At the same time, a woman removes her shoes and pokes her feet at a large yellow rattler she has placed on the floor. The serpent coils, raises its tail, and rattles menacingly, but does not strike. Another devotee, holding two rattlesnakes, one in each hand, close to his body at about waist level, slowly lifts and turns his hands so that the reptiles' swaying heads are brought to within a few inches of his face.[16]

There is no trickery involved in any of these occasions, and no simple explanation for why the snakes do not usually try to bite the handlers. Snakebites, sometimes leading to death, do occur at services, but they are rarer than might be expected, given what is done with the snakes. But it is the human experience that is more relevant to our study.

152 Snake-handling at a Pentecostalist service in Kentucky in 1946. Note the cymbals being played.

Various psychological studies of snake-handlers in recent years have used the sermons and the testimony of handlers to try to understand their motivation.[17] But snake-handling, like ancient mystery cults, cannot be fully explained in terms of following religious texts or obeying religious injunctions. One anthropologist has suggested:

> Serpent-handlers may be said to be achieving an epiphany, that is, an intuitive grasp of reality, a perception of the essential nature or the meaning of themselves, religion, and God.[18]

This is approaching the kind of experience we have found in mystery cults. Another anthropologist, Steven Kane, in fieldwork carried out in the 1970s, identified snake-handlers as entering into a 'possession trance'. He interviewed people who had experienced this trance during snake-handling services and records answers that are not given in biblical or even specifically Christian terms:

> Worshippers describe the trance experience as follows: 'It makes a different person out of me'; 'I feel queer all over'; 'It's like sweet honey poured down my throat'; 'It's like a good cold shower'; 'I get drunk in the spirit'; 'It's like a bolt of lightning goes through me'; 'My hands and sometimes my whole body gets numb. It's the best feeling there is'; 'It's like sticking my finger in electricity'; 'It's so wonderful. I can feel it in my flesh. All the pain leaves, and everything looks just beautiful.'[19]

There is a strong physical element in these descriptions, and there is nothing (aside from the reference to sticking a finger in an electrical socket) that might not have been said by someone experiencing ecstatic cults in other times and other religious circumstances.

It is clear that the noise and music of the services help to make the trance possible:

> The sound of furiously strummed guitars, crashing cymbals and tambourines, hand clapping and foot stamping, and fervent singing is the usual immediate stimulus for inducing a state of dissociation.[20]

However, it is equally clear that these are not enough. Kane argues that the snake-handlers' particular experience is the result of a combination that includes not only the external stimuli and internal physiological conditions, such as increased adrenaline flow, but also 'psychological variables (beliefs, motivation, expectations, needs, range of experience).'[21] In other words, to reach the state that snake-handlers experience, it is necessary to belong to that community and to share fully its approach to religion.[22] And the same would have been true for ancient ecstatic cult practice.

Finding the Sacred

More than 1,600 years of religious and intellectual development separate us from the world in which mystery cults flourished, and that is too vast a gap to bridge. For that reason, we will never be able to experience the closeness to the gods that initiates found in those cults. For most people, the gap between the modern world and Appalachian Mountain religion is also too great to cross. But not for all. Dennis Covington is a journalist and writer from Alabama, brought up in a Southern Methodist tradition, who became interested in snake-handling churches. Open to the possibility that their members might indeed be moved by the Holy Spirit, he was accepted into churches and drawn into their practices. His account can stand at the end of this book to show that what the fictional Lucius experienced when he was initiated into the cult of Isis can still be felt today:

> I turned to face the congregation and lifted the rattlesnake up toward the light. It was moving like it wanted to get up even higher, to climb out of that church and into the air. And it was exactly as the handlers had told me. I felt no fear. The snake seemed an extension of myself. And suddenly there seemed to be nothing in the room but me and the snake. Everything else had disappeared. Carl, the congregation, Jim — all gone, all faded to white. And I could not hear the earsplitting music. The air was silent and still, and filled with that strong, even light. And I realized that I, too, was fading into white. I was losing myself by degrees, like the incredible shrinking man. The snake would be the last to go, and all I could see was the way the scales shimmered one last time in the light, and the way the head moved from side to side, searching for a way out. I knew then why the handlers took up serpents. There is power in the act of disappearing; there is victory in the loss of self. It must be close to our conception of paradise, and it's like before you're born or after you die.[23]

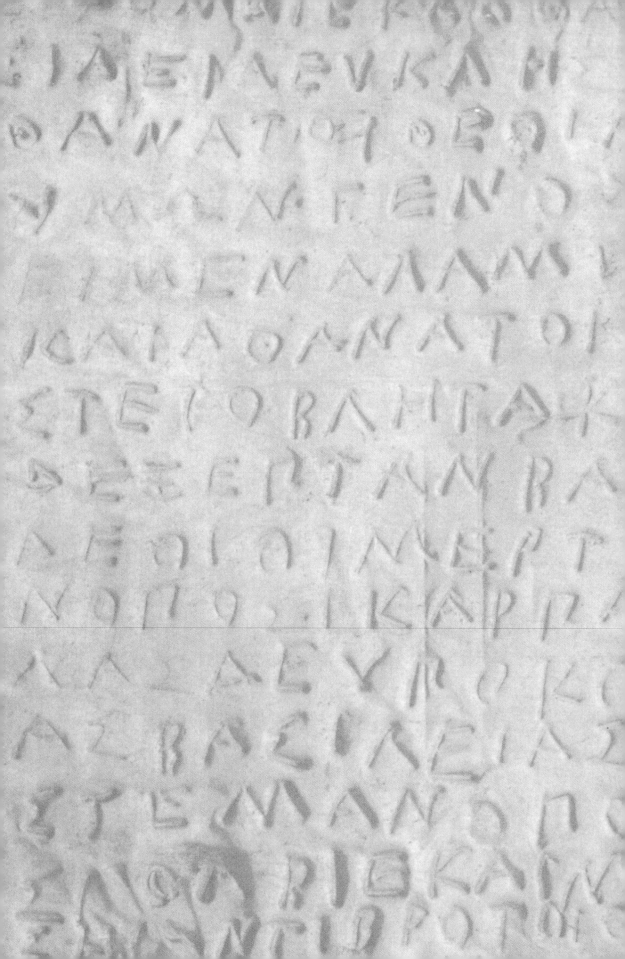

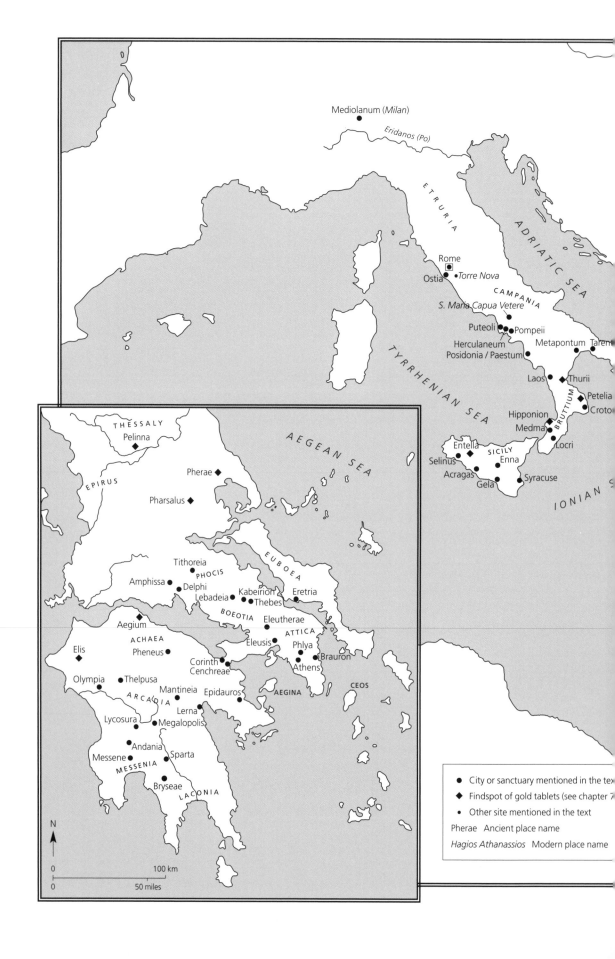

Mediolanum (*Milan*)

Eridanos (Po)

ETRURIA

ADRIATIC SEA

Rome
Ostia • •*Torre Nova*

CAMPANIA
S. Maria Capua Vetere
Puteoli• •Pompeii
Herculaneum
Posidonia / Paestum
Metapontum Taren
Laos• •Thurii
Petelia
Croto
Hipponion
Medma•
Locri
Entella•
SICILY
Enna
Selinus•
Acragas• •Syracuse
Gela

TYRRHENIAN SEA

BRUTTIUM

IONIAN S

AEGEAN SEA

THESSALY
Pelinna♦

Pherae♦

EPIRUS

Pharsalus♦

EUBOEA

Tithoreia
Amphissa• •PHOCIS
•Delphi
Lebadeia
Kabeirion
•Thebes
Eretria
BOEOTIA
Eleutherae
Aegium♦
ACHAEA
ATTICA
Eleusis• •Phlya
Elis•
Pheneus•
Corinth• •Brauron
Cenchreae
Athens
Olympia• •Thelpusa
Mantineia
Epidauros
ARCADIA
AEGINA
CEOS
Lerna•
Lycosura• •Megalopolis
Andania•
Sparta
Messene•
MESSENIA
Bryseae•
LACONIA

N

0 ———— 100 km
0 ———— 50 miles

• City or sanctuary mentioned in the tex
♦ Findspot of gold tablets (see chapter 7
• Other site mentioned in the text
Pherae   Ancient place name
Hagios Athanassios   Modern place name

Olbia

BLACK SEA

Istros (Danube)

PAEONIA

Hagios
Athanassios
opos Pella Amphipolis
NIA
Aegae
ethone *Derveni*

Byzantium

Proconessus

GALATIA

Apollonia SAMOTHRACE

IMBROS Cyzicus

Ilium / Troy

Pessinus

SSALY

LEMNOS

LESBOS Pergamum

PHRYGIA

Erythrae Cyme
Phocaea
CHIOS Smyrna LYDIA
Chios Colophon Sardis
Clazomenae Teos Ephesus
SAMOS Magnesia-on-the-Meander

COMMAGENE

Nemrut Dag

Euphrates

CILICIA

Samos Miletus
DELOS Physcus
NAXOS
COS

Dura
Europos

RHODES

CYPRUS

Orontes

Eleutherna
CRETE
Gortyn

MEDITERRANEAN SEA

Alexandria

Memphis

N

0   400 km
0   250 miles

Nile

RED SEA

Abydos

Notes

Abbreviations

1 Cor. Paul's First Epistle to the Corinthians

1 Tim. Paul's First Epistle to Timothy

2 Macc. Second Book of Maccabees

2 Thess. Paul's Second Epistle to the Thessalonians

Amm. Marc. Ammianus Marcellinus

Andoc. Andocides

Anth. Pal. *Anthologia Palatina* (*Palatine Anthology*)

Apollod. Apollodorus

Ap. Rhod. Apollonius Rhodius
  Argon. *Argonautica*

App. Appian
  BC *Bellum Civile* (*Civil War*)

Apul. Apuleius
  Apol. *Apologia*
  Met. *Metamorphoses* (*The Golden Ass*)

Ar. Aristophanes
  Eccl. *Ecclesiazusae* (*Assemblywomen*)
  Lys. *Lysistrata*
  Ran. *Ranae* (*Frogs*)
  Vesp. *Vespae* (*Wasps*)

Arist. Aristotle
  Pol. *Politica* (*Politics*)
  Rhet. *Rhetorica* (*Rhetoric*)

[Arist.] attributed to Aristotle

Arnob. Arnobius
  Ad. Nat. *Adversus Nationes* (*Against the Heathen*)

Ath. Athenaeus
  Deip. *Deipnosophistae* (*The Learned Banqueteers*)

Ath. Pol. *Athenaion Politeia* (*Constitution of the Athenians*)

Carm. Contr. Pag. *Carmen contra Paganos* (*The Song against the Pagans*)

Catull. Catullus

CCCA M.J. Vermaseren, *Corpus cultus Cybelae Attidisque* (1977–89)

CD *Choisir Dionysos* (= Jaccottet (2003: vol. 2))

Cic. Cicero
  De nat. deo. *De natura deorum* (*On the nature of the gods*)
  De re pub. *De re publica* (*Republic*)
  Leg. *De Legibus* (*Laws*)
  Ver. *Verrine Orations*

CIMRM *Corpus Inscriptionum et Monumentorum Religionis Mithriacae* (= Vermaseren (1956–60))

Clem. Al. Clement of Alexandria
  Protr. *Protrepticus* (*Exhortation to the Greeks*)
  Str. *Stromateis* (*Carpets*)

Coloss. Paul's Epistle to the Colossians

COP *Corpus des ordonnances des Ptolémées*

Dan. Daniel

Dem. Demosthenes

Derv. *Derveni Papyrus* (= Kouremenos et al. (2006: 62–125))

Dig. *Digestae Iustiniani* (*Digest of Justinian*)

Dio Chrys. Dio Chrysostom

Diod. Diodorus Siculus

Dion. Hal. Dionysius Halicarnassius

D.L. Diogenes Laertius

Eccls Ecclesiasticus

Emped. Empedocles

Eph. Paul's Epistle to the Ephesians

Eur. Euripides
  Ba. *Bacchae*
  Hel. *Helen*
  Hipp. *Hippolytus*
  Tro. *The Trojan Women*

Firm. Mat. Firmicus Maternus
  Err. prof. rel. *de Errore Profanum Religionum* (*On the error of profane religions*)

Fr. *Fragment*

Hdt. Herodotus

Hes. Hesiod
  Th. Theogony
Hipp. Hippolytus
  Haer. Refutatio Omnium Haeresium
  (*Refutation of all heresies*)
Hom. Homer
  Il. Iliad
  Od. Odyssey
Hom. Hymn Dem. *Homeric Hymn*
  to Demeter
Hom. Hymn Mo. *Homeric Hymn*
  to the Mother of the Gods
Iamb. Iamblichus
ID Inscriptions de Délos (1926–92)
IE K. Clinton, *Eleusis: the Inscriptions*
  on Stone (2005)
IG Inscriptiones Graecae (1873–)
  de Myst. de Mysteriis
  (*On the Mysteries*)
Isoc. Isocrates
  Aegin. Aegineticus (*Aiginetan*
  Oration)
Jer. Jerome
  Ep. Epistolae (*Letters*)
Jos. Josephus
  AJ Antiquitates Judaicae
  (*Jewish Antiquities*)
  BJ De Bello Judaico (*Jewish War*)
Jud. Judith
Jul. Julian
  Ep. Epistolae (*Letters*)
  Or. Orationes
Just. Justinus Martyr
  Apol. Apologiae
Juv. Juvenal
Lact. Lactatius
  Div. Inst. Epit. Divinarum
  Institutionum Epitome (*Summary*
  of the Divine Institutions)
LIMC Lexicon Iconographicum
  Mythologiae Classicae (1981–99)
LSAM F. Sokolowski, *Lois sacrées*
  de l'Asie Mineure (1955)
Luc. Lucan
Lys. Lysias
Mart. Martial

Matt. Gospel of Matthew
Obs. Julius Obsequens
  Lib. Prod. Liber Prodigiorum
  (*Book of Prodigies*)
OF A. Bernabé, *Poetae Epici Graeci*
  Testimonia et Fragmenta Pars II:
  Orphicorum et Orphicis Similium
  Testimonia et Fragmenta (2004–5)
Ov. Ovid
  Fas. Fasti
  Met. Metamorphoses
Paus. Pausanias
Petron. Petronius
Pind. Pindar
Pl. Plato
  Cri. Crito
  Euthyd. Euthydemus
  Gor. Gorgias
  Leg. De Legibus (*Laws*)
  Phd. Phaedo
  Phdr. Phaedrus
  Prt. Protagoras
  Resp. Respublica (*Republic*)
  Symp. Symposium
  Tht. Theaetetus
  Tim. Timaeus
Plaut. Plautus
  Mil. Miles Gloriosus
  (*The Braggart Soldier*)
Plut. Plutarch
  Alc. Life of Alkibiades
  Alex. Life of Alexander
  Ant. Life of Antony
  Arist. Life of Aristeides
  Demetr. Life of Demetrius
  Mor. Moralia (*Philosophical essays*)
  Nic. Life of Nikias
  Per. Life of Perikles
  Pom. Life of Pompey
  Them. Life of Themistokles
Polyb. Polybius
Porph. Porphyry
  de Abstin. de Abstinentia
  (*On Abstinence*)
  de Antro de Antro Nympharum
  (*On the cave of the Nymphs*)

Prud. Prudentius
Lib. Per. *Liber Peristephanon*
(*Crowns of Martyrdom*)
Rev. Revelation
RICIS *Recueil des inscriptions concernant les cultes isiaques*
Rom. Paul's Epistle to the Romans
RTA *Ritual texts for the afterlife*
(= Graf & Johnston (2007: 1–49))
Sap. Sal. Sapientia Salomonis
(Wisdom of Solomon)
schol. scholion (ancient commentary)
SEG *Supplementum Epigraphicum Graecum* (1923–)
Sol. Solon
Soph. Sophocles
Ant. *Antigone*
Stob. Stobaeus
Strab. Strabo
Suet. Suetonius
Dom. *Life of Domitian*

Tac. Tacitus
Ann. *Annales* (*Annals*)
Hist. *Historiae* (*Histories*)
Taurob. *Taurobolium*
(= Duthoy (1969: 5–53))
Tert. Tertullian
Ad Nat. *ad Nationes* (*To the nations*)
de Cor. *de Corona Militis*
(*On the soldier's crown*)
Val. *Adversus Valentinianos*
(*Against the Valentinians*)
Theophr. Theophrastus
Char. *Characters*
Thuc. Thucydides
Tob. Tobit
Val. Max. Valerius Maximus
Vir. Virgil
G. *Georgica*
Vitruv. Vitruvius

Introduction

1 Apul. *Met.* 11.23.
2 On Greek religion in general: Gould (1985), Sourvinou-Inwood (1990b, 1988a), Bruit Zaidman & Schmitt Pantel (1992), Price (1999); on Roman religion: Beard, North & Price (1998), Rives (2007), Rüpke (2007).
3 Boyer (1994, 2001), Knight & Smith (2008).
4 West (1997); Hdt. 2.50–52.
5 Bowman (1990).
6 Sherwin-White & Kuhrt (1993).
7 Sourvinou-Inwood (1990b).
8 Woolf (1998: 206–37).
9 Hurwit (2004: 146–54).
10 See for example Gradel (2002: 4–5): 'The most useful definition, in my view, interprets the concept of "religion" as defined by action of dialogue – sacrifice, prayer, or other forms of establishing and constructing dialogue – between humans and what they perceive as "another world," opposed to and different from the everyday sphere in which men function.'
11 Booty: Pritchett (1971: 93–100). Burkert (1987b).
12 Vernant (1981).
13 Osborne (1987: 174–84).
14 Sourvinou-Inwood (1990b: 303).
15 Hdt. 2.53.
16 Edmunds (1990), Dowden (1992), Graf (2004).
17 Bowden (2007).
18 Johnston & Struck (2005). Bowden (2003, 2005).
19 E.g. Acts 1.7: 'And he said to them, It is not for you to know times or seasons, which the Father has set within His own authority.'
20 A rare report of a meeting when the god was not in disguise: Hdt. 6.105.
21 Whitehouse (2000, 2004).
22 Barth (1975).

23 Mithen (1996: 171–210).

24 Gellner (1988).

25 Plut. *Fr.* 168 (= Stob. 4.52.46): translation from Burkert (1987b).

26 Lewis (2003).

27 Larson (2001: 12–13).

28 Anderson, R. M. (1979), Anderson, A. (2004).

29 On snakes in mystery cult and Christianity: Bremmer (1984: 268–9).

30 Acts 2.

31 Acts 2.13.

32 Makris (2007: 152–3).

33 E.g. in the *Odyssey* Athena appears to Telemachus as the wise advisor Mentor (Hom. *Od.* 2.399–404).

34 Hom. *Il.* 5.124–31.

35 Eur. *Ba.* 1–10; Apollod. 3.4.3.

36 *Hom. Hymn. Dem.* 276–80.

37 Eur. *Ba.* 576–603.

38 Burkert (1987a: 21–7), Albinus (2000), Sourvinou-Inwood (2003).

39 *Hom. Hymn Dem.* 470–82: translation from West (2003).

40 Hom. *Od.* 4.565–8.

41 Paus. 1.14.3, 1.38.7, 8.15.2, 8.25.7.

42 Strab. 10.3.21.

43 See Chapters 1 and 5.

44 As well as Alcibiades (see Chapter 1) there was also Diagoras of Melos (Lys. 6.17).

45 Hipp. *Haer.* 5.8.39–40; Tert. *Val.* 1.

46 Burkert (1972: 125–32), Zhmud (1997: 105–28).

47 Pl. *Tht.* 156a.

48 Scheid (2003: 186–8).

49 E.g. Goodman (1997: 315): 'from the perspective of the ancient world it can be seen as a peculiarly successful oriental cult, in many ways similar to Mithraism and (most obviously) Judaism.'

Chapter 1

1 Crinagoras. Greek Anthology 11.42: first century BC.

2 Richardson (1974), Parker (1991), Foley (1994).

3 *Hom. Hymn Dem.* 1–89.

4 *Hom. Hymn Dem.* 90–300.

5 *Hom. Hymn Dem.* 301–471.

6 *Hom. Hymn Dem.* 472–82: adapted from West (2003).

7 *Hom. Hymn Dem.* 483–95.

8 For a list of other significant versions: Foley (1994: 30–31).

9 Nixon (1995: 88–92). Alternative reading: Burkert (1983: 260–61).

10 Mylonas (1961), Clinton (1974, 1992, 2003, 2005), Burkert (1983: 248–97), Cavanaugh (1996), Sourvinou-Inwood (1997, 2003), Binder (1998), Parker (2005: 327–68).

11 Roman attitudes: Oliver (1981), Spawforth & Walker (1985), Clinton (1989, 1997).

12 *IE* 19 (= *IG* i³ 6).

13 Hipp. *Haer.* 5.8.39–40.

14 Mylonas (1961: 273–6), Sourvinou-Inwood (2003: 35–7).

15 Plut. *Demetr.* 26.

16 Pl. *Gor.* 497c.

17 Diod. 4.14.3.

18 Parker (2005: 344–6).

19 Clinton (2003: 50–60), Parker (2005: 345 n. 78).

20 Clinton (2003).

21 Exclusion: Isoc. 4.157. For the festival programme: Mylonas (1961: 245–80), Clinton (1993), Robertson (1998).

22 Robertson (1998). Clinton (1993) suggests that the Epidauria was the third day of the festival and the fourth was a day of rest.

23 Paus. 1.38.7.

24 Evans (2002).

25 Clinton (1992: 126–32).

26 Richardson (1974: 344–8).

27 Mylonas (1961: 261–74).

28 Hipp. *Haer.* 5.8.40.

29 Clem. Al. *Protr.* 2.

30 Andoc. 1.11–12: translation from Maidment (1968).

31 Plut. *Alc.* 19.1.

32 Lys. 6.51.

33 Hdt. 6.75.3, 9.65.2.

34 Thuc. 6.15.4.

35 Plut. *Fr.* 168 (=Stob. 4.52.46): translation from Burkert (1987b).

36 Lact. *Div. Inst. Epit.* 23; (Sourvinou-Inwood 2003: 30).

37 Clem. Al. *Protr.* 2.12.

38 Clinton (1993: 118–19, slightly modified); cf. Sourvinou-Inwood (2003).

39 Graves (1964: 106–7).

40 Wasson, Hoffman & Ruck (1978), Ruck (2006).

41 For the most recent reports: Ruck (2006: 171–86).

42 Ruck (2006: 184): 'Drugs often produce unsatisfactory or meaningless experiences, whereas something as simple as a piece of toast and a cup of black coffee in a religious setting might open the door to the divine.'

43 E.g. Barth (1975).

44 Burkert (1983: 275). Barth (1975).

45 Clem. Al. *Str.* 5.70.7–71.1: translation from Roberts et al. (1885).

46 Clinton (1993: 58–60).

47 Whitehouse (2004: 70–74).

48 Whitehouse (2004: 70) says that practices with imagistic features are 'low frequency (rarely performed)'. Obviously the Eleusinian Mysteries were performed every year, but for all but the presiding figures, the events within the sanctuary were experienced only twice (from different perspectives) in a lifetime.

49 Whitehouse (2004: 71).

50 E.g. Just. *Apol.* 1.66.

51 Whitehouse (2004: 65–70).

52 In the early church some information was withheld until after the convert had been baptized and received communion for the first time, but then taught (Maza & Alvar 1995: 521).

53 *Hom. Hymn Dem.* 270–74.

54 *Hom. Hymn Dem.* 473–6.

55 *Hom. Hymn Dem.* 284–91.

56 *Hom. Hymn Dem.* 236–8, 263–4.

57 *Hom. Hymn Dem.* 265–7; see Richardson (1974: 245–8).

58 Pind. *Fr.* 137a: translation from Burkert (1985).

59 Soph. *Fr.* 837, from *Triptolemos*: translation from Burkert (1985).

60 Ar. *Ran.* 440–59.

61 *Hom. Hymn Dem.* 371–413.

62 Clinton (1992).

Chapter 2

1 Published excavations: Lehmann (1957–98). See also Roux (1981), Cole (1984b), Ehrhardt (1985), Lehmann (1985), Burkert (1993b).

2 Hdt. 2.51.

3 Plut. *Alex.* 2.1.

4 Carney (2006: 88–103).

5 Cole (1989).

6 Hdt. 2.51. Cole (1989).

7 Clinton (2003).

8 Hdt. 2.51: translation adapted from Godley (1920).

9 Diod. 5.48.4–49.6.

10 Clinton (2003: 67), quoting Ephorus (FGrH 70 F 120) from a commentary on Euripides. The information that initiates at Samothrace search for Harmonia may be provided by the commentator rather than Ephorus himself.

11 Nonnus, *Dionysiaca* 3.35–4.248.

12 Strab. 10.3.21.

13 On the Kabeiroi in general: Hemberg (1950), Daumas (1998). Delos: Bruneau (1970).

14 Levi (1964), Beschi (1997, 1998, 2000), Beschi et al. (2004); 'Assembly of the initiates': Cargill (1995: 181–2).

15 Published excavation: Wolters &
   Bruns (1940), Schmaltz (1972),
   Heyder & Mallwitz (1978), Braun &
   Haevernick (1981), Heimberg (1982).
   See Schachter (1986: 66–110).
   Dining: Cooper & Morris (1990: 66–8).
   Rocks: Schachter (2003: 115).
16 Paus. 9.25.5: translation from
   Jones & Ormerod (1918).
17 Ov. *Met.* 10.686–94: translation from
   Miller (1984). See Schachter (1986: 90).
18 Heimberg (1982).
19 Daumas (1998).
20 Paus. 9.25.6: translation from
   Jones & Ormerod (1918).
21 Strab. 10.3.21.
22 Origins of the name: Hemberg
   (1950), Beekes (2004).
23 Hdt. 2.51.2.
24 Schol. Ap. Rhod. *Argon.* 1.917:
   translation from Lehmann (1957–98).
25 Strab. 7 *Fr.* 50: translation from
   Jones (1917–32).
26 Hdt. 2.53: translation adapted
   from Godley (1920).
27 Paus. 8.25.7.
28 Bowden (2007).
29 E.g. *ID* 1902.
30 Delos inscriptions: *ID* 1562, 1574,
   1581, 1582, 1898–1902; *SEG* 40: 657.
   Syros coins: *LIMC* 8.2: 560.
31 Ar. *Pax* 277–8 with Scholia; Ap. Rhod.
   Argon. 1.915–18; Diod. 4.43.1–2,
   4.48.5–7, 5.94.5; Cic. *De nat. deo.* 3.37.
32 Tac. *Ann.* 2.54.2–4.
33 Hdt. 2.52.
34 Diod. 5.47.3.

Chapter 3
1 Graf (2003a).
2 Guarducci (1934), Georgountzos
   (1979), Meyer (1987), Zunino (1997:
   301–34), Deshours (2006).
3 Text: *IG* 5.1.1390: translation in
   Meyer (1987).
4 Paus. 10.32.14–17.

5 Paus. 4.33.5.
6 Paus. 4. Ogden (2004), Luraghi (2008).
7 Paus. 4.1.5–9, 4.2.6, 4.26.6–8.
8 Robertson (1988: 239–54).
9 Jost (1970, 1985, 1994, 2003).
10 Paus. 8.9.8.
11 See Vout (2007: 52–135).
12 Paus. 8.15.2.
13 Paus. 8.25.7, 8.37.9.
14 Paus. 8.37.1–10.
15 Kourouniotos (1912), Jost (2003:
   148–50).
16 Paus. 8.37.8.
17 Jost (2003: 157–64).
18 Paus. 1.31.4, 9.27.2, 9.30.12, cf. 4.1.5;
   Plut., *Them.* 1.3. Parker (1996: 305).
19 Hdt. 1.141–51. Vitruv. 4.1.4–5. Thuc.
   3.104.3. Kleiner et al. (1967), Gorman
   (2001: 121–8).
20 Evidence in Graf (1985: 69–73,
   273–82, 388, 418), Sfameni Gasparro
   (1986: 333–8). Thesmophoria:
   Burkert (1985: 242–6). Eleusinia:
   Strabo 14.1.3, Hdt. 9.97 (cf. 9.65, 9.101).
21 Tac. *Hist.* 4.83.3.
22 Fraser (1972: 1.200–201).
23 Plut. *Ant.* 58.5.
24 Sfameni Gasparro (1986: 336–7),
   Bohtz (1981).
25 Bowden (2007).
26 Sfameni Gasparro (1986: 333–8).
27 Hinz (1998).
28 Cic. *Ver.* 5.187.
29 Hdt. 7.153.
30 Holloway (1991: 55–63).
31 White (1967), Holloway (1991: 61–3).
32 Giannelli (1963).
33 Lissa Caronna, Sabbione & Vlad
   Borrelli (1999–2003). The third part
   of their work, with the scenes of
   Hades and Persephone, and the
   woman with the child in the basket,
   is not yet published.
34 Sourvinou-Inwood (1978), Redfield
   (2003: 346–85).
35 Bowden (2007).

36 In Thessaly and Macedonia there is evidence for rites of passage for girls and boys, associated with Demeter and Dionysus respectively, but these are not the same as the mystery cults we have been discussing: Hatzopoulos (1994).

Chapter 4

1 Hdt. 4.7: translation adapted from Godley (1920).
2 Roller (1999: 131–8, 145–9).
3 Sol. *Fr.* 36.4–5 West.
4 Hes. *Th.* 453–8.
5 Eur. *Ba.* 58–9, cf. 128.
6 Eur. *Hel.* 1301–18.
7 Roller (1999: 44–71).
8 *Derv.* 22.7.
9 *Hom. Hymn Mo.*
10 See Roller (1999: 127–8).
11 Ap. Rhod. *Argon.* 1.1079–1152.
12 Ap. Rhod. *Argon.* 1.1132–9: translation from Seaton (1912).
13 Roller (1999: 332–4); Schwertheim (1978: 809–12) has epigraphic material.
14 Hasluck (1910), Mitchell (1999: 130).
15 Strab. 12.11 (575); Paus. 8.46.4.
16 Pind. *Pythian* 3.138–40.
17 For a more general discussion of cult of the Mother, see Roller (1999: 144–61).
18 Roller (1999: 121–41).
19 Graf (1985: 107–20, 317–18, 388–9, 419–20); Roller (1999: 119, 137–9).
20 Roller (1999: 202–3).
21 Roller (1999: 162–9), Borgeaud (2004: 11–30), Munn (2006).
22 Parker (2005: 164, 185).
23 Bremmer (1984: 268–9). The vase is discussed, with some differences of emphasis, by Roller (1999: 151–5).
24 Ustinova (1998).
25 Strab. 10.3.20–21.
26 Graf (1985: 319–34), Parker (1983: 244–8), Ustinova (1998).
27 Eur. *Hipp.* 143, Ar. *Lys.* 558, *Eccl.* 1069.

28 Pl. *Euthyd.* 277d.
29 Ar. *Vesp.* 8, Pl. *Symp.* 215e.
30 Ar. *Vesp.* 119, Pl. *Leg.* 790d.
31 Pl. *Cri.* 54d, *Phdr.* 228b, *Ion* 534a, 536c.
32 Pl. *Phdr.* 244d–e, Arist. *Pol.* 1341b–1342a.
33 Roller (1999: 206–12).
34 Roller (1999: 206), Lawall (2003: 95–7).
35 Mitchell (1993).
36 Livy 29.10.
37 Livy 29.11.
38 Ov. *Fas.* 4.264–72
39 Allen (1983).
40 Roller (1999: 267–8).
41 Roller (1999: 263–320), Beard (1994).
42 E.g. Beard (1994: 164).
43 Lane (1996a), Roller (1999: 105).
44 Roller (1999: 252–4).
45 Polyb. 21.6.7, Diod. 36.13, Hdt. 4.76.
46 Plut. *Marius* 17.5–6; Diod. 36.13. Val. Max. 7.7.6 for a eunuch being forbidden to speak in public.
47 Antiphanes *Fr.* 154 (Kock 2.74).
48 Arist. *Rhet.* 1405a.
49 Photius, s.v. *Metragyrtes.*
50 Jul. *Or.* 5.159a.
51 Apul. *Met.* 8.24–9.4. Lightfoot (2002).
52 *Anth. Pal.* 6.217–20, 237.
53 *Anth. Pal.* 6.234.
54 E.g. Polyb. 21.6.7, 21.37.4–7. Livy 37.9.9, 38.18.9–10.
55 *CCCA* 3 401–2.
56 Mart. 3.81: translation by Simon Pembroke from Beard (1994).
57 Dion. Hal. 2.19.1–2: translation adapted from Cary (1937–50).
58 Dion. Hal. 2.19.4–5: translation adapted from Cary (1937–50).
59 Hales (2002). An inscription of April 383 honours a woman who is *sacerdus maxima* of Magna Mater who is daughter and wife of senators (*Taurob.* 15).
60 Lucretius *De rerum natura* 2.608–23.

61 Cic. *Leg.* 2.21.

62 For eunuchs in the ancient world see Tougher (2002).

63 Obs. *Lib. Prod.* 44a; Val. Max. 7.7.6.

64 Brown (1988: 169).

65 Roller (1999: 237–59).

66 Dem. 18.260.

67 Roller (1999: 177–82).

68 Ov. *Fas.* 4.221–44.

69 Catull. 63.1–11: translation from Sisson (1967).

70 Paus. 7.17.10–12, Arnob. *Ad. Nat.* 5.5–7.

Chapter 5

1 Seaford (2006).

2 Goldhill (1987).

3 Ath. *Deip.* 5.197c–203b. Rice (1983).

4 Burkert (1993a).

5 Hdt. 4.79–80.

6 Dubois (1996).

7 Seaford (1996).

8 Zeitlin (1986).

9 Eur. *Ba.* 20–22, 39–42.

10 Eur. *Ba.* 73–82.

11 Soph. *Ant.* 1117–25: translation from Jebb (1891).

12 Eur. *Ba.* 465–6, 469–76: translation adapted from Buckley (1850).

13 E.g. Seaford (1981, 1998).

14 Jaccottet (2003), École française de Rome (1986).

15 *CD* 146. See Henrichs (1978: 123–37), from where the translation is taken.

16 Soph. *Ant.* 1146–50; Plut. *Mor.* 953d.

17 Plut. *Mor.* 249e.

18 Paus. 10.4.3. McInerney (1997).

19 *CD* 149: translation from Henrichs (1978).

20 *CD* 153: translation from Beard et al. (1998).

21 Diod. 4.3.3.

22 Paus. 3.20.3.

23 *CD* 150.

24 Cave: *CD* 31, 58, 61; temple: *CD* 1–3, 31, 54, 126 etc.

25 *CD* 54.

26 Eur. *Ba.* 32–8: translation adapted from Buckley (1850).

27 Eur. *Ba.* 1051–7.

28 *CD* 150.2.

29 Zeitlin (1982: 133–8).

30 Cole (1984a, 1998), Sourvinou-Inwood (1988b, 1990a), Perlman (1989).

31 Versnel (1992).

32 *CD* 171.

33 Pailler (1988, 1998), Takács (2000), North (1979), Gruen (1990: 34–78).

34 Livy 39.8.

35 Livy 39.13.

36 Diod. 4.3.3.

37 Livy 39.13.11–13: translation adapted from Roberts (1912–24).

38 Livy 39.13.14.

39 Walsh (1996).

40 Livy 39.17–18. Cf. Cic. *De re pub.* 2.37.

41 Livy 39.8.1.

42 *CD* 188.

43 Plaut. *Mil.* 1016–17.

44 *Mystai*: *CD* 12, 19, 22, 23, 28 etc.; *arkhimystai*: *CD* 24, 36, 37, 46 etc.

45 Seaford (1981, 1998).

46 Paus. 8.26.1.

47 Seaford (1981).

48 Maiuri (1967), Sauron (1998), Veyne et al. (1998). Gazda (2000) has earlier bibliography.

49 Livy 39.9.

50 Nilsson (1957), Henrichs (1978).

51 Segal (1997: 215).

Chapter 6

1 *COP* 29.

2 Dem. 18.259–60.

3 Pl. *Resp.* 364b–e: translation adapted from Storey (1969).

4 Guthrie (1935), Linforth (1941), West (1983), Borgeaud (1991), Parker (1995).

5 Theophr. *Char.* 16.12.

6 Eur. *Hipp.* 952–5.

7 Hdt. 7.6.3.

8 Bowden (2003).

9 Isoc. *Aegin.* 5–6.

10 Jourdan (2003), Betegh (2004),
Kouremenos et al. (2006), all with text,
translation and earlier bibliography.

11 *Derv.* 2.3, 2.7, 3.5, 4.9.

12 *Derv.* 20.1–12: translation adapted
from Kouremenos et al. (2006).

13 Themelis & Touratsoglou (1997: 193).

14 Themelis & Touratsoglou (1997: 206).

15 Plut. *Nic.* 23.2–3.

16 Pl. *Meno* 81b: translation from
Lamb (1967).

17 Lloyd-Jones (1985).

18 Emped. B112 DK.

19 Pl. *Prt.* 316d.

20 Pl. *Tim.* 40d6–41a3: translation
from Lee (1971).

21 Burkert (1972, 1982), Kahn (2001),
Bremmer (1999), Riedweg (2005).

22 Hdt. 2.81.

23 D.L. 8.8.

24 Polyb. 2.39.1–3.

25 Plut. *Per.* 6.2–4.

26 Arist. *Rhet.* 1419a.

27 Burkert (2006: 34–6).

Chapter 7

1 Burkert (1975, 1977, 1998), Cole (1980,
1993, 2003), Graf (1993), Edmonds
(2004), Graf & Johnston (2007),
Bernabé & Jiménez San Cristóbal
(2008).

2 *RTA* 19, 39.

3 *RTA* 1.

4 Hom. *Od.* 11.1–50.

5 Hom. *Od.* 4.561–8.

6 Pl. *Meno* 81b (see Chapter 6).

7 *RTA* 2.

8 Pind. *Olympian* 2.68–80: translation
from Perseus Project (1990),
www.perseus.tufts.edu.

9 Hom. *Od.* 4.565–8.

10 Lloyd-Jones (1985).

11 *RTA* 10–14.

12 *RTA* 29.

13 *RTA* 5.

14 *RTA* 6–7.

15 Bernabé & Jiménez San Cristóbal
(2008: 102–5).

16 Bernabé & Jiménez San Cristóbal
(2008: 106).

17 *RTA* 3.

18 *RTA* 26a–b.

19 *RTA* 28: translation from Parker &
Stamatopoulou (2007).

20 *RTA* 4.

21 *RTA* 20–22.

22 *RTA* 24.

23 *RTA* 31–7.

24 *RTA* 9.

25 Edmonds (2004: 102–4), Bernabé &
Jiménez San Cristóbal (2008: 231–3).

26 Graf & Johnston (2007), Bernabé &
Jiménez San Cristóbal (2008: 179–205).

27 Burkert (1982: 3–12).

28 Parker & Stamatopoulou (2007).
Graf & Johnston (2007: 50–65) and
Bernabé & Jiménez San Cristóbal
(2008: 266).

29 *OF* 652 T.

30 Bernabé & Jiménez San Cristóbal
(2008: 4).

31 Edmonds (2004: 104–8), Bernabé &
Jiménez San Cristóbal (2008: 233–6).

32 Janko (1984) argues that the
differences between the texts are the
result of the oral transmission of the
original written poem (or part of it).
He suggests that the texts on the
tablets were written down from
memory when needed, although he is
vague about who was doing the writing.

33 Bernabé & Jiménez San Cristóbal
(2008: 2).

Chapter 8

1 Meyer (1987: 172–4), Bianchi (1980),
Beck (1996: 137–40): translation from
Meyer (1987).

2 Bianchi (1980: 9–23).

3 Bommas (2005), Donalson (2003), Bricault (2001), Solmsen (1979), Dunand (1973), Witt (1971).

4 Plut. *Mor.* 351c–384c.

5 Plut. *Mor.* 356c, 358a–b.

6 David (1981, 1998: 107–8), Assmann (2005: 225–30), Bommas (2005: 9–11).

7 Hdt. 2.42.1, 59.2, 144.2, 156.5; 2.47.2, 48.2.

8 Diod. 1.13.5, 22.7–23.7, 29.2–5.

9 Bommas (2005: 72–5).

10 Bianchi (1980).

11 Apul. *Met.* 11.30.

12 Donalson (2003), Malaise (1972).

13 Tert. *Ad Nat.* 1.10.17–18, Dio 40.47.4, Val. Max. 1.3.4.

14 Dio 47.15.4.

15 Val. Max. 7.3.8, App. *BC* 4.47.

16 Tac., *Hist.* 3.74.1, Suet. *Dom.* 1.4.

17 Dio 50.25.4.

18 Dio 53.2.4, cf. 54.6.6.

19 Jos. *AJ* 18.65–79.

20 Luc. 8.831.

21 Jos. *BJ* 7.123.

22 Suet. *Otho* 12.1.

23 Lembke (1994).

24 Donalson (2003: 115–82), Takács (1995), Stambaugh (1972).

25 Paus. 1.41.3, 2.2.3, 2.4.6, 2.13.7, 2.32.6, 2.34.1, 2.34.10, 3.22.13, 4.32.6, 7.25.9, 10.32.12–18.

26 Paus. 10.32.12–18.

27 Parker (2005: 272–4).

28 Clinton (1993: 113, 118).

29 Vir. *G.* 4.295–314.

30 Bricault (2005), Vidman (1970).

31 *RICIS* 112/0701.

32 *RICIS* 101/0206, 101/0210 etc.

33 *RICIS* 204/0103.

34 *RICIS* 202/0276.

35 Heyob (1975).

36 Harrison (2000), Griffiths (1976).

37 Apul. *Met.* 11.23.

38 Serious: Nock (1933: 138). Satirical: Winkler (1985: 215–27), Harrison (2000: 238–52), Murgatroyd (2004).

39 Apul. *Met.* 8.24–9.

40 Porph. *de Abstin.* 4.6–8; Van der Horst (1984: 16–23, 56–61).

41 Plut. *Mor.* 352b–c.

42 Apul. *Met.* 9.10.

43 Apul. *Met.* 11.17.

44 Apul. *Met.* 11.29.

45 Apul. *Met.* 11.27, 11.30.

46 *RICIS* 512/0201.

47 *RICIS* 114/0703.

48 *RICIS* 104/0109–11.

49 e.g. *RICIS* 501/0161.

50 Apul. *Apol.* 55.8.

51 Livy 39.9 (see Chapter 5).

52 Apul. *Met.* 11.5.

53 Apul. *Met.* 11.22.

Chapter 9

1 This chapter follows closely the interpretative approaches of Roger Beck (see Beck 2004a, 2006) and Richard Gordon (see Gordon 1996). The subtlety and complexity of their arguments are difficult to get across within the available space, and I have certainly oversimplified elements. Other important recent scholarship includes Merkelbach (1984).

2 Clauss (2000: 42–61).

3 Clauss (2000: 48–60).

4 Hom. *Od.* 13.102–12.

5 Beck (2006: 102–18).

6 e.g. *CIMRM* 1014, 1083, 1118.

7 e.g. *CIMRM* 810.

8 *CIMRM* 368.

9 Beck (2006: 190–227).

10 Clauss (2000: 62–101).

11 Clauss (2000: 108–13).

12 Martens & De Boe (2004).

13 Jer. *Ep.* 107.2.

14 Gordon (1980), Beck (2006), Clauss (2000: 131–40), Merkelbach (1984: 86–133).

15 Clauss (1990, 2000: 131–3), Gordon (1994: 465–7).

16 Tert. *de Cor.* 15.3.

17 Porph. *de Antro* 15: translation from Seminar Classics 609 (1969).
18 Porph. *de Abstin.* 4.16.
19 Francis (1975, esp. 440–45).
20 Clauss (2000: 102–5), Vermaseren (1971, esp. 24–42).
21 Beck (2006).
22 Plut. *Pom.* 24.5.
23 Gordon (1996).
24 Clauss (2000: 21–2).
25 Sherwin-White & Kuhrt (1993).
26 Facella (2006), Sullivan (1977).
27 Beck (1999, 2006: 227–39). I owe the suggestions about Babylonian influence to Christopher Farrell.
28 Beck (1998).
29 Clauss (1992, 2000: 33–41).

Chapter 10

1 *CD* 191 (= *CIMRM* 523 = *Taurob.* 20).
2 *CD* 193 (= *RICIS* 501/0208 = *CIMRM* 514 = *Taurob.* 17).
3 *RICIS* 501/0210 (= *Taurob.* 29).
4 *Taurob.* 1, 2, 4.
5 Duthoy (1969), Borgeaud (2004: 110–19).
6 Prud. *Lib. Per.* 10.1036–40, 1046–50: translation from Barrett (1998).
7 Sfameni Gasparro (2003: 291–327), McLynn (1996), Kahlos (2007: 115–19).
8 *Carm. Contr. Pag.* 57–62.
9 *CIMRM* 1698.
10 *CIMRM* 400–405.
11 Gordon (1972), Griffith (2000).
12 Kahlos (2002), Matthews (1973).
13 Witschel (1999), Millar (1967: 239–48).
14 Turcan (1996: 328–41), Van den Heever (2005).
15 Paus. 1.37–8, 2.30.2, 2.36.7.
16 Amm. Marc. 22.12.6, 22.14.3.
17 Jul. *Ep.* 49.
18 Bowersock (1978: 97–105), Browning (1975: 177–86).
19 Clarke (2001).
20 Iamb. *de Mysteriis* 3.
21 Iamb. *de Mysteriis* 3.9.

22 Iamb. *de Mysteriis* 6.5–7.
23 Iamb. *de Mysteriis* 10.5 (translation from Clarke, Dillon & Hershbell 2003).
24 Pl. *Phd.* 107c–115a.
25 Apul. *Met.* 11.23.
26 E.g. Eur. *Tro.* 326.
27 Clem. Al. *Protr.* 2.12.2.
28 Dem. 18.260.
29 Firm. Mat. *Err. prof. rel.* 26.
30 Smith (1990), Lease (1980). See also Metzger (1955), Maza & Alvar (1995).
31 Rom. 11.25, 16.25; 1 Cor. 2.1, 2.7, 4.1, 13.2, 14.2, 15.51; Eph. 1.9, 3.3, 3.4, 3.9, 5.32, 6.19; Coloss. 1.26, 1.27, 2.2, 4.3; 2 Thess. 2.7; 1 Tim. 3.9, 3.16; Rev. 1.20, 10.7, 17.5, 17.7; Matt. 13.11; Mark 4.11; Luke 8.10.
32 Dan. 2.18–19, 2.28–30, 2.47, 4.9; Jud. 2.2; Tob. 12.11, Eccls 22.22, 27.16–17, 27.21; Sap. Sal. 2.22, 6.22; 2 Macc. 13.21.
33 Sap. Sal. 14.23, cf. 12.4, 14.15.
34 Lampe (1961: 891–3, esp. 893); Bornkamm (1967: 826–7).
35 See Eusebius, *Demonstratio evangelica* 1.10.32 (*mysterion*), 3.4.48 (*mystai*), 4.7.1 (*mystagogos*).
36 Johnston (2004: 449–51).
37 E.g. Livy 39.9.

Chapter 11

1 Athenian documents refer to the Eleusinian Mysteries simply as *ta mysteria*, but to the 'Lesser Mysteries' as *ta pros Agran mysteria* (The Mysteries at Agrae): e.g. *IG* ii2 661. Cf. [Arist.] *Ath. Pol.* 57.1.
2 Livy 39.13.12–13: translation adapted from Roberts (1912–24).
3 Petron. 21.
4 Wasson, Hoffman & Ruck (1978), Ruck, Hoffman & Staples (2004), Nencini (2002).
5 Pl. *Phdr.* 250b–c.
6 Dio Chrys. 12.33.
7 Burkert (1987a: 89–114).

8 Kane (1974), Burton (1993), Kimborough (1995).

9 Kimborough (1995: 29–34).

10 Kimborough (1995: 16–17). See also Burton (1993: 146–8).

11 Kane (1974: 295).

12 Covington (1995: 63, 67–80). For an unconvincing attempt to draw such direct parallels see La Barre (1962: 71–4).

13 Hood & Kimborough (1995: 312–14).

14 Covington (1995: 99).

15 Kimborough (1995: 17).

16 Kane (1974: 296).

17 Burton (1993: 126–37), Hood & Kimborough (1995), Hood (1998), Poloma (1998), Williamson & Pollio (1999).

18 Burton (1993: 134).

19 Kane (1974: 296).

20 Kane (1974: 299).

21 Kane (1974: 301).

22 See also Makris (2007: 153) on Sufic breathing practices: 'This use of hyperventilation I have also observed among the participants in spirit-possession rituals. It is a powerful technique for guiding the self into ecstasy in particularly designed contexts *among people for whom spirits and sufi saints are experientially real*.' (Emphasis mine.)

23 Covington (1995: 169–70).

Bibliography

Albinus, L. (2000), *The House of Hades: studies in ancient Greek eschatology*, Aarhus.

Allen, R. E. (1983), *The Attalid Kingdom: a constitutional history*, Oxford.

Alvar, J., Blázquez, J. M., Ardanaz, S. F., Monteagudo, G. L., Lozano, A., Maza, C. M. and Piñero, A. (1995), *Cristianismo primitivo y religiones mistéricas*, Madrid.

Anderson, A. (2004), *An Introduction to Pentecostalism*, Cambridge.

Anderson, R. M. (1979), *Vision of the Disinherited: the making of American Pentecostalism*, Oxford.

Assmann, J. (2005), *Death and Salvation in Ancient Egypt*, Ithaca.

Barrett, C. K. (1998), *The New Testament Background: selected documents*, rev. edn, London.

Barth, F. (1975), *Ritual and Knowledge among the Baktaman of New Guinea*, New Haven.

Beard, M. (1994), 'The Roman and the foreign: the cult of the Great Mother in imperial Rome' in Thomas & Humphrey (1994: 164–90).

Beard, M., North, J. and Price, S. (1998), *Religions of Rome*, 2 vols, Cambridge.

Beck, R. (1996), 'Mystery religions, aretalogy and the ancient novel' in Schmeling (1996: 131–50).

—— (1998), 'The mysteries of Mithras: a new account of their genesis', *Journal of Roman Studies* 88: 115–28 (= Beck (2004a: 31–44)).

—— (1999), 'The astronomical design of Karakush, a royal burial site in ancient Commagene: an hypothesis', *Culture & Cosmos* 3: 10–34 (= Beck (2004a: 297–322)).

—— (2004a), *Beck on Mithraism: collected works with new essays*, Aldershot.

—— (2004b), 'Four men, two sticks, and a whip: image and doctrine in a Mithraic ritual' in Whitehouse & Martin (2004: 87–103).

—— (2006), *The Religion of the Mithras Cult in the Roman Empire*, Oxford.

Beekes, R. S. P. (2004) 'The origin of the Kabeiroi', *Mnemosyne* 57: 465–77.

Bernabé, A. and Jiménez San Cristóbal, A. I. (2008), *Instructions for the Netherworld: the Orphic gold tablets*, Leiden.

Beschi, L. (1997), 'Cabirio di Lemno: Testimonianze letterarie ed epigrafiche', *Annuario della Scuola archeologica di Atene* 74–5: 7–192.

—— (1998), 'Imagini dei Cabiri di Lemno', in Capecchi (1998: 45–58).

—— (2000), 'Lo scavo del Cabirio di Chloi' in *Un ponte tra l'Italia e la Grecia: Scritti in onore di A. Di Vita, Ragusa*, Padova, 75–84.

Beschi, L., Monaco, M. C., Zarkadas, A. and Gorini, G. (2004), 'Il Telesterio ellenistico del Cabirio di Lemno', *Annuario della Scuola archeologica di Atene* 82, 225–341.

Betegh, G. (2004), *The Derveni Papyrus: cosmology, theology and interpretation*, Cambridge.

Bianchi, U. (1980), 'Iside dea misterica. Quando?' in *Perennitas: Studi in onore di Angelo Brelich*, Rome, 9–36.

Binder, J. (1998), 'The early history of the Demeter and Kore sanctuary at Eleusis' in Hägg (1998: 131–9).

Blundell, S. and Williamson, M. (eds) (1998), *The Sacred and the Feminine*, London.

Bohtz, C. H. (1981), *Altertümer von Pergamon XIII: Das Demeter Heiligtum*, Berlin.

Bommas, M. (2005), *Heiligtum und Mysterium: Griechenland und seine ägyptischen Gottheiten*, Mainz.

Borgeaud, P. (ed.) (1991), *Orphisme et Orphée*, Genève.

—— (2004), *Mother of the Gods: from Cybele to the Virgin Mary*, Baltimore.

Bornkamm, G. (1967), '*Mysterion*' in Kittel (1967: 4.802–27).

Bowden, H. (2003), 'Oracles for sale' in Derow & Parker (2003: 256–74).

—— (2005), *Classical Athens and the Delphic Oracle: divination and democracy*, Cambridge.

—— (2007), 'Cults of Demeter Eleusinia and the transmission of religious ideas', *Mediterranean Historical Review* 22: 71–83.

—— (2008), 'Before superstition and after: Theophrastus and Plutarch on *Deisidaimonia*' in Knight & Smith (2008).

Bowersock, G. (1978), *Julian the Apostate*, London.

Bowman, A. K. (1990), *Egypt after the Pharaohs 332 BC–AD 642: from Alexander to the Arab Conquest*, rev. edn, Oxford.

Boyer, P. (1994), *The Naturalness of Religious Ideas: a cognitive theory of religion*, Berkeley.

—— (2001), *Religion Explained: the human instincts that fashion gods, spirits and ancestors*, London.

Braun, K. and Haevernick, T. E. (1981), *Bemalte Keramik und Glas aus dem Kabirenheiligtum bei Theben (Das Kabirenheiligtum bei Theben 4)*, Berlin.

Bremmer, J. N. (1984), 'Greek Maenadism reconsidered', *Zeitschrift für Papyrologie und Epigraphik* 55: 267–86.

—— (1999) 'Rationalisation and disenchantment in ancient Greece: Max Weber among the Pythagoreans and Orphics' in Buxton (1999: 71–83).

Bricault, L. (2001), *Atlas de la diffusion des cultes isiaques (IVe s. av. J.-C. – IVe s. apr. J.-C.)*, Paris.

—— (2005), *Recueil des inscriptions concernant les cultes isiaques*, 3 vols, Paris.

Brown, P. (1988), *The Body and Society: men, women, and sexual renunciation in early Christianity*, New York.

Browning, R. (1975), *The Emperor Julian*, Berkeley.

Bruit Zaidman, L. and Schmitt Pantel, P. (1992), *Religion in the Ancient Greek City*, Cambridge.

Bruneau, P. (1970), *Recherches sur les cultes de Délos à l'époque hellénistique et à l'époque impériale*, Paris.

Buckley, T. A. (1850), *The Tragedies of Euripedes*, London.

Burkert, W. (1972), *Lore and Science in Ancient Pythagoreanism*, Cambridge, Mass.

—— (1975), 'Le laminette Auree: da Orfeo a Lampone' in Convegno di studi sulla Magna Grecia (1975: 81–104) (= Burkert 2006: 21–36).

—— (1977), *Orphism and Bacchic Mysteries*, Berkeley (= Burkert 2006: 37–46).

—— (1982), 'Craft versus sect: the problem of Orphics and Pythagoreans' in Meyer & Sanders (1982: 1–22) (= Burkert 2006: 191–216).

—— (1983), *Homo Necans: the anthropology of ancient Greek sacrificial ritual and myth*, Berkeley.

—— (1985), *Greek Religion: archaic and classical*, Oxford.

—— (1987a), *Ancient Mystery Cults*, Cambridge, Mass.

—— (1987b), 'Offerings in perspective: surrender, distribution, exchange' in Linders & Nordquist (1987: 43–50).

—— (1993a), 'Bacchic teletai in the Hellenistic Age' in Carpenter & Faraone (1993: 259–75) (= Burkert 2006: 120–36).

—— (1993b), 'Concordia discors: the literary and the archaeological evidence on the sanctuary of Samothrace' in Marinatos & Hägg (1993: 178–91) (= Burkert 2006: 137–51).

—— (1998), 'Die neuen orphischen Texte: Fragmente, Varienten, "Sitz im Leben"', in Burkert et al. (1998: 387–400) (=Burkert 2006: 47–61).

—— (2006), *Kleine Schriften*, vol. 3: *Orphica et Pythagorica*, Göttingen.

Burkert, W., Gemelli Marciano, L., Mantelli, E. and Orelli, L. (eds) (1998), *Fragmentsammlungen philosophischer Texte der Antike*, Göttingen.

Burton, T. (1993), *Serpent-Handling Believers*, Knoxville.

Buxton, R. (ed.) (1999), *From Myth to Reason? studies in the development of Greek thought*, Oxford.

—— (ed.) (2000), *Oxford Readings in Greek Religion*, Oxford.

Capecchi, G. (ed.) (1998), *Scritti in memoria di E. Paribeni*, Rome.

Cargill, J. (1995), *Athenian Settlements of the Fourth Century BC*, Leiden.

Carney, E. (2006), *Olympias: mother of Alexander the Great*, London.

Carpenter, T. H. and Faraone, C. A. (eds) (1993), *Masks of Dionysus*, Ithaca.

Cary, E. (1937–50), *Dionysius of Halicarnassus Roman Antiquities*, 7 vols, Loeb Classical Library, London.

Cavanaugh, M. (1996), *Athens and Eleusis: documents in finance, religion and politics in the fifth century B.C.*, Atlanta.

Clarke, E. C. (2001), *Iamblichus' de Mysteriis: a manifesto of the miraculous*, Aldershot.

Clarke, E. C., Dillon, J. M. and Hershbell, J. P. (2003), *Iamblichus' de Mysteriis*, Atlanta.

Clauss, M. (1990), 'Die sieben Grades des Mithraskultes', *Zeitschrift für Papyrologie und Epigraphik* 82: 183–94.

—— (1992), *Cultores Mithrae: die Anhängerschaft des Mithras-Kulte*, Stuttgart.

—— (2000), *The Roman Cult of Mithras: the god and his mysteries*, Edinburgh.

Clinton, K. (1974), *The Sacred Officials of the Eleusinian Mysteries*, Philadelphia.

—— (1989), 'The Eleusinian mysteries: Roman initiates and benefactors, second century BC to AD 267', *Aufsteig und Niedergang der römischen Welt* 2.18.2: 1499–1539.

—— (1992), *Myth and Cult: the iconography of the Eleusinian mysteries*, Stockholm.

—— (1993), 'The sanctuary of Demeter and Kore at Eleusis' in Marinatos & Hägg (1993: 110–24).

—— (1997), 'Eleusis and the Romans: late republic to Marcus Aurelius' in Hoff & Rotroff (1997: 161–81).

—— (2003), 'Stages of initiation in the Eleusinian and Samothracian mysteries' in Cosmopoulos (2003: 50–78).

—— (2005), *Eleusis, the Inscriptions on Stone: documents of the sanctuary of the two goddesses and public documents of the deme*, vol. 1 (2 parts), Athens.

Cole, S. G. (1980), 'New evidence for the mysteries of Dionysos', *Greek Roman and Byzantine Studies* 21: 223–38.

—— (1984a), 'The Social Function of Rituals of Maturation: the Koureion and Arkteia', *Zeitschrift für Papyrologie und Epigraphik* 55, 233–44.

—— (1984b), *Theoi Megaloi: the cult of the Great Gods at Samothrace*, Leiden.

—— (1989), 'The mysteries of Samothrace during the Roman period', *Aufsteig und Niedergang der römischen Welt* 2.18.2: 1564–98.

—— (1993), 'Voices from beyond the grave: Dionysos and the dead' in Carpenter & Faraone (1993: 276–95).

—— (1998), 'Domesticating Artemis' in Blundell & Williamson (1998: 27–43).

—— (2003), 'Landscapes of Dionysos and Elysian fields' in Cosmopoulos (2003: 193–217).

Convegno di studi sulla Magna Grecia (1975), *Orfismo in Magna Grecia*, Napoli.

Cooper, F. A. and Morris, S. (1990), 'Dining in round buildings' in Murray (1990: 66–85).

Cosmopoulos, M. B. (ed.) (2003), *Greek Mysteries: the archaeology and ritual of ancient Greek secret cults*, London.

Covington, D. (1995), *Salvation on Sand Mountain: snake handling and religion in southern Appalachia*, New York.

Daumas, M. (1998), *Cabiriaca: Recherches sur l'iconographie du culte des Cabires*, Paris.

David, R. A. (1981), *A Guide to Religious Ritual at Abydos*, Warminster.

—— (1998), *The Ancient Egyptians: beliefs and practices*, rev. edn, Brighton.

Derow, P. and Parker, R. (eds) (2003), *Herodotus and his World*, Oxford.

Deshours, N. (2006), *Les mystères d'Andania: étude d'épigraphie et d'histoire religieuse*, Bordeaux.

Dodd, D. B. and Faraone, C. A. (eds) (2003), *Initiation in Ancient Greek Rituals and Narratives: new critical perspectives*, London.

Donalson, M. D. (2003), *The Cult of Isis in the Roman Empire: Isis Invicta*, Lewiston.

Dowden, K. (1992), *The Uses of Greek Mythology*, London.

Dubois, L. (1996), *Inscriptions grecques dialectales d'Olbia du Pont*, Geneva.

Dunand, F. (1973), *Le culte d'Isis dans la bassin oriental de la Méditerranée*, 3 vols, Leiden.

—— (1986), 'Les associations dionysiaques au service du pouvoir lagide (IIIe s. av. J.-C.)' in École française de Rome (1986: 85–104).

Duthoy, R. (1969), *The Taurobolium: its evolution and terminology*, Leiden.

Easterling, P. E. and Muir, J. V. (eds) (1985), *Greek Religion and Society*, Cambridge.

École française de Rome (1986), *L'association dionysiaque dans les sociétés anciennes*, Rome.

Edmonds, R. G. (2004), *Myths of the Underworld Journey: Plato, Aristophanes and the 'Orphic' gold tablets*, Cambridge.

Edmunds, L. (ed.) (1990), *Approaches to Greek Myth*, Baltimore.

Ehrhardt, H. (1985), *Samothrake: Heiligtümer in ihrer Landschaft und Geschichte als Zeugen antiken Geisteslebens*, Stuttgart.

Euben, J. P. (ed.) (1986), *Greek Tragedy and Political Theory*, Berkeley.

Evans, N. A. (2002), 'Sanctuaries, sacrifices, and the Eleusinian mysteries', *Numen* 49: 227–54.

Facella, M. (2006), *La dinastia degli Orontidi nella Commagene ellenistico-romana*, Pisa.

Foley, H. P. (ed.) (1994), *The Homeric Hymn to Demeter: translation, commentary, and interpretive essays*, Princeton.

Francis, E. D. (1975), 'Mithraic Graffiti from Dura-Europos' in Hinnells (1975: 424–45).

Fraser, P. M. (1972), *Ptolemaic Alexandria*, 3 vols, Oxford.

Gazda, E. K. (2000), *The Villa of the Mysteries in Pompeii: ancient ritual, modern muse*, Ann Arbor.

Gellner, E. (1988), *Plough, Sword and Book: the structure of human history*, London.

Georgountzos, P. K. (1979), 'τὰ μυστήρια τῆς 'Ανδανίας', *Platon* 31: 3–43.

Giannelli, G. (1963), *Culti e Miti della Magna Grecia: contributo alla storia più antica delle colonie greche in occidente*, 2nd edn, Firenze.

Godley, A. D. (1920), *Herodotus*, 4 vols, Loeb Classical Library, London.

Golden, M. and Toohey, P. (eds) (1997), *Inventing Ancient Culture: historicism, periodization and the ancient world*, London.

Goldhill, S. (1987), 'The great Dionysia and civic ideology', *Journal of Hellenic Studies* 107: 58–76.

Goodman, M. (1997), *The Roman World: 44 BC–AD 180*, London.

Gordon, R. (1972), 'Mithraism and Roman society', *Religion* 2: 92–121 (= Gordon 1996: ch. III).

—— (1980), 'Reality, evocation and boundary in the mysteries of Mithras', *Journal of Mithraic Studies* 3: 19–99 (= Gordon 1996: ch. V).

—— (ed.) (1981), *Myth, Religion and Society*, Cambridge.

—— (1994), 'Who worshipped Mithras?', *Journal of Roman Archaeology* 7: 459–74.

—— (1996), *Image and Value in the Graeco-Roman World: studies in Mithraism and religious art*, Aldershot.

Gorman, V. B. (2001), *Miletos: the ornament of Ionia*, Ann Arbor.

Gould, J. (1985), 'On making sense of Greek religion' in Easterling & Muir (1985: 1–33).

Gradel, I. (2002), *Emperor Worship and Roman Religion*, Oxford.

Graf, F. (1974), *Eleusis und die orphische Dichtung Athens in vorhellenistischer Zeit*, Berlin.

—— (1985), *Nordionische Kulte: Religionsgeschichtliche und epigraphische Untersuchungen zu den Kulten von Chios, Erythrai, Klazomenai und Phokaia*, Zürich.

—— (1993), 'Dionysian and Orphic eschatology: new texts and old questions' in Carpenter & Faraone (1993: 239–58).

—— (2003a), 'Lesser mysteries – not less mysterious' in Cosmopoulos (2003: 241–62).

—— (2003b), 'Initiation: a concept with a troubled history' in Dodd & Faraone (2003: 3–24).

—— (2004), 'Myth' in Johnston (2004: 45–58).

Graf, F. and Johnston, S. I. (2007), *Ritual Texts for the Afterlife: Orpheus and the Bacchic gold tablets*, London.

Graves, R. (1964), *Difficult Questions, Easy Answers*, Garden City.

Griffith, A. B. (2000), 'Mithraism in the private and public lives of 4th-c. senators in Rome', *Electronic Journal of Mithraic Studies* 1 (www.uhu.es/ejms/papers.htm, consulted 22 July 2008).

Griffiths, J. G. (1976), *Apuleius, the Isis Book (Metamorphoses xi)*, Leiden.

Gruen, E. S. (1990), *Studies in Greek Culture and Roman Policy*, Leiden.

Guarducci, M. (1934), 'I culti di Andania', *Studi e Materiali di Storia delle Religioni* 10: 174–204.

Guthrie, W. K. C. (1935), *Orpheus and Greek Religion*, Oxford.

Hägg, R. (ed.) (1983), *The Greek Renaissance of the Eighth Century BC*, Stockholm.

—— (ed.) (1998), *Ancient Greek Cult Practice from the Archaeological Evidence*, Stockholm.

Hales, S. (2002), 'Looking for eunuchs: the *galli* and Attis in Roman art' in Tougher (2002: 87–102).

Harrison, S. J. (2000), *Apuleius: a Latin sophist*, Oxford.

Hasluck, F. W. (1910), *Cyzicus*, Cambridge.

Hatzopoulos, M. B. (1994), *Cultes et rites de passage en Macedoine*, Athens.

Hawley, R. and Levick, B. (eds) (1995), *Women in Antiquity: new assessments*, London.

Heimberg, U. (1982), *Die Keramik des Kabirions (Das Kabirenheiligtum bei Theben 3)*, Berlin.

Hemberg, B. (1950), *Die Kabiren*, Lund.

Henrichs, A. (1978), 'Greek maenadism from Olympias to Messalina', *Harvard Studies in Classical Philology* 82: 121–60.

—— (1982), 'Changing Dionysiac identities' in Meyer & Sanders (1982: 137–60).

—— (2003), '*Hieroi logoi* and *hierai bibloi*: the (un)written margins of the sacred in ancient Greece', *Harvard Studies in Classical Philology* 101: 207–66.

Heyder, W. and Mallwitz, A. (1978), *Die Bauten im Kabirenheiligtum bei Theben (Das Kabirenheiligtum bei Theben 2)*, Berlin.

Heyob, S. K. (1975), *The Cult of Isis among Women in the Graeco-Roman World*, Leiden.

Hinnells, J. R. (ed.) (1975), *Mithraic Studies: proceedings of the First International Congress of Mithraic Studies*, 2 vols, Manchester.

Hinz, V. (1998), *Der Kult von Demeter und Kore auf Sizilien und in der Magna Graecia*, Wiesbaden.

Hoff, M. C. and Rotroff, S. I. (eds) (1997), *The Romanization of Athens*, Oxford.

Holloway, R. R. (1991), *The Archaeology of Ancient Sicily*, London.

Hood, R. W. (1998), 'When the spirit maims and kills: social psychological considerations for the history of serpent handling sects and the narrative of handlers', *International Journal for the Psychology of Religion* 8: 71–96.

Hood, R. W. and Kimborough, D. L. (1995), 'Serpent-handling holiness sects: theoretical considerations', *Journal for the Scientific Study of Religion* 34: 311–22

Hurst, A. (ed.) (1985), *Pindare*, Genève.

Hurwit, J. M. (2004), *The Acropolis in the Age of Pericles*, Cambridge.

Jaccottet, A.-F. (2003), *Choisir Dionysos: les associations dionysiaques ou la face chachée du dionysisme*, Zürich.

Janko, R. (1984), 'Forgetfulness in the golden tablets of memory', *Classical Quarterly* 34: 89–100.

Jebb, R. (1891), *The Antigone of Sophocles*, Cambridge.

Johnston, S. I. (ed.) (2004), *Religions of the Ancient World: a guide*, Cambridge, Mass.

Johnston, S. I. and Struck, P. T. (eds) (2005), *Mantike: studies in ancient divination*, Brill.

Jones, H. L. (1917–32), *Strabo Geography*, 8 vols, Loeb Classical Library, London.

Jones, W. H. S. and Ormerod, H. A. (1918), *Pausanias Description of Greece*, 4 vols, Loeb Classical Library, London.

Jost, M. (1970), 'Les Grandes Déesses d'Arcadie', *Revue des Études Anciennes* 77: 138–51.

—— (1985), *Sanctuaires et cultes d'Arcadie*, Paris.

—— (1994), 'Nouveau regard sur les Grandes Déesses de Mégalopolis: influences, emprunts, syncrétismes religieux', *Kernos* 7: 119–29.

—— (2003), 'Mystery cults in Arcadia' in Cosmopoulos (2003: 143–68).

Jourdan, F. (2003), *Le papyrus de Derveni*, Paris.

Kahlos, M. (2002), *Vettius Agorius Praetextatus: a senatorial life in between*, Rome.

—— (2007), *Debate and Dialogue: Christian and pagan cultures c. 360–430*, Aldershot.

Kahn, C. H. (2001), *Pythagoras and the Pythagoreans: a brief history*, Indianapolis.

Kane, S. M. (1974), 'Ritual possession in a southern Appalachian religious sect', *Journal of American Folklore* 87: 293–302.

Kimborough, D. L. (1995), *Taking up Serpents: snake handling believers of Eastern Kentucky*, Chapel Hill.

Kittel, G. (1967), *Theological Dictionary of the New Testament*, 10 vols, Grand Rapids.

Kleiner, G., Hommel, P. and Müller-Wiener, W. (1967), *Panionion und Melie*, Berlin.

Knight, A. and Smith, S. (eds) (2008), *The Religion of Fools: superstition past and present*, Oxford.

Kouremenos, T., Parássoglou, G. M. and Tsantsanoglou, K. (2006), *The Derveni Papyrus*, Firenze.

Kourouniotos, K. (1912), 'Το εν Λυκοσουρα Μεγαρον της Δεσποινης', *Archeologike Ephemeris* 142–61.

La Barre, W. (1962), *They Shall Take up Serpents: psychology of the southern snake-handling cult*, Prospect Heights.

Lamb, W. R. M. (1967), *Plato*, vol. 3, Loeb Classical Library, London.

Lampe, G. W. H. (1961), *A Patristic Greek Lexicon*, Oxford.

Lane, E. N. (1996a), 'The name of Cybele's priests the "galloi"' in Lane (1996b: 117–33).

—— (ed.) (1996b), *Cybele, Attis and Related Cults: essays in memory of M. J. Vermaseren*, Leiden.

Larson, J. (2001), *Nymphs: myth, cult, lore*, New York.

Lawall, M. L. (2003), '"In the sanctuary of the Samothracian Gods": myth, politics and mystery cult at Ilion' in Cosmopoulos (2003: 79–111).

Lease, G. (1980), 'Mithraism and Christianity: borrowings and transformations', *Aufsteig und Niedergang der römischen Welt* 2.32.2: 1306–32.

Lee, H. D. P. (1971), *Plato Timaeus and Critias*, Harmondsworth.

Lehmann, K. (ed.) (1957–98), *Samothrace: excavations conducted by the Institute of Fine Arts of New York University*, 11 vols, Princeton.

—— (1985), *Samothrace: a guide to the excavations and the museum*, 5th edn, Locust Valley.

Lembke, K. (1994), *Das Iseum Campense in Rom: Studie über den Isiskult unter Domitian*, Heidelberg.

Levi, D. (1964), 'Il Cabirio di Lemno', Χαριστήριον εἰς Ἀ. Ὀρλάνδον III: 110–32.

Lewis, I. M. (2003), *Ecstatic Religion: a study of shamanism and spirit possession*, 3rd edn, London.

Lightfoot, J. L. (2002), 'Sacred eunuchism in the cult of the Syrian goddess' in Tougher (2002: 71–86).

Linders, T. and Nordquist, G. (eds) (1987), *Gifts to the Gods*, Uppsala.

Linforth, I. M. (1941), *The Arts of Orpheus*, Berkeley.

Lissa Caronna, E., Sabbione, C. and Vlad Borrelli, L. (eds) (1999–2003), *I pinakes di Locri Epizefiri* (2 parts, 9 vols), Rome.

Lloyd-Jones, H. (1985), 'Pindar and the after-life' in Hurst (1985: 245–79) (= Lloyd-Jones 1995: 80–103).

—— (1995), *Greek Epic, Lyric and Tragedy*, Oxford.

Luraghi, N. (2008), *The Ancient Messenians: constructions of ethnicity and memory*, Cambridge.

Maidment, K. J. (1968), *Minor Attic Orators*, 2 vols, Loeb Classical Library, Cambridge, Mass.

Maiuri, A. (1967), *La villa dei misteri*, 3rd edn, Rome.

Makris, G. P. (2007), *Islam in the Middle East: a living tradition*, Oxford.

Malaise, M. (1972), *Les conditions de pénétration et de diffusion des cultes égyptiens en Italie*, Leiden.

Marinatos, N. and Hägg, R. (eds) (1993), *Greek Sanctuaries: new approaches*, London.

Martens, M. and De Boe, G. (eds) (2004), *Roman Mithraism: the evidence of the small finds*, Brussels.

Martin, L. H. (2005), 'Aspects of "religious experience" among the Hellenistic mystery religions', *Religion and Politics* 12: 349–69.

Matthews, J. F., (1973), 'Symmachus and oriental cults', *Journal of Roman Studies* 63: 175–95.

Maza, C. M. and Alvar, J. (1995), 'Cultos mistéricos y cristianismo' in Alvar et al. (1995: 515–36).

McInerney, J. (1997), 'Parnassus, Delphi, and the Thyiades', *Greek Roman and Byzantine Studies* 38: 263–83.

McLynn, N. (1996), 'The fourth-century *taurobolium*', *Phoenix* 50: 312–30.

Merkelbach, R. (1984), *Mithras*, Königstein.

Metzger, B. M. (1955), 'Considerations of methodology in the study of the mystery religions and early Christianity', *Harvard Theological Review* 48: 1–20.

Meyer, B. F. and Sanders, E. P. (eds) (1982), *Jewish and Christian Self-definition*, vol. 3, *Self-definition in the Graeco-Roman world*, London.

Meyer, M. W. (1987), *The Ancient Mysteries: a source book of sacred texts*, Philadelphia.

Millar, F. (1967), *The Roman Empire and its Neighbours*, London.

Miller, F. J. (1984), *Ovid Metamorphoses*, 2nd edn, 2 vols, Loeb Classical Library, Cambridge, Mass.

Mitchell, S. (1993), *Anatolia: land, men, and gods in Asia Minor*, 2 vols, Oxford.

—— (1999), 'Archaeology in Asia Minor 1990–98', *Archaeological Reports* 45: 125–91.

Mithen, S. (1996), *The Prehistory of the Mind: a search for the origins of art, religion and science*, London.

Munn, M. (2006), *The Mother of the Gods, Athens, and the Tyranny of Asia: a study of sovereignty in ancient religion*, Berkeley.

Murgatroyd, P. (2004), 'The ending of Apuleius' *Metamorphoses*', *Classical Quarterly* 54: 319–21.

Murray, O. (ed.) (1990), *Sympotika: a symposium on the symposion*, Oxford.

Murray, O. and Price, S. (eds) (1990), *The Greek City from Homer to Alexander*, Oxford.

Mylonas (1961), *Eleusis and the Eleusinian Mysteries,* Princeton.

Nencini, P. (2002), 'The shaman and the rave party: social pharmacology of ecstacy', *Substance Use and Misuse* 37: 923–39.

Nilsson, M. P. (1957), *The Dionysiac Mysteries of the Hellenistic and Roman Age*, Lund.

Nixon, L. (1995), 'The cults of Demeter and Kore' in Hawley & Levick (1995: 75–96).

Nock, A. D. (1933), *Conversion: the old and the new in religion from Alexander the Great to Augustine of Hippo*, Oxford.

North, J. (1979), 'Religious toleration in Republican Rome', *Proceedings of the Cambridge Philological Society* 25: 85–103.

Ogden, D. (2004), *Aristomenes of Messene: legends of Sparta's nemesis*, Swansea.

Oliver, J. H. (1981), 'Roman emperors and Athens', *Historia* 30: 412–23.

Osborne, R. (1987), *Classical Landscape with Figures*, London.

Pailler, J.-M. (1988), *Bacchanalia: la répression de 186 av. J.-C. à Rome et en Italie*, Rome.

—— (1998), 'Les Bacchanales, dix ans après', *Pallas* 48: 67–86.

Parker, R. (1983), *Miasma: pollution and purification in early Greek religion*, Oxford.

—— (1991), 'The "Hymn to Demeter" and the "Homeric Hymns"', *Greece & Rome* 38: 1–17.

—— (1995), 'Early Orphism' in Powell (1995: 483–510).

—— (1996), *Athenian Religion: a history*, Oxford.

—— (2005), *Polytheism and Society at Athens*, Oxford.

Parker, R. and Stamatopoulou, M. (2007), 'A new funerary gold leaf from Pherai', *Archeologike Ephemeris* 2004: 1–32.

Perlman, P. (1989), 'Acting the she-bear for Artemis', *Arethusa* 22: 111–33.

Poloma, M. M. (1998), 'Routinization and Reality: reflections on serpents and the spirit', *International Journal for the Psychology of Religion* 8: 101–5.

Powell, A. (ed.) (1995), *The Greek World*, London.

Price, S. R. F. (1999), *Religions of the Greeks,* Cambridge.

Pritchett, W. K. (1971), *The Greek State at War*, part I, Berkeley.

Pyysiäinen, I. and Anttonen, V. (eds) (2002), *Current Approaches in the Cognitive Science of Religion*, London.

Redfield, J. M. (2003), *The Locrian Maidens: love and death in Greek Italy*, Princeton.

Rice, E. E. (1983), *The Grand Procession of Ptolemy Philadelphus*, Oxford.

Richardson, N. J. (1974), *The Homeric Hymn to Demeter*, Oxford.

Riedweg, C. (2005), *Pythagoras: his life, teaching and influence*, Ithaca.

Rives, J. B. (2007), *Religion in the Roman Empire*, Oxford.

Roberts, A., Donaldson, J. and Coxe, A. C. (1885), *The Ante-Nicene Fathers*, vol. 2, Buffalo.

Roberts, W. M. (1912–24), *Livy: the history of Rome*, 6 vols, London.

Robertson, N. (1988), 'Melanthus, Codrus, Neleus, Caucon: ritual myth as Athenian history', *Greek Roman and Byzantine Studies* 29: 201–61.

Robertson, N. D. (1998), 'The two processions to Eleusis and the programme of the Mysteries', *American Journal of Philology* 119: 547–75.

Roller, L. E. (1999), *In Search of God the Mother: the cult of Anatolian Cybele*, Berkeley.

Roux, G. (1981), 'Samothrace, le sanctuaire des Grand Dieux et les mystères', *Bulletin Budé* 2–23.

Ruck, C. A. P. (2006), *Sacred Mushrooms of the Goddess: the secrets of Eleusis*, London.

Ruck, C. A. P., Hoffman, M. A. and Staples, B. D. (2004), 'The brotherhood of the warriors of Mithras', *New England Classical Journal* 31: 225–62.

Rüpke, J. (2007), *Religion of the Romans*, Cambridge.

Şahin, S., Schwertheim, E. and Wagner, J. (eds) (1978), *Studien zur Religion und Kultur Kleinasiens*, Leiden.

Sauron, G. (1998), *La grande fresque de la villa des Mystères à Pompéi: mémoires d'une dévote de Dionysos*, Paris.

Schachter, A. (1986), *Cults of Boeotia 2. Bulletin of the Institute of Classical Studies*, Supplement 38, London.

—— (2003), 'Evolution of a mystery cult: the Theban Kabiroi' in Cosmopoulos (2003: 112–42).

Scheid, J. (2003), *An Introduction to Roman Religion*, Edinburgh.

Schmaltz, B. (1972), *Terrakotten aus dem Kabirenheiligtum bei Theben: menschenähnliche Figuren, menschliche Figuren und Gerät (Das Kabirenheiligtum bei Theben 5)*, Berlin.

Schmeling, G. (ed.) (1996), *The Novel in the Ancient World*, Leiden.

Schwertheim, E. (1978), 'Denkmäler zur Meterverehrung in Bithynien und Mysien' in Şahin, Schwertheim & Wagner (1978: 791–837).

Seaford, R. (1981), 'Dionysiac drama and Dionysiac mysteries', *Classical Quarterly* 31: 252–75.

—— (1996), *Euripides Bacchae*, Warminster.

—— (1998), 'In the mirror of Dionysos' in Blundell & Williamson (1998: 128–46).

—— (2006), *Dionysos*, London.

Seaton, R. C. (1912), *Apollonius Rhodius Argonautica*, Loeb Classical Library, London.

Segal, C. (1997), *Dionysiac Poetics and Euripides' Bacchae*, expanded edn, Princeton.

Seminar Classics 609 (1969), *The Cave of the Nymphs in the Odyssey: a revised text with translation*, *Arethusa* Monograph 1, Buffalo.

Sfameni Gasparro, G. (1986), *Misteri e culti mistici di Demetra*, Rome.

—— (2003), *Misteri e teologie: per la storia dei culti mistici e misterici nel mondo antico*, Rome.

Sherwin-White, S. M. and Kuhrt, A. (1993), *From Samarkhand to Sardis: a new approach to the Seleucid empire*, London.

Sisson, C. H. (1967), *The Poetry of Catullus*, New York.

Smith, J. Z. (1990), *Drudgery Divine: on the comparison of early Christianity and the religions of late antiquity*, London.

Solmsen, F. (1979), *Isis among the Greeks and Romans*, Cambridge, Mass.

Sourvinou-Inwood, C. (1978), 'Persephone and Aphrodite at Locri: a model for personality definitions in Greek religion', *Journal of Hellenic Studies* 98: 101–21.

—— (1983), 'A trauma in flux: death in the 8th century and after' in Hägg (1983: 33–48).

—— (1988a) 'Further aspects of polis religion', *Annali dell'instituto universitario orientale di Napoli; Sezione di archeologia e storia antica* 10: 259–74 (= Buxton 2000: 38–55).

—— (1988b), *Studies in Girls' Transitions: aspects of the* arkteia *and age representation in Attic iconography*, Athens.

—— (1990a), 'Ancient rites and modern constructs: on the Brauronian Bears again', *Bulletin of the Institute of Classical Studies* 37: 1–14.

—— (1990b), 'What is polis religion?' in Murray & Price (1990: 297–322) (= Buxton 2000: 13–37).

—— (1997), 'Reconstructing change: ideology and ritual at Eleusis' in Golden & Toohey (1997: 132–64).

—— (2003), 'Festivals and mysteries: aspects of the Eleusinian cult' in Cosmopoulos (2003: 25–49).

Spawforth, A. J. S. and Walker, S. (1985), 'The world of the Panhellenion I: Athens and Eleusis', *Journal of Roman Studies* 75: 78–104.

Stambaugh, J. E. (1972), *Sarapis under the Early Ptolemies*, Leiden.

Storey, P. (1969), *Plato*, vols 5–6, Loeb Classical Library, London.

Sullivan, R. D. (1977), 'The dynasty of Commagene', *Aufsteig und Niedergang der römischen Welt* 2.8: 732–98.

Takács, S. A. (1995), *Isis and Sarapis in the Roman World*, Leiden.

—— (2000), 'Politics and religion in the Bacchanalian affair of 186 BCE', *Harvard Studies in Classical Philology* 100: 301–10.

Themelis, P. G. and Touratsoglou, G. P. (1997), *I taphi tou Derveniou*, Athens.

Thomas, N. and Humphrey, C. (eds) (1994), *Shamanism, History and the State*, Ann Arbor.

Tougher, S. (ed.) (2002), *Eunuchs in Antiquity and Beyond*, London.

Turcan, R. (1996), *The Cults of the Roman Empire*, Oxford.

Ustinova, Y. (1998), 'Corybantism: the nature and role of an ecstatic cult in the Greek polis', *Horos* 10–12: 503–20.

Van den Heever, G. (2005), 'Making mysteries: from the *Untergang der Mysterien* to imperial mysteries – social discourse in religion and the study of religion', *Religion and Theology* 12: 262–307.

Van der Horst, P. W. (1984), *Chaeremon: Egyptian priest and stoic philosopher*, Leiden.

Vermaseren, M. J. (1956–60), *Corpus Inscriptionum et Monumentorum Religionis Mithriacae*, 2 vols, The Hague.

—— (1971), *Mithriaca I: the Mithraeum at Santa Maria Capua Veter*, Leiden.

Vernant, J.-P. (ed.) (1974), *Divination et rationalité*, Paris.

—— (1981), 'Sacrificial and alimentary codes in Hesiod's myth of Prometheus' in Gordon (1981: 57–79).

Versnel, H. S. (1992), 'The festival for Bona Dea and the Thesmophoria', *Greece & Rome* 39: 31–55.

Veyne, P., Lissarrague, F. and Frontisi-Ducroux, F. (1998), *Les mystères du gynécée*, Paris.

Vidal-Naquet, P. (1981), 'Land and sacrifice in the Odyssey: a study of religious and mythical meanings' in Gordon (1981: 80–94).

Vidman, S. (1970), *Isis und Sarapis bei den Griechen und Römern*, Berlin.

Vout, C. (2007), *Power and Eroticism in Imperial Rome*, Cambridge.

Walsh, P. G. (1996), 'Making a drama out of a crisis: Livy on the Bacchanalia', *Greece & Rome* 43: 188–203.

Wasson, G. R., Hoffman, A. and Ruck, C. A. P. (1978), *The Road to Eleusis: unveiling the secret of the mysteries*, New York.

Wellman, T. J. (2005), 'Ancient *mysteria* and modern mystery cults', *Religion and Theology* 12: 308–48.

West, M. L. (1983), *The Orphic Poems*, Oxford.

—— (1997), *The East Face of Helicon: West Asiatic elements in Greek poetry and myth*, Oxford.

—— (2003), *Homerica Hymns, Homerica Apocrypha, Lives of Homer*, Loeb Classical Library, Cambridge, Mass.

White, D. (1967), 'The post-classical cult of Malophoros at Selinus', *American Journal of Archaeology* 71: 335–52.

Whitehouse, H. (2000), *Arguments and Icons: divergent modes of religiosity*, Oxford.

—— (2004), *Modes of Religiosity: a cognitive theory of religious transmission*, Walnut Creek.

Whitehouse, H. and Martin, L. H. (eds) (2004), *Theorizing Religions Past: archaeology, history and cognition*, Walnut Creek.

Williamson, W. P. and Pollio, H. R. (1999), 'The phenomenology of religious serpent handling: a rationale and thematic study of extemporaneous sermons', *Journal for the Scientific Study of Religion* 38: 203–18.

Winkler, J. J. (1985), *Auctor and Actor: a narratological reading of Apuleius'* The Golden Ass, Berkeley.

Wiseman, T. P. (2004), *The Myths of Rome*, Exeter.

Witschel, C. (1999), *Krise – Rezession – Stagnation? Der Westen des römischen Reiches im 3. Jahrhundert n. Chr.*, Frankfurt am Main.

Witt, R. E. (1971), *Isis in the Ancient World*, Baltimore.

Wolters, P. H. A. and Bruns, G. (1940), *Das Kabirenheiligtum bei Theben*, Berlin.

Woolf, G. (1998), *Becoming Roman: the origins of provincial civilization in Gaul*, Cambridge.

Zeitlin, F. I. (1982), 'Cultic models of the female: rites of Dionysus and Demeter', *Arethusa* 15: 129–57.

—— (1986), 'Thebes: theater of self and society in Athenian drama', in Euben (1986: 101–41).

Zhmud, L. (1997), *Wissenschaft, Philosophie und Religion im frühen Pythagoreismus*, Berlin.

Zunino, M. L. (1997), *Hiera Messeniaka. La storia religiosa della Messenia dall' età micenea all'età ellenistica*, Udine.

Acknowledgments

Many people have helped me to write this book. The list of those whose scholarship I have relied on but whom I have never met is vast, and the bibliography will have to stand as a sign of my debt to them. I am equally indebted to those people with whom I have discussed areas of the subject, including Kirsten Bedigan, Joan Connelly, Matthew Dickie, Radcliffe Edmonds, Chris Farrell, Elizabeth Gebhard, Richard Gordon, Alan Griffiths, John North, Robin Osborne, Robert Parker, Richard Seaford, Julia Shear, Maria Stamatopoulou, Mike Trapp and Froma Zeitlin. Versions of some of the chapters were delivered at seminars in London, Cardiff, Edinburgh and Dublin, and the book has benefited enormously from what I learned on those occasions. Since starting work on this book I have also given a course on mystery cults for several years for the MAs in Classics and Ancient History at the University of London: the students who took it taught me much. While I was completing the manuscript, two scholars died who in different ways had a great impact on the book. It was a remark by Mary Douglas that led me to the cognitive science of religion, and a new approach to mystery cults. The other scholar was Christiane Sourvinou-Inwood, whose expertise in all areas of Greek religion, critical advice and intellectual acuity I always valued, and will always miss.

In Greece I was given great help by Helen Clarke, Christy Constantakopoulou, Fanis Constantakopoulos and the staff of the Ninth Ephoria of Prehistoric and Classical Antiquities in Thebes. I have for many years been blessed with the friendship and support of my colleagues in the Departments of Classics and History at King's College London. Research would also be impossible without the expertise and unstinting support of the Library staff of the Institute of Classical Studies in London.

This book would not exist without the encouragement of Colin Ridler and the dedication of my editor Nina Shandloff, as well as the work of Pauline Hubner and Rowena Alsey at Thames & Hudson, and Rob Tempio at Princeton University Press, and the support of my agent Vivien Green. Finally I must acknowledge above all my gratitude to my family, my children, Isabel and Clare, and my wife Jill, to whom I dedicate this book.

Sources of Illustrations

Museo Archeologico Regionale di Agrigento 18; akg-images 83; akg-images/Bildarchiv Steffens 93; akg-images/Gérard Degeorge XXVII; akg-images/John Hios 24; akg-images/Erich Lessing 103, 150, XIV, XV; The Art Archive/Archaeological Museum Brauron (Vravron), Greece/Gianni Dagli Orti XI; Antalya Museum, Turkey 72; Acropolis Museum, Athens 7; Agora Excavations, American School of Classical Studies, Athens 16, 61; Epigraphic Museum, Athens 5; French School of Archaeology, Athens 109; National Archaeological Museum, Athens 20, 25, 28, 34, 39, 44, 66, 97, III; Antikenmuseum, Basel 1; Staatliche Museen, Berlin 8, 57, 76, 98, X; Hugh Bowden 21, 37, 47, 60, 131–8; Royal Museums of Art and History, Brussels 26, 27; Museo Nazionale, Reggio Calabria 56, 84; Archaeological Museum, Capua XXIII, XXIV; Giovanni Caselli 46, 144, XXII, XXVIII; The International Catacomb Society/Photo Estelle Brettman 146; Photo © Chuck Conner 151; Ny Carlsberg Glyptotek, Copenhagen 85; © Scott Houston/Sygma/Corbis 149; © Mimmo Jodice/Corbis 92; © Massimo Listri/Corbis 143; © Adam Woolfitt/Corbis 102; Photo Giovanni Dall'Orto 122, 123; Dickins, G. (1906–7), 'Damphon of Messene II', *Annual of the British School at Athens* 13 (fig. 16) 49; Staatliche Kunstsammlungen, Dresden 148; Trinity College Library, Dublin 129; Archaeological Museum, Eleusis 17, 19; Museo Archeologico Nazionale, Ferrara 14, 62–5; Alinari Archives, Florence 32; Prof. Dr. A. de Franciscis, Naples 75; Museo Archeologico Regionale di Gela 52; Cristina Quicler/AFP/Getty Images 2; Kaveh Kazemi/Hulton Archive/Getty Images 11; Glyn Goodrick 12; Gordion Excavation Project 58; © J. Matthew Harrington 51; photo Hirmer 23, 55, 108; © Sven von Hofsten 54; www.iStockphoto.com 79; Deutsches Archäologisches Institut, Istanbul 59; Badische Landesmuseum, Karlsruhe 128; Photo Andonis Katanos 50; Giovanni Lattanzi/archart.it 142; © Jürgen Liepe 105, 106; British Museum, London 3, 6, 80, 86, 110, 117, 141; The Trustees of the British Museum, London 4; Museum of London 127; University of Southern California, Institute for Creative Technologies, Los Angeles, CA II; Direktion Landesarchäologie, Mainz 139, 140, XXV, XXVI; from Martens, M. and De Boe, G. (eds) (2004), *Roman Mithraism: the evidence of the small finds*, Instituut voor het Archeologisch Patrimonium/Museum Het Toreke, Brussels (fig. 10) 130; Esther Millea 119; Staatliche Antikensammlungen und Glyptothek, Munich 9, 77 (photo Hirmer), 82 (photo Hirmer); Museo Archeologico Nazionale, Naples 94, 116, XVIII; US National Archives and Records Administration, Photo Russell Lee 152; Samothrace Excavations, Institute of Fine Arts, New York University 33; Courtesy Pennsylvania-Yale-Institute of Fine Arts, New York University (PYIFA) Expedition to Abydos 107 (drawing by Laurel Bestock), XX; © Marie-Lan Nguyen 29, 95, 96, 124, XII; Museo Ostiense, Ostia 73; Ashmolean Museum, Oxford 41, 42, 88–90; Museo Archeologico Regionale di Palermo 53; © Georg Gerster/Panos Pictures 15; Cabinet des Médailles, Bibliothèque Nationale, Paris V; Louvre, Paris 99, 145; Musée Gustave Moreau, Paris IV; Josh Reynolds/AP/Press Association Images 10; Soprintendenza Archeologica di Roma 70, 71; Deutsches Archäologisches Institut, Rome 112, 113; Musei Capitolini, Rome 68, 74, 78, 91, 114; Museo Gregoriano Egizio, Rome 115; Archivio SAIA 35, 36; Photo 1990 Scala, Florence – courtesy of the Ministero Beni e Att. Culturali 125; Photo 2008 Scala, Florence – courtesy of the Ministero Beni e Att. Culturali I; Photo 1990 Scala, Florence/Fondo Edifici di Culto – Min. dell'Interno 147; Photo 2008 The Metropolitan Museum of Art/Art Resource/Scala, Florence 13, IX; Shepherd, J. (1998), *The temple of Mithras, London*, English Heritage, London (fig. 51) 120; Samuel Magal/Sites & Photos 31, 67, 111, VI, VII, VIII, XIII, XXI; Alan Sorrell 121; Photo Amy A. Sowder 104; Photo Heidi Grassley © Thames and Hudson Ltd, London 48; Themelis, P. G. and Touratsoglou, G. P. (1997), *I taphi tou Derveniou*, Athens 101; Archaeological Museum, Thessaloniki 100, XVI; from *Vestnik Drevnei Istorii* 143 (p. 89: fig. 6) 81; Sistema Bibliotecario Vibonese XVII; Kunsthistorisches Museum, Vienna 87; Volos Archaeological Museum XIX; Städtisches Museum, Wiesbaden 126; http://en.wikipedia.org/wiki/File:Plan_Samothrace_sanctuary-en.svg (after Lehmann, K. (1985), *Samothrace: a guide to the excavations and the museum*) 30; Wolters, P. H. A. and Bruns, G. (1940), *Das Kabirenheiligtum bei Theben*, de Gruyter, Berlin (pl. 33, 1) 40, (pl. 33, 3) 43, (p. 107, fig. 5) 45

Drawings by Dražen Tomic: 22 (after Travlos, J. (1988), *Bildlexikon zur Topographie des antiken Attika*, Tübingen, p. 115, fig. 125 and p. 154, fig. 187); 38 (Wolters, P. H. A. and Bruns, G. (1940), *Das Kabirenheiligtum bei Theben*, de Gruyter, Berlin); 69 (after Pensabene, P., *Archeologia Laziale* 9 (1988), fig. 1); 118; 224–5

Index